taiwan

NATIONAL GEOGRAPHIC

TRAVELER

taiwan

by Phil Macdonald

National Geographic
Washington, D.C.

CONTENTS

Pages 2–3: Taiwan's north coast beckons with rock formations and richly blue waters.
Opposite: A robed boy partakes in a ritual celebration marking the birthday of Confucius.

TRAVELING WITH EYES OPEN

Alert travelers go with a purpose and leave with a benefit. If you travel responsibly, you can help support wildlife conservation, historic preservation, and cultural enrichment in the places you visit. You can enrich your own travel experience as well.

To be a geo-savvy traveler:

- Recognize that your presence has an impact on the places you visit.

- Spend your time and money in ways that sustain local character. (Besides, it's more interesting that way.)

- Value the destination's natural and cultural heritage.

- Respect the local customs and traditions.

- Express appreciation to local people about things you find interesting and unique to the place: its nature and scenery, music and food, historic villages and buildings.

- Vote with your wallet: Support the people who support the place, patronizing businesses that make an effort to celebrate and protect what's special there. Seek out shops, local restaurants, inns, and tour operators who love their home—who love taking care of it and showing it off. Avoid businesses that detract from the character of the place.

- Enrich yourself, taking home memories and stories to tell, knowing that you have contributed to the preservation and enhancement of the destination.

That is the type of travel now called geotourism, defined as "tourism that sustains or enhances the geographical character of a place—its environment, culture, aesthetics, heritage, and the well-being of its residents." To learn more, visit National Geographic's Center for Sustainable Destinations at *www .nationalgeographic.com/travel/sustainable.*

taiwan

ABOUT THE AUTHORS

Phil Macdonald moved to Hong Kong from Sydney, Australia, in 1989 to continue a career in journalism that had begun eight years earlier in the west coast city of Perth. He worked for the *Hong Kong Standard* and the *South China Morning Post* for a number of years before settling—by way of Singapore and Laos—in Phuket, Thailand, in 1996. He now lives in Bangkok, working as a freelance journalist and writer, and contributing to a number of regional and international publications. His interests include Southeast Asian politics and recent history, and the beaches of southern Thailand. He is author of *National Geographic Traveler: Hong Kong* and co-author of *National Geographic Traveler: Thailand* guidebooks.

Rick Charette wrote the Muzha tea plantation, Jiufen, and Sun Moon Lake entries, and also updated and wrote additional new features for this edition. A Taiwan resident for more than two decades, Charette's work is featured in numerous local, regional, and international publications.

Brent Hannon contributed several features.

Charting Your Trip

The image of Taiwan as one vast factory belching out Made in Taiwan goods is far off the mark. This is a subtropical land blessed by nature. The diversity of terrain is remarkable: White-sand beaches fringed with palms are almost always within sight of towering peaks clad in soaring pine and cypress. The variety of adventures is impressive, each day's experience a world away from yesterday's.

Today it's a hot-springs soak in the high hills. Tomorrow it's a yacht tour along mangrove-lined river and coast. Then it's thrilling white-water rafting. Gentle teahouse visits in plantation-patchwork mountain valleys. Coral diving and snorkeling. Mountain hiking. Surfing and windsurfing on windswept offshore islands. Remote aboriginal areas. Whale-watching. Trekking deep marble-lined gorges. Bright, ornate temples in grand mountainside settings. Quaint towns clinging to hilltops. Welcome to Taiwan.

How to Get Around

Almost all overseas travelers enter Taiwan in the north, via Taiwan Taoyuan International Airport, and use nearby Taipei, 40 minutes away by vehicle, as a base. Touring this city—the capital—and other major cities is viable by taxi, which are inexpensive and driven by honest individuals who speak little if any English; be sure to have your destination and hotel written down in Chinese. In Taipei and Kaohsiung mass rapid transit—MRT—subway systems are the best way to go, with most major sites near stations and with good English signage.

Travel between cities is made easy by inexpensive and very efficient domestic airlines—Mandarin Airlines (*www.mandarin-airlines.com*) and UNI Airways (*www.uniair.com.tw*)—and new high-speed rail services (*www.thsrc.com.tw/en*). The regular train system is also efficient, but the many service options and lack of clear and usable English makes it difficult to navigate for newcomers. Because of language difficulties, a weblike road system, and sometimes untrustworthy and/or confusing English road signage and maps, bus tours are recommended for all forays outside cities. The Taiwan Tourism Bureau (see sidebar opposite) works with local agencies to provide quality English-language tours to myriad destinations and on a wealth of themes, and you will be accompanied at all times by an English-speaking guide. Customized tours are also an option.

A note of caution: For its population Taiwan is exceedingly small (about one-tenth the size of the state of California) and has comparatively

A red lantern riding the wind signals tradition and celebration.

little flat and/or accessible land. Expect many co-visitors to whichever sites you visit, save for such activities as high-elevation hiking and coastal diving. To avoid the crowds, visit sites on weekdays when locals are at work; sites will be quieter, though it's rare anywhere on Taiwan's main island to ever find yourself alone.

How to Visit in One Week

Taipei is the country's political, economic, cultural, and transportation hub. Until just the past decade or so it was overwhelmingly dominant in all areas of interest to travelers save for nature's beauties. It remains by far the most popular base for overseas visitors to begin their explorations. There is more than enough to do in the city itself to fill an entire week. Here's how the most important Taipei sites rank: historic **Longshan Temple,** the grandiose **Chiang Kai-shek Memorial,** the buzzing **Shilin Night Market** food emporium, the skyscraping and not long ago record-setting **Taipei 101** tower, the valley-bound **Beitou hot-springs** resort area, and the **National Palace Museum.** Each can fill up a half day or an evening, though a full visit to the museum can easily fill two days. The first five are short walks from MRT stations; the museum is a five-minute taxi ride and longer shuttle-bus ride from MRT Shilin station.

Yangmingshan National Park takes up much of a massif of extinct volcanoes on the city's north side. It is Taipei's crown jewel of the natural realm, a world of hot springs, fumaroles, nature trails, and farm restaurants. The most developed and visited area—the south side—is within city limits, reached within 20 minutes by taxi from MRT Shilin station; park-bound buses with clearly marked English also head uphill from here.

NOT TO BE MISSED:
Shilin Night Market   67
Religious practice at Taipei's Longshan Temple   68–71
The National Palace Museum's Chinese treasures   80–85
Hot-springs soaking and hiking on Yangmingshan   98–101
Taroko Gorge and the drive along the thrilling Central Cross Island Highway   134–137
Surf and turf fun at Kenting National Park   172–183
Sunrise at Alishan   227–229

Taiwan Visitor Information

For a wealth of timely information on Taiwan, from sights to events, hotels to sporting activities, visit the excellent **Taiwan Tourism Bureau** online at *www.taiwan.net .tw.* Another reliable source of up-to-the-minute information is the **Ministry of Transportation and Communications** *(9F, 290 Zhongsiao E. Rd., Sec.4, Taipei, Taiwan 106, Republic of China, tel 02/2349-1500, fax 02/2771-7036, e-mail: tbroc@ tbroc.gov.tw).*

A wide-ranging menu of rewarding day trips is available from Taipei. None of the destinations is more than an hour or two from downtown Taipei, and English signage in the north is comparatively good, so renting a car is an option. However, since roads outside the cities can still be quite congested, especially in the north, and Taiwan drivers tend to be aggressive, that carefree road-trip feeling can be quickly snatched away. All places recommended here are regular destinations for tour-bus agencies serving international tourists, so leaving the driving to them is the best option.

A visit to the north coast or the northeast coast encompasses mountains falling down to the sea, picturesque temples, crashing surf, bizarre rock formations, tucked-away fishing villages, fresh-from-the-dock seafood restaurants, and surfside cafés. The old gold-rush town of **Jiufen** clings to a high mountain crest off the northeast coast overlooking the Pacific, today a place of old redbrick structures housing artist galleries, mining museums, 24-hour teahouses, and traditional eateries. Spectacular **Wulai** is hidden away in a deep gorge south of Taipei, an angelic waterfall hurtling down from high above, natural hot springs in the riverbed below, the northernmost settlement of Taiwan's northernmost tribe, the Atayal, who offer cultural displays and song-and-dance shows. The towns of **Sanxia** and **Yingge** are close by each other southwest of Taipei, and are usually visited together. Sanxia is an old coal-mining and market center famed for one of the Chinese world's most ornate and colorful temples, along with a nearby renovated Old Street of shop houses. Yingge is stuffed with ceramics factories and working kilns, its cobblestoned Old Street lined with scores of shops selling practical and artistic works, and a first-rate ceramics museum.

If You Have More Time

Tour-bus service makes sense for the following trips. **Sun Moon Lake,** high in the central mountains, about three hours from Taipei, is by far Taiwan's largest freshwater lake. Ringed by peaks and magisterially picturesque, it is Taiwan's honeymoon capital. A sightseeing yacht tour is a must, as is the long cable-car ride to **Formosan Aboriginal Culture Village** to see the superb mock-ups of nine traditional aboriginal villages.

Alishan, a great hiking and see-the-sunrise spot, is about 40 minutes south of Sun Moon Lake, an old lumbering area reachable only by a narrow-gauge railway. Take the three-hour plunge to the plains on one of the world's great—and few—alpine tracks.

Kenting National Park takes up the entire southern tip of the island. A lush oasis

After dusk, Taipei's Ximending quarter bustles with shoppers, theatergoers, and bar-hoppers.

of protected coastal forest areas, bird-watching spots, sand beaches, and coral reefs popular with divers, this is Taiwan's tropical playground. Six hours from Taipei by car—90 minutes by shuttle bus from Kaohsiung International Airport—the coast is lined with resorts and the small main town likes to party into the wee hours each night.

The rugged **Central Mountain Range** cuts off the east coast from the rest of the main island, creating a sense of peaceful isolation. A recommended outing (three days minimum) is to fly to small **Hualien City,** rent a vehicle, and travel 30 minutes up-coast to **Taroko Gorge,** which though smaller in scale than the Grand Canyon rivals it in grandeur. Using Hualien as base, next day travel south along the east coast's simple two-highway road grid through a California-style Big Sur environment offering beach action, whale-watching, unusual geological formations, fishing-village seafood eateries, and, if time is sufficient, bicycling. After checking out the small city of **Taitung** with its heavy aboriginal population (don't miss the National Museum of Prehistory, based on local digs) loop back up to Hualien through the bucolic East Rift Valley, a long garden of tea farms, aborigine villages, small hot-springs resorts, and white-water rafting on the **Xiuguluan River.** Hmmm; best make that minimum four days.

For more off-the-beaten-track zones, Taiwan's many offshore islands can't be beat. While not remote in terms of ease of getting there, they are decidedly remote in terms of distance from the style and pace of life on the main island. Flights from Taipei Songshan Airport are direct to the **Kinmen, Penghu, and Matsu** island groups.

What to Pack

April through October, take summer clothes, along with a waterproof jacket (or umbrella) for the almost daily showers. Smart, casual slacks and a light dress jacket for men and smart dress for women is suitable for dining in the better restaurants. Bring a warm pullover or jacket if you plan to visit mountain areas, even in summer. For the cooler months, pack warmer clothing. Note: Long sleeves are rarely worn by locals, even in cooler weather. Finally, don't forget sunglasses and a wide-brimmed hat for sun protection.

History & Culture

In Taiwan, stylized stone lions often serve as Taoist temple guardians. Opposite: Volcanic rock along Taiwan's coast couples with clouds for dazzling sunrises and sunsets.

Taiwan Today

On an island as densely populated as Taiwan, you might think that the last thing
a local would want to see is another outsider coming in. Yet the Taiwanese are
exceptionally welcoming to foreign visitors, sometimes disarmingly so. Speak
to any traveler, businessperson, or expatriate who has spent time on the island,
and the talk will likely drift to Taiwanese hospitality.

A stranger to Taiwan (officially, the Republic of China) is automatically taken in
as a guest, and the locals—who pride themselves on being good hosts—treat their
guests as guests should be treated, often going out of their way to make them feel
at ease. So be prepared for largesse, take it all in stride, and accept it graciously.
The notion of payback rarely enters the picture, although the conscientious guest
should attempt to show generosity in return.

A common example of this hospitality comes when it's time to pay the bill at a
restaurant. Forget about sharing. Dividing up the bill over the dining table is considered
demeaning, and asking you, the guest, to pay your share is not even a consideration.
In the West we settle for a coffee and polite conversation as an after-meal ritual; in Taiwan, the hosts argue over who will have the honor of paying the bill—with the host almost always winning the argument.

A Culture of Cash & Community

A healthy portion of Taiwan's economic activity still remains off official books. The most popular financial vehicle for individuals is the *huzhuhui*, or "mutual help association." Each month members give a set amount, usually NT$10,000 (U.S. $312), to an organizer—less the "interest" bid by a member who wants to borrow all the money that month, usually at 10–15 percent. Because none of this is reported for tax purposes, there is no legal recourse if a member fails to pay monthly contributions after borrowing. People generally minimize this risk by making sure they know all the other members in a start-up association.

Beautiful Island

This hospitality exists in one of the most crowded places on Earth. Some 23 million souls jam into just 14,015 square miles (36,300 sq km) of land. That's an area slightly larger than Massachusetts and Connecticut combined. Factor in the chains of towering mountains that can't support human settlement and the squeeze is accentuated. The shortage of elbowroom means that about 1,600 people jostle for space on each square mile of land (640 people per sq km). In the capital, Taipei, the situation is even more extreme, with 25,000 residents crowding into each square mile (10,000 people per sq km).

In the 16th century, Portuguese explorers were so impressed by the towering, green, mountainous island they saw from the decks of their ships that they called the place Ilha Formosa, meaning "beautiful island." Even allowing for the hyperbole of early explorers, these Portuguese seafarers were not far off the mark. The appellation stuck, particularly

A mere backwater just decades ago, Taipei has emerged as a modern, sophisticated city.

EXPERIENCE: Wedding Pics with Help from Pros

On any visit to Taipei's Chiang Kai-shek Memorial Hall you are almost sure to see a young woman and man decked out in full wedding attire having their photos taken. You may well see multiple couples. The East Asia custom is to have all wedding photos done before the big event, with everything handled by the pros at what are called "wedding salons."

These are businesses that combine a portrait studio, beauty parlor, and dress shop. In Taipei there are two renowned clusters of wedding salons, along Aiguo East Road and along Zhongshan North Road, Sec. 3. A package of about 30 portraits costs about NT$50,000 (U.S. $3,120) and includes all styling, selection of gowns and other attire, an album and framed photos, and a disk of photos with music and other special effects. Attire can be Western, Chinese imperial costume, Japanese geisha, samurai, and more. Competition is fierce, with over 1,000 salons on the island, so discounts can be had and extras are common.

Taiwan's prices are about half those at wedding salons in Singapore and Japan; a solid percentage of customers comes from overseas. The Tourism Bureau works with salons to set up preferential package deals for international travelers; two Taipei salons that regularly work with foreigners are **France Paris & Salomant** (tel 02/2560-1361) and **Royal** (tel 02/2597-5777), both on Zhongshan North Road.

Many locals also use the salons for individual and family portraits. If outside shoots are involved the photographer serves as tour guide, too.

in the United States, and the names Taiwan and Formosa were interchangeable as recently as the early 1970s.

Areas of the island's wild beauty that so awed early explorers are still intact. Those who imagine Taiwan as a crowded, clamorous, urban land are only partly correct. To be sure, the island's headlong rush into modernization has left its environmental scars, particularly on the heavily populated central west plains, but it has not totally eradicated the land's natural glory, nor overwhelmed Taiwan's traditional culture.

The grandeur of the jagged peaks and alpine scenery of the Central Mountain Range matches that of mountains in better known regions of the world. And in many cases, Taiwan's mountains are more accessible than those elsewhere. The Central Cross Island Highway cuts its way through the Central Mountain Range in such a miraculous fashion as to leave you wondering how the government managed to build it in the first place. You will be searching the rest of your life to find a more spectacular road.

While lacking the sheer drama of the Central Mountain Range, the island's east coast—the most isolated and unspoiled region of Taiwan proper—imparts a rare feeling of solitude in an otherwise crowded island. It's a place of spectacular gorges (its most famous, the stunning marble canyon of Taroko Gorge, is a world-class attraction), precipitous cliff faces rising from the Pacific Ocean, fertile hillsides, and bucolic valleys. Kenting, at the southern tip of the island, is Taiwan's tropical playground, with sparkling beaches, abundant offshore corals, and pristine coastal scenery.

About 85 percent of the people living on the main island of Taiwan and its offshore islands consider themselves native Taiwanese, or benshengren (this province people), and they take pride in their unique culture and traditions. The Taiwanese dialect is heard in the lyrics of pop songs, on television and radio, and at the movies alongside the official Mandarin Chinese.

The two million people who followed Chiang Kai-shek's Nationalist government to Taiwan when it was evacuated from the mainland in 1949, as well as their descendants, are referred to as *daluren* (mainlanders). Until the lifting of martial law in 1987, the benshengren harbored a great deal of resentment toward the *daluren,* who occupied positions of power and privilege and suppressed the Taiwanese language and culture after the Nationalists took power. Not surprisingly, the end to martial law was pivotal socially, politically, and economically for the island. But the resentment still lingers, albeit to a lesser extent and at a level that is hardly noticeable to the visitor, except during the country's major elections.

Taiwan's indigenous minorities, referred to as aborigines and called *yuanzhumin,* or original inhabitants, account for 1.5 percent of the population. Fourteen officially recognized tribes live in communities around the country.

The Ami is the largest group, with 180,000 members. They live in the mountains and valleys of Hualien and Taitung counties, while smaller groups like the Dahwu on Orchid Island and the Thao—who live around Sun Moon Lake—number only a few thousand or fewer. Other groups include the Atayal, Bunun, Paiwan, Puyuma, Rukai, Saisiat, Kavalan, Truku, Sakizaya, Sediq, and Tsou.

The Hakka, a Chinese minority group whose ancestors came primarily from the Chinese province of Guangdong, make up about 10 percent of the Taiwanese population.

Bride and groom (plus helper) pose in front of Chiang Kai-shek Memorial Hall in Taipei.

Every October 10, crowds turn out across the island to celebrate Double Tenth National Day.

Along with the indigenous groups, they tend to refer to themselves as Taiwanese.

Most trips to Taiwan will begin and end in the modern capital of Taipei, a flat, urban sprawl contained within a ring of mountains that forms the Taipei Basin. Taipei is the social, business, cultural, and political hub of the island. Its three million smartly dressed and confident inhabitants go about their business along wide avenues and tree-lined boulevards, parting with cash across counters in gleaming shopping malls, trendy Japanese department stores, and brand-name fashion boutiques. They relax by surfing the World Wide Web on their wireless laptop computers and sipping on lattes in Starbucks, and by ordering drinks and being seen in chic-this-week nightclubs, restaurants, and bars.

"Economic miracle" is the tag used to describe the transformation of some Asian cities and territories from underdeveloped outposts in the 1970s to modern and affluent urban centers that now demand to be taken seriously. Taipei is where Taiwan's economic miracle is most vigorously on show, and Taipei's affluent citizens have no qualms about showing off their economic status.

The economic growth of Taiwan over the past five decades has been phenomenal. The island has emerged as one of the region's strongest economies, one of a group including Hong Kong, Singapore, and South Korea that has come to define Asia's economic success since the 1980s. It has proved itself resilient in the face of the disastrous Asian financial crisis of 1997–98 and the global recession of the late 2000s.

Like its Asian counterparts, Taiwan learned early that its future prosperity lay in shifting its focus away from producing and exporting inexpensive consumer goods, products that made the label "Made in Taiwan" synonymous with cheap and disposable.

After China opened up politically in the late 1970s and began to embrace a market economy, factories making low-cost consumer items started to move across the Taiwan Strait to the mainland, where labor was plentiful and inexpensive. Taiwan looked for a market niche and found it in the manufacture of computers and other high-tech electronics.

Now the island rolls out computers, computer peripherals, and components like no other place on Earth. It makes more than a quarter of the world's desktop computers and well over half of its laptops. In the city of Hsinchu, to the southwest of Taipei, the sprawling Hsinchu Science Park rivals California's Silicon Valley.

> **In the city of Hsinchu, to the southwest of Taipei, the sprawling Hsinchu Science Park rivals California's Silicon Valley.**

The outstanding economic and political achievements of Taiwan stand out because many of them have taken place in difficult circumstances. For six decades, the country's powerful neighbor mainland China (officially, the People's Republic of China) has regarded Taiwan as a renegade province that one day must return to the fold. In recent times, China has reclaimed Hong Kong and the former Portuguese enclave of Macau and would like to add Taiwan to its holdings. Relations between the two lands are often hostile.

While most Taiwanese were once resigned to—and in many cases in favor of—one day officially becoming part of China, that is less the case today. Democratic changes that began in the 1990s have brought a political maturity to the island. This, coupled with increasing affluence and economic prosperity, has given the Taiwanese enough confidence to defy their huge neighbor, at least in word if not in deed. Today, more Taiwanese than ever before favor independence over reunification with mainland China. However, this is something that the People's Republic of China has strongly opposed.

One would think such a threatening political scenario would be oppressive, but this is far from the case. If the Taiwanese are afraid for their future, they certainly don't

Weekend Outdoor Cultural Creativity Markets

Two of Taipei's most eclectic markets are weekend celebrations of creative energy, filled with booths displaying the work of independent designers selling everything from clothing to baked goods, designer hairpins to oil-paper purses. Many items are one of a kind; both markets feature live musical entertainment.

Tianmu Market (Fri. 4 p.m.–10 p.m., Sat. 9 a.m.–3 p.m. & 4 p.m.–10 p.m., Sun. 3 p.m.–9 p.m.) sets up in the large parklike traffic circle where Tianmu Road and Zhongshan North Road, Section 7, meet. It started as an expatriate flea market and expanded from there. Hundreds of kiosks sell all manner of objects.

The smaller **Red House** market (10 Chengdu Rd., Sat. 2 p.m.–10 p.m., Sun. 2 p.m.–9:30 p.m.) is held at a landmark redbrick octagonal building, a former opera house that now hosts small theater productions, a teahouse, and the market.

Of course, an early start to browsing brings the best rewards at both markets.

show it. Perhaps it's denial, but Taiwan and its people roll along their day-to-day lives with a palpable vibrancy and assuredness.

While some Asian countries rail against Western culture gnawing away at their traditions and values, Taiwan takes a more pragmatic view. It accepts elements of Western culture, but generally not at the expense of its own. As a decades-old ally of the United States, Taiwan harbors very little anti-Western sentiment, making Western culture more acceptable.

But the modern gloss of Taiwan can be seen as a veneer covering a culture deeply rooted in Buddhist, Taoist, and Confucian beliefs, which are intertwined and often presented in riotously ornate temples. The Taiwanese honor many dozens of deities, integrate folk and ancestral worship in their religions, and add in soothsaying to create a compelling spiritual mix.

People gather in thousands of temples around the country—from makeshift shrines to astonishing achievements in religious architecture—to pray, burn incense, and offer

Carp Lake in central Taiwan's Puli Township offers natural beauty on an island teeming with factories.

food to myriad deities. Taiwanese religion (and Chinese religion in general) incorporates around one hundred deities of varying popularity and spiritual influence. A student cramming for exams will find time to visit a temple honoring a scholarly god; sharp-suited businessmen will lay food offerings before the image of a god who will bestow riches; a person worn down by sickness will pay homage to a deity that can restore health; while a fisherman faced with weeks at sea will visit a temple that honors a deity who will ensure a good catch and a safe return. Fortune-tellers have co-opted this religious hodgepodge and linger outside temples, lending counsel to those impatient to see if their prayers will be answered. The Taiwanese do not like to leave things to chance.

Temples erupt with color and noise around the time of a particular deity's birthday. The sounds of beating drums, crashing cymbals, and earsplitting firecrackers provide accompaniment to the throngs of devotees who follow the deity's icon as it is carried on a sedan chair through city streets.

Superstition pervades and informs daily life in Taiwan. Certain dates and numbers portend success or failure.

Superstition pervades and informs daily life in Taiwan. Certain dates and numbers portend success or failure. There are good days to do things, and there are bad days to do things. To make sure a marriage is a long and happy one, young couples choose a suitable time and date for the ceremony as ordained by tradition or confirmed by a soothsayer. A businessman well versed in the ways of international wheeling and dealing may attribute his latest success to the way his *feng shui* master arranged his office. Families may not travel during Ghost Month because they are more likely to run into trouble when angry ghosts are about, and should a family member be killed in an accident, passage to the afterlife will be fraught with peril.

Early Christian missionaries had some success converting the locals, especially the aborigines, who were more amenable to the religion's tenets than the Chinese. Just over a million Taiwanese are Christians, about three-quarters of them Protestant, and they worship in some 3,000 churches around the island.

Like other Asians, people in Taiwan take the concept of "face" seriously. The customs, hierarchies, and rules that apply can vary from country to country in Asia, but they share the theme of showing respect and avoiding embarrassing others.

Being rich and powerful will earn you a lot of respect (and therefore allow you to gain face) in Taiwan. The reason is very simple: To become rich, you must be diligent and hardworking, qualities that will necessarily command respect.

Obviously no one is going to give you the respect you deserve as a rich or powerful person if they don't know you are rich and powerful. This explains the common and ostentatious displays of wealth you may see in the country (luxury cars, expensive jewelry and watches, designer clothing, etc.).

"Face" works at all levels of society and exists in part to maintain harmony. Raising your voice in anger or frustration causes much embarrassment—and hence loss of face—for the person at whom your ire is directed. The result is invariably negative and potentially dangerous.

Compliment freely and you will give people face, but even the slightest personal criticism, even one that would be considered harmless or even helpful in the West, can cause loss of face, embarrassment for the target, and a period of uncomfortable silence. Even in the most frustrating moments, a smile and some patience will get you a lot further than a scowl and fist-thumping.

The peculiarly Chinese concept of *guanxi* also pervades interpersonal relationships. In mainland China, for example, a stifling bureaucracy can make it impossible to get anything done, so individuals need to form relationships with the people who can get wheels turning. However, the person who turns the wheels for you will, at some point, want to have the favor returned.

To accumulate guanxi, you need to do things for people: Give them gifts, take them to dinner, lend them your car, and so on. Once you have built up guanxi, an unspoken understanding develops that favors will be returned repeatedly in an ongoing relationship. Visitors to Taiwan will rarely become involved in guanxi, unless they are there often on business.

Most Taiwanese people, especially in the cities, dress well and expect you to do the same. The way you dress often says a lot about your character and can determine how you are treated. Always dress neatly. For men, clean T-shirts, shorts, and sandals are the minimum dress standards for streetwear. Don't wear skimpy shirts or flip-flops. Women should always dress modestly.

A Taiwanese peculiarity that can confuse visitors is the use of different English translations for Chinese. The problem stems from the number of transliteration systems that follow different criteria and the inability of governments and municipal authorities to agree on a single one. The same major road may be called Zhongxiao, Chunghsiao, and Chung Hsiao; another Zhongshan and Chungshan; and another Ta an, Da an, and Daan. Applying some logic will usually solve the problem, although it is sometimes a little tricky (e.g., Pateh Road at

EXPERIENCE:
Learning Chinese

In Taiwan, Mandarin is the official language, imposed by the Nationalists after their arrival following World War II. It is the lingua franca in schools, so almost everyone speaks it to greater or lesser degree—noticeably "lesser" in rural areas, where the older generation often speaks only Taiwanese.

A good place to start when looking for short-term tutoring, language exchanges, and formal classes is *www .tealit.com.* **Hess Educational Organization** *(www.hess.com.tw/careers/eng lish/podcasts)* has good Survival Guide CDs and podcasts that let you pick, choose, and learn at your own pace.

Private schools in major cities offer short, intensive Mandarin classes geared toward conversation; some offer Taiwanese courses.

A researcher at one of Taiwan's many biotechnology firms "pipettes," or transfers, materials to a tray. The country reigns as one of Asia's leaders in high technology.

times is also called Bade Road and Pate Road). Among the main transliteration systems are Wade-Giles, Tongyong, and Hanyu; however, the situation can become frustrating when individual sign writers and mapmakers add their own interpretations. This guidebook uses the Hanyu method, now the official one, though only Taipei has to date applied it systematically and almost eliminated non-Hanyu signage.

The transformation of Taiwan over the past 30-plus years from a backwater into an Asian economic powerhouse has generally not been at the expense of its traditional culture and values. A trip to a Taoist temple to burn incense and make offerings of food is still as much a part of everyday life as a trip to a shopping mall to buy the latest brand-name fashion. Seeking counsel from a fortune-teller is no more unusual than meeting with a stockbroker to discuss investment opportunities. Burning paper "hell money" to appease wandering spirits is as run-of-the-mill as handing over a wad of notes in a trendy bar for overpriced cocktails. Indeed, much of Taiwan's appeal for the visitor lies in this unaffected blend of a modern, consumer-driven, Western-influenced lifestyle with the vitality of a culture whose values are richly steeped in tradition. ■

Food & Drink

The flood of immigrant civilians and Nationalist soldiers to Taiwan after China's civil war ended in 1949 brought with it a wide variety of culinary traditions, which have been maintained and refined. Today, Taiwan can boast the best Chinese food in the world and find little argument. The island's restaurants run the gamut of major Chinese regional cuisines, providing a rich culinary tour.

Food is very much a part of Chinese culture. Confucius, who believed social ritual taught virtue, laid down the ground rules for customs and etiquette at the dining table. In classical Chinese teaching, a true scholar not only mastered the arts of poetry, calligraphy, music, and strategy, but also needed to be an accomplished

Taiwan serves up no end of restaurants to satiate the local appetite for food and company.

hand in the kitchen, able to turn out a superb meal for family, friends, and guests.

While lofty ideals of aligning food and fine art may have dissipated, the Taiwanese—like all ethnic Chinese—still take food quite seriously. Food and eating play a far more important role in ritual, language, symbolism, and social interaction than they do in even the most gregarious of Western cultures.

To the Chinese, the most important elements of the taste experience are color, aroma, flavor, and texture, all of which must be combined into one harmonious whole. Herein lies the art of Chinese cuisine. Dishes will have a main ingredient and a number of supplementary ones that bring it into a coordinated whole. Furthering this conceit, traditionally dishes are brought to the table in a sequence that reflects a particular harmonic relationship and order among the foods.

> While lofty ideals of aligning food and fine art may have dissipated, the Taiwanese—like all ethnic Chinese—still take food quite seriously.

Taiwanese Cuisine

Taiwanese food combines local ingredients with the culinary influences of the nearby Chinese province of Fujian and ex-colonial master Japan. Oyster omelets are popular, as are fried taro cakes doused with pork-based sauce. Other offerings include squid balls, fried fish with peanuts, and simmered cuttlefish. Taiwanese food is often eaten as a snack and sold at night markets. Shilin Night Market (see p. 67) is one of the best places to sample a variety of the dishes.

Cantonese Cuisine

To Westerners, Cantonese cuisine—from the southern Chinese province of Guangdong—is the most familiar style of Chinese food. The vast majority of Chinese restaurants found in the West are Cantonese, but this probably has more to do with the Cantonese propensity for migration than anything else.

Cantonese cuisine emphasizes freshness and natural flavor; food is lightly seasoned. Many dishes are stir-fried or steamed to allow the foods to retain their natural taste. Guangdong's tropical climate encourages abundant, varied produce. Cantonese dishes often include seafood along with tropical fruits, rice, and a wide array of vegetables. Beef, chicken, and pork are the typical meats. Popular Cantonese offerings include steamed sea bass, stir-fried garoupa, steamed chicken, beef with oyster sauce, and fried rice. Vegetable dishes come in wide variety. Elaborately prepared shark's-fin

Food markets offer an abundance of fresh, locally grown produce—the hallmark of Chinese cuisine.

soup and bird's-nest soup are two of the most exotic (and expensive) dishes on offer.

Cantonese cuisine is also famous for its roast meats, such as pork and duck, as well as the assortment of treats known as dim sum, usually enjoyed from early morning to early afternoon.

Beijing-style Cuisine

Beijing-style cuisine reflects its origins in the northern Chinese provinces. These cooler climes prohibit the growing of rice as a staple, so the emphasis has shifted to wheat-based foods. The cuisine, therefore, is characterized by a variety of dumplings, baked and steamed breads, and buns and noodles. A typical meal consists of several; vegetable dishes, soups, tofu (soybean curd), and fish, often prepared with garlic or vinegar. Meats may be braised or stewed, and in general the food is tasty though not heavily spiced.

The variety of buns, dumplings, and noodles makes Beijing cuisine ideal for snacks. Round flat buns filled with meat are pan-fried or baked. Dumplings traditionally hold a mixture of minced meat or vegetables (or sometimes both) and are steamed, boiled, or fried. Noodle-making at some Beijing-style restaurants is fun to watch, with chefs expertly twisting and twirling the dough while peeling off strands.

Peking duck, the most famous Beijing dish, is often served at banquets. Slices of oven-roasted duck with crispy brown skin are wrapped in thin pancakes and served with sauce and scallions.

Shanghainese Cuisine

Shanghai cuisine comes from the central coastal region of China. The area's coast and lakes provide saltwater and freshwater seafood, while both rice- and wheat-based dishes, such as buns and noodles, are available as accompaniments. Sauces are rich and slightly sweet. Shanghai cuisine tends to be heavier than Cantonese, lightly spiced and relatively oily. Popular Shanghainese dishes include fried prawns, drunken chicken, and steamed crab. Its West Lake vinegar fish (a whole carp is sliced open and splayed, lightly poached, then smothered with minced ginger and sweet-and-sour sauce) can be superb.

Sichuanese Cuisine

The cuisine of southwestern China's Sichuan Province features generous sprinklings of garlic, peppercorns, fennel, anise, coriander, and chilies, making it the spiciest of all Chinese foods. Traditionally prepared Sichuan food—often soaked and simmered in chili oil—can be too fiery for the unprepared Western palate, although milder dishes are available. Popular ingredients include chicken, pork, and river fish. Bean curd with spicy minced pork is a favorite dish, along with tasty stir-fried diced chicken with tiny, dry, and extremely hot chilies.

Dim Sum

Originally a Cantonese custom, these days dim sum is found throughout greater China, although the Cantonese still serve up the best.

Dim sum consists of a variety of steamed or fried dumplings stuffed with an assortment of either savory or sweet mixtures, along with bite-size items ranging from spareribs and meatballs to egg custard tarts. Most people eat dim sum mid to late morning, similar to brunch in the West, although restaurants may open as early as 6:30 a.m. and not close until mid-afternoon.

Once you are seated, waiters with food-laden trolleys push their way around the restaurant. You choose the snacks you want from the trolley and share them with others at the table. It is best to go with a group, as that way you can try a greater variety of treats. You wash the food down with an endless supply of green tea.

Dim sum favorites worth sampling include spring rolls, shrimp and pork dumplings, steamed pork spareribs, sesame-seed balls filled with a sweet potato paste, egg custard tarts, and mango pudding.

Chopsticks Etiquette

While waiting for food to arrive, don't play with your chopsticks, and never leave them standing upright in your rice bowl, as it evokes the funerary tradition of burning incense. Don't use your own chopsticks to take food from communal plates; use the spoons provided. And don't root around for the tastiest morsel or repeatedly return to the same dish; it's seen as selfish. Lazy Susans are always turned clockwise, slowly—not spun. Chopsticks laid across your rice bowl indicate you're full. Never point your chopsticks at others or at things; they are symbolic of a knife, inviting ill fortune.

Tea

You might never believe that tea could taste so good until you visit Taiwan. Even the most uncompromising coffee drinker could be converted to the delights of Taiwanese teas during a visit to the island. The mountains and mild climate, along with Chinese tradition and expertise in cultivation, have collaborated to produce some of the world's finest brews: delightfully aromatic and renowned for their sweet and pure flavor (see pp. 96–97).

> Dining—whether at home or in a restaurant—fulfills an important cultural function in ethnic Chinese communities.

Alcohol

Taiwan Beer is Taiwan's best known locally made brew; it is an acceptable beer, not a great one, but cheaper than imported beers. The selection of imported beers is reasonably varied, with ubiquitous global brands Heineken and Carlsberg widely available. U.S. beers Budweiser and Miller can be found in most bars, as can China's well-known Tsingtao.

Local liquor falls into the firewater category, with powerful Kaoliang (sorghum liquor) coming in at 58.5 percent alcohol. The most popular liquor is Shaohsing, a rice wine with a much more moderate alcohol content. The island also produces several decent grape wines, as well as more exotic plum wine.

Dining out and drinking are often combined into one convivial social event involving a great deal of toasting. To impress, hosts may splurge on an expensive bottle of brandy, and you will be required to have some even if you have not been drinking beforehand. Diluting even expensive brands with cola, however, is perfectly acceptable.

At the Table

Dining—whether at home or in a restaurant—fulfills an important cultural function in ethnic Chinese communities. That being the case, there are a number of rules

The Beer House Tradition

Taiwanese beer houses were the favorite nighttime venue before discos and Western-style pubs emerged on the scene. Called *pijiu wu*, they are inexpensive, cavernous places enlivened with over-the-top theme decorations. Some seat over a thousand patrons. The food is night-market style, a mix of seafood snacks and spicy Sichuan-type dishes that have evolved into a distinctive cuisine. Frosty kegs of draft are placed beside tables, then the dishes roll in: grilled oysters, chili clams, deep-fried bean curd, spareribs, crab stir-fried in garlic and onion, fried squid, steamed mussels, and dozens of other dishes. Beer houses are friendly spots where groups of friends relax after a hard day's work with food, beer, and chatter.

The island's iconic beer house, quickly known to all foreigners setting up in the country, is Taipei's **Indian Beer House** *(196 Bade Rd., Sec. 2, tel 02/2741-0550).* On the roof is its famous giant dinosaur skeleton, lit up at night, and inside is a bizarre multistory cavelike world of Indian heads, gargoyle-shaped urinals, and other visual entertainment. If looking to entertain newfound local acquaintances on an informal night out, this is the spot.

Taiwan's younger set has enthusiastically embraced the nightclub scene.

attached. As a foreigner you will be graciously given some leeway—but just because no one says anything (that would be impolite), don't think you are not breaking any rules. Try to become familiar with some basic etiquette for formal meals.

Waiters place dishes of food on the table throughout the meal. Many dishes come with their own serving spoons or chopsticks. Diners get their own rice bowl—which is refilled by waiters during the meal—and sometimes an empty plate to place food on before transferring to their rice bowl.

There are a number of things that you can do that would be considered impolite in the West. It's okay to spit bones on the table, slurp the noodles and soup, and even let out a discrete burp now and again. Holding your rice bowl close to your lips and rapidly shoveling the food into your mouth with chopsticks is an accepted mode of eating.

The host and others will interrupt dining with toasts, and your glass will regularly be topped up. You are expected to join in the toasts, but it's fine to just touch the glass with your lips. You may choose soft drinks over alcohol, although it is polite to accept a glass of alcohol if offered.

Lingering at the table after a meal for coffee, tea, or a chat is not a Taiwanese habit. When the host signals the end of a meal—sometimes by standing and offering a toast—it's over. As a guest, you are not expected to pay the bill, or even to offer to do so. Just sit back and enjoy the ritual argument over who pays. It will always end up being the one who made the invitation, or the boss, who pays. Never suggest splitting the bill, as this will demean the occasion. ■

History of Taiwan

In the mid-16th century, Jan Huygen van Linschoten, a Dutch navigator, was traveling on a Portuguese ship to Japan when the vessel came upon the island of Taiwan. Van Linschoten was enthralled by the lovely island, and in the centuries to come, the Dutch, Portuguese, Spanish, and Japanese would all attempt to settle this scenic but strife-torn land.

By the time the first European visitors arrived, indigenous peoples had been living on Taiwan for thousands of years. Finds at more than 500 prehistoric sites in Taiwan—some of which date back 10,000 years—offer clues to the origins of Taiwan's first settlers, but not enough evidence has been discovered to provide any definite conclusions. Digs have unearthed dwelling areas, tombs, shell mounds, megaliths, flat axes, red unglazed pottery, and decorated bronze implements, indicating that

A 19th-century oil painting of Takow, Formosa, captures Taiwan's sublime beauty.

the island's earliest peoples were likely from Malayan-Polynesian groups of Southeast Asia and the Pacific. Other sites have yielded implements that suggest some of Taiwan's earliest settlers might also have come from the Chinese mainland. These various indigenous groups—14 are now officially recognized in Taiwan—operated independently and were often hostile.

Chinese immigrants, mainly from the province of Fujian, began arriving in relatively large numbers in the 17th century. They found two indigenous groups. One had settled mostly in the southwest, hunting, fishing, and farming. The other, whose practices of tattooing and headhunting pointed to Pacific-island origins, lived in the mountains.

Piracy

From the 14th to 16th centuries, marauding Chinese and Japanese pirates used Taiwan as a stronghold, retreating to the island after attacking Chinese and Japanese trading ships and pillaging coastal towns on the mainland. The Ming dynasty (1368–1644) government could do little to stop this piracy, and warships would rarely chase the opportunistic pirates beyond the Ming outpost on the Penghu Islands (known to Europeans as the Pescadores) in the Taiwan Strait.

The Portuguese established a trading settlement in the north of the island in 1590, but left soon after. The Dutch, the next European power to try its luck, proved more resilient. They originally set up fortifications on the Penghu Islands in 1622. However, after an overpowering Ming fleet threatened them in 1624 and forced a truce, they moved to Anping (now part of Tainan) on the southwest coast of Taiwan. It proved a convenient arrangement for both parties. The Ming had little interest in the island and held no sovereign claim to it.

The Dutch & Spanish

The Dutch East India Company, which managed Holland's colonial business, gained exclusive rights to sugarcane and camphor, along with anything else it could trade. Local Chinese were herded into villages and farming cooperatives and burdened with heavy taxes, while missionaries—with a marked degree of success—set about converting aborigines to Christianity. (The Aborigines who refused to be converted often ended up on the wrong end of a musket.)

The Spanish looked on the success of the Dutch in Taiwan with envy, seeing the island as a perfect midway trade point between the Philippines—which they had conquered in the 1560s—and Japan, with which they were trying to establish trade. In 1626, the Spanish launched a small fleet from Manila, landing in the north of Taiwan and establishing posts at Keelung and, in 1628, Danshui. The fort at Keelung was christened

A panel of an 1859 triptych portrays Koxinga, who expelled the Dutch from Taiwan in 1662.

Fort San Salvador, while the smaller fort at Danshui was named Fort San Domingo.

The Dutch made two attempts to drive out the Spanish in 1630 and 1641, but both times failed. Feisty local aborigines were also a thorn in the side of the Spanish, while many soldiers succumbed to illness and died. Finally, a threatened rebellion in the Philippines forced the recall of three-quarters of the Spanish garrison. The Dutch overran Fort San Salvador in the summer of 1642. By 1650, nearly 300 Chinese and aboriginal villages were under the direct jurisdiction of the Dutch East India Company. Chinese immigrant farmers were organized into collectives, with leaders responsible for keeping local law and order. Areas of land under cultivation continued to increase and new crops were introduced.

By this time, Taiwan had become one of the most profitable outposts of the Dutch East India Company in the Far East. Spices, amber, kapok, and opium arrived from Southeast Asia through Batavia (Java in Indonesia), silver from Japan, and silk, pottery, herbs, and gold from China. All this was exchanged for sugar, camphor, venison, and deer hides from Taiwan. Sporadic uprisings by both aborigines and Chinese living on the island were swiftly and severely dealt with.

Meanwhile, turmoil had erupted in mainland China, with Manchu armies in the north threatening to overthrow the Ming dynasty. Mainland Chinese began pouring across the Taiwan Strait to escape the fighting. At first the Dutch welcomed the new settlers and provided them with oxen, seeds, and agricultural tools. The Chinese cleared new land, agriculture continued to flourish, and the Dutch landowners profited handsomely from the rents and taxes paid by their industrious Chinese tenants.

But the Chinese farmers became dissatisfied and asked to be allowed to buy land and pay taxes in lieu of rent. The Dutch were not interested. The situation came to a head in 1652 after the Dutch introduced a poll tax. The Chinese revolted, but the uprising was easily suppressed. Up to 6,000 poorly armed Chinese peasants were slaughtered.

Koxinga

On mainland China, the Ming dynasty was crumbling under a relentless southward push by the Manchu, who had by now built up a huge army. After the Manchu took Beijing, Ming loyalists headed south and continued to resist. Among these resistance fighters was the pirate Zheng Zhi-long, who led a formidable mercenary army. One of his sons, Zheng Cheng-gong, known in the West by his title Koxinga, eventually took over his father's army and pledged to use it to reestablish Ming rule.

From 1646 to 1658, with an army of 100,000 men and a flotilla of 3,000 ships, Koxinga was a scourge to cities along the Chinese coast. The Manchu eventually forced the inhabitants of coastal towns to move inland, robbing Koxinga of his safe havens and supplies. With the Manchu pressing in on his base, Koxinga set off to Taiwan to regroup.

In 1661, Koxinga's army laid siege to Fort Zeelandia at Anping. The Dutch managed to hang on for eight months before surrendering and eventually leaving the island. Koxinga chose Anping as his capital and set about transforming the Ming enclave into a base from which one day to defeat the Manchu, who had by now established control over almost all of China. However, Koxinga's rule was short-lived. Just a few months after defeating the Dutch, at the age of 38, he succumbed to illness and died.

Qing Dynasty Rule

Koxinga's son Zheng Jing succeeded his father and ruled for the next 19 years until his death, when his son, only 12 years old, was placed on the throne. Two years later, in 1683, the Zheng navy was all but wiped out near the Penghu Islands. The Manchu, or Qing, took control of Taiwan. It became a part of China's Fujian Province.

Initially, the Qing were intent on seeing that Taiwan did not become a haven for pirates and antigovernment forces. One hundred thousand Chinese were repatriated to the mainland and immigration was banned. Other Chinese were prohibited from living in aboriginal territories lest they foment revolt and form alliances; intermarriage was also forbidden. But concerted resistance continued. During the 212 years of Qing rule on Taiwan, there were over a hundred uprisings and revolts, as the people railed against an undisciplined army and bald-faced corruption and mismanagement by officials.

Despite all this, Taiwan thrived. Farms, which were previously owned by the state and the army, fell into private hands. The immigration ban had little effect, and Chinese continued to pour across from the mainland. Camphor became a major cash crop, sugar plantations expanded, and rice fields and tea plantations sprang up.

Taiwan's newfound wealth and strategic position didn't escape the notice of foreign powers. In the 19th century the British, in almost constant conflict with China since the establishment of Hong Kong in 1841, sent their warships out to patrol the coast of Taiwan, searching for movements by Qing forces. Matthew Perry, commander of the U.S. East India Squadron, which had earlier forced Japan to open up to trade after two centuries of peaceful isolation, also realized the strategic importance of Taiwan, and pushed for it to become a protectorate of the United States.

The grisly fate awaiting shipwrecked sailors who frequently washed up onto Taiwan's shores did not help matters. These unfortunate souls were subject to beatings, imprisonment, and sometimes beheading by the Chinese or hostile aborigines. Calls for justice were met with shrugs in the Chinese capital of Beijing,

Hanyu & Tongyong Pinyin: Language Battles

The politically charged war over how best to anglicize Chinese sounds continues to rage in Taiwan. The old Wade-Giles and Yale systems were rejected by China's Communists, who championed Hanyu Pinyin. This was rejected by Taiwan's Democratic Progressive Party after winning national power in 2000, considering China a foreign place, introducing the homegrown Tongyong Pinyin; differing about 10 percent from Hanyu, it is said to better reflect Taiwanese pronunciation. The Kuomintang, retaking power in 2008, promptly reinstated Hanyu. Since not obligatory, you'll see both systems in use, depending on political leanings, though Hanyu is slowly winning.

whose official influence over Taiwan remained minimal. Europeans often resorted to gunboat diplomacy, bombarding coastal settlements in retribution for the attacks.

The Treaty of Nanjing, signed after the end of the Second Opium War in 1858, led to the opening of four Taiwanese ports, Anping, Danshui, Dagou (Kaohsiung), and Keelung, to foreign trade. Trading companies quickly established themselves, trade boomed, and expatriate communities expanded. But skirmishes continued. In 1866, American warships bombarded a tribal area in southern Taiwan in revenge for the murder of two shipwrecked American sailors. In 1869, British warships attacked Anping and demanded better terms for the camphor trade. In 1884, France attacked and temporarily shut down the ports of Keelung, Danshui, and the Penghus to challenge Qing power. Taiwan remained an unruly place, virtually ignored by the central government in Beijing and the provincial leaders in Fujian, which left it sorely lacking in law and order. Much of Taiwan was still in the hands of the aborigines, who begrudgingly shared the island so long as others did not encroach on their territory. The Chinese who did—often in search of new land to farm—were often killed by the land's original inhabitants.

> **In 1884, France attacked and temporarily shut down the ports of Keelung, Danshui, and the Penghus to challenge Qing power.**

Western Powers and Japan Eye Taiwan

In 1871 the Japanese ship *Miyako* foundered off the southeast coast of Taiwan. Sixty-six men came ashore to be met by a particularly hostile group of Botan aborigines, who duly slaughtered 54 of them. Japan was set for retaliation, but Foreign Minister Soyeshima Taneomi convinced the Meiji government that a diplomatic solution would be in its best interests. He set off for Beijing with Meiji adviser Charles Le Gendre, a retired American consul from Amoy (Xiamen) and an American Civil War hero, who had previously negotiated settlements of similar incidents between aborigines and American sailors.

The Qing government sought to escape responsibility for the incident by claiming that China's sovereign rights did not extend to the eastern and southern part of the island inhabited by aborigines. So on May 17, 1874, 2,500 Japanese troops left Nagasaki and headed to Hengchun in the south of Taiwan to confront the Botan. After a few attacks on the tribe to teach them a lesson, the Japanese showed no signs of leaving. Negotiations ended with Beijing paying compensation to the families of the victims and for construction expenses of the Japanese during their six-month occupation.

The affair shook the Chinese into action as they realized that the Western powers and Japan were eyeing the island. Shen Bao-zhen, the administrator of shipping affairs, was put in charge of Taiwan's defense in 1874. He organized local militias and constructed cannon emplacements along the coast. A law prohibiting contact between immigrants and aborigines was lifted, and immigration from the mainland encouraged.

In 1885 the Qing government made Taiwan China's 22nd province. Its new governor, Liu Ming-chuan, continued to modernize Taiwan's defenses and implemented tax reforms in an effort to make the island financially independent. Telegraph lines soon linked Taipei, Keelung, Danshui, and Tainan. A submarine cable between Danshui and Fuzhou in Fujian was completed in 1888, the same year, China opened its first post office. A railroad connected Keelung and Hsinchu in 1893. The government established a trade office to encourage foreign trade, and Western-style schools sprang up.

Japanese Occupation

War between China and Japan broke out in 1894 when the Japanese invaded the Chinese vassal state of Korea. It ended in a humiliating defeat for the Chinese, and the ensuing Treaty of Shimonoseki forced China to cede Taiwan and the Penghu Islands to Japan. The move, naturally enough, shocked the people of Taiwan. In a futile act of defiance, Qing officials on the island boldly declared a new country, the Taiwan Republic, on May 25, 1895, and pledged to resist the Japanese takeover. It was a disaster. Between June 6, 1895, when Japanese troops formally entered Taipei, and October 21, when they took Tainan, 7,000 Chinese soldiers died, along with thousands of civilians. The Tapani Incident, another uprising in 1915, proved even more calamitous, resulting in the death of thousands of Chinese.

Japan set about modernizing and remodeling Taiwan in its own image. It built roads and railways linking major towns and cities; constructed dams for hydroelectric power; and created irrigation systems that greatly increased the productivity of land for rice and sugarcane cultivation. Schools, hospitals, and public buildings sprang up, industry developed, agricultural methods were modernized, and public health improved tremendously.

Taiwan's first census in 1905 found 3,040,000 people living on the island, 97.8 percent of whom were Chinese and 1.9 percent Japanese. But the census neglected to count aborigines and "bandits," both groups with sizable populations.

The Japanese also managed to do something all previous administrations had failed to

Chiang Kai-shek, Franklin Roosevelt, and Winston Churchill allied to defeat Japan in World War II.

Chiang Kai-shek and his wife, Soong Mayling, wave to followers at a mass rally in Taipei in 1970.

accomplish: bring law and order. They established administrative mechanisms, monopolized important industries, and suppressed armed resistance. Strict police controls were brought to bear; the infamous Bandit Penalties and Punishments Decree resulted in the executions of more than 10,000 Chinese and aborigines between 1898 and 1920. Later the occupiers introduced compulsory Japanese education and forced cultural assimilation. Economic development began to focus on building the Japanese war machine and providing a launchpad for its forays to the south. In the later years of Japanese rule, Taiwan's residents were forced to become Japanese subjects and adopt Japanese names. They had to wear Japanese-style clothing, eat Japanese food, and observe Japanese religious rites. Japan drafted tens of thousands of young Taiwanese men into the Imperial Japanese Army, and many thousands were killed.

Retrocession

After the Japanese surrender in World War II, Taiwan was officially restored to Chinese rule, as agreed to by Chiang Kai-shek and the other Allied powers. At war's end, Taiwan's population consisted of 6.7 million Taiwanese, 285,000 Japanese civilians, and 158,000 Japanese military personnel; about 200,000 Japanese wanted to remain in Taiwan, but only 28,000 technical personnel were allowed to stay. Each departing Japanese was allowed to take two rucksacks worth of personal belongings and 1,000 yen. All property and real estate once owned by the Japanese was co-opted by the incoming Kuomintang (KMT) government.

In October 1945, 12,000 Chinese military personnel and 200 officials landed on the island. The joyous welcome was soon replaced by despair, as undisciplined troops and officials were more intent on plundering than governing. The Republic of China installed a brutal administrator, Chen Yi, who appointed only mainland officials. The Taiwanese soon came to feel they'd traded one colonial government for another.

Newly liberated Taiwan was suffering food shortages, skyrocketing unemployment, and rampant inflation. Its people became second-class citizens in their own land as corrupt KMT officials took what they could and did what they liked. Festering anger and resentment came to a head on February 27, 1947, when a street vendor in Taipei was beaten by officials for selling contraband cigarettes. In the ensuing melee, a bystander was accidentally shot dead. The following day a crowd gathered in front of government offices to protest. Sentries fired on the crowd and many were killed. Shops and factories closed in protest, and students went on strike. Governor Chen Yi declared martial law (which was to remain in place for 40 years) and unleashed a wave of oppression that became known as the White Terror. Within a few months the number of deaths ran into the thousands, with students, lawyers, and intellectuals the main targets. Between 18,000 and 28,000 people were killed, and in the ensuing decades thousands more were imprisoned. The incident that sparked the killings, which occurred on February 28, became known as "er er ba" or 2-2-8, and remained a taboo subject until the lifting of martial law in 1987. On February 28, 1997, the day was named a national holiday.

The Republic of China

Chiang Kai-shek, an ardent Nationalist, had earlier joined Sun Yat-sen in his revolutionary activities in China in a bid to overthrow the Qing dynasty. Sun became first president of the Republic of China in 1912. After Sun's death in Beijing in 1925, Chiang set about consolidating power, leading expeditions into northern China and shattering the control of powerful warlords. He then turned to fighting the Communists before joining Communist leader Mao Zedong to fight the Japanese during World War II—under United States pressure.

Following the war, the Communists and Nationalists took up where they left off and unleashed a bloody civil war that ended with Mao proclaiming the People's Republic of China in October 1949. Chiang, who a year earlier had had been elected president of the Republic of China by the National Assembly, was forced to flee to Taiwan with his army, where he set up a Nationalist base and vowed one day to retake the mainland—an ideal not officially abandoned until 1991.

At first the United States refused to support Chiang, seeing his KMT party as brutal and corrupt. But with the advent of the Korean War in 1950, Truman declared: "In these circumstances the occupation of Formosa by Communist forces would be a direct threat to the security of the Pacific area and to the United States forces performing their lawful and necessary functions in that area. Accordingly I have ordered the 7th Fleet to prevent any attack on Formosa." In January 1951, military aid was provided for the KMT, with the proviso that Chiang root out corruption within the KMT.

Millions of Chiang's supporters had followed him to the island, and Taiwan's new leader—who had an affection for the title "Generalissimo"—set about reforming the KMT and planting the seeds for Taiwan's phenomenal economic growth over the

> In the later years of Japanese rule, Taiwan's residents were forced to become Japanese subjects and adopt Japanese names.

Influence of Madame Chiang

Western-educated, shrewd in politics, and charming as could be, Soong Mayling was one of the 20th century's pivotal figures in the struggle between Nationalists and Communists for control of post imperial China. Married to Chinese Nationalist leader Chiang Kai-shek in 1927, Madame Chiang, as she became known, rose to prominence during World War II. In 1943 she became the first Chinese and the second woman to address a joint session of the U.S. Congress. Her influence in Washington during those years played a big part in the close relationship that exists today between the United States and Taiwan. After her husband's death in 1975, Madame Chiang moved to New York; she was left shattered by President Jimmy Carter's announcement in 1978 that the United States was breaking off diplomatic ties with Taiwan and establishing relations with China. She lived in seclusion in New York until her death at the age of 106 in October 2003.

ensuing decades. Chiang instituted liberal economic reforms, dismantling state monopolies and encouraging free enterprise and freeing up the entrepreneurial spirit of the island's people in the process. However, political freedom did not come as quickly and challenging the authority of the KMT was not an option.

The Republic of China's insistence that it was the representative of all of China led to the loss of its seat in the United Nations in 1971. In 1972, President Richard Nixon made a historic visit to mainland China, giving de facto recognition to the Communist regime. In December 1978, President Jimmy Carter ordered a shift of the United States Embassy from Taipei to Beijing. From the time Chiang took control of Taiwan in 1949 until his death on April 5, 1975, the population of Taiwan more than doubled to 16 million. The island had reached new heights of prosperity, and it enjoyed a standard of living well above that of most economies in the region, certainly far above that of the mainland.

But all this came at a price. Chiang was a ruthless dictator and the KMT monopolized power at national and provincial levels. Dissent was not countenanced. The government commonly imposed long jail terms and executed citizens without trial. Citizens were not allowed to leave the country without government permission (a law not repealed until the lifting of martial law in 1987), and the Taiwanese language and customs were suppressed, as were those of the Hakka and aboriginal populations.

Road to Democracy

Chiang's son Chiang Ching-kuo took over as head of the KMT and was elected president in 1978. He was a more personable figure than his father, willing to listen to the growing opposition forces within Taiwan. Eventually he gave tacit approval for opposition parties to operate openly. In 1979, in the southern city of Kaohsiung—a stronghold of antigovernment dissent—150,000 people rallied to protest against the government. Police swamped the demonstrators with tear gas, and the rally soon became a riot. When the dust settled, organizers were arrested and charged with sedition, and a number received long jail sentences. The Kaohsiung Incident, as it became known, proved to be a watershed in Taiwan's movement toward democracy.

Chiang Ching-kuo died in 1988. His vice president, Lee Teng-hui, a Taiwanese, succeeded him and legalized opposition parties, giving more credence to the increasingly popular pro-independence Democratic Progressive Party formed in 1986. He outmaneuvered KMT hardliners to cement his position as KMT chairman. Lee then turned his attention toward mainland China. He boldly announced his pro-independence feelings (shared by much of the population), and further inflamed the situation by lobbying for a seat at the United Nations and making a high-profile visit to the United States in 1995.

Taiwan's first democratic presidential elections were held the following year. China, in an unsubtle attempt to dissuade people from voting for pro-independence Lee, began lobbing missiles near the island as part of "military exercises." The bullying backfired; the Taiwanese, fed up with the mainland's belligerence, elected Lee with an overwhelming majority. Lee fired a final political salvo at the mainland when he declared that China and Taiwan were two separate states, going against his previous statements that the two were one country with two different governments.

The Future

After 55 years in power, the KMT lost the presidency in 2000. Pro-independence Democratic Progressive Party leader Chen Shui-bian was elected and then narrowly reelected in 2004. But the Kuomintang retook power in 2008 and Ma Ying-jeou immediately moved to improve relations with China. Travel, trade, and tourism continue to be strengthened, and, as this book went to press in late 2010, a free-trade agreement was being negotiated.

Mainland China sees Hong Kong's "one country, two systems" handover in 1997— which guarantees 50 years of autonomy for the territory—as a precursor to a similar political solution for Taiwan. But the mainland's often overt political interference in Hong Kong since the 1997 handover has convinced many Taiwanese that a similar agreement would not their best option. A solution to the "one China" problem remains far off. ∎

Supporters of Ma Ying-jeou celebrate after Ma won the presidential election in 2008.

The Land

Much of Taiwan's natural beauty is found in the Central Mountain Range that runs for 167 miles (270 km) along much of the island's length. Visitors are often surprised at the pervasive presence and majesty of these heavily forested mountains. More than 200 peaks rise above 10,000 feet (3,000 m), and the towering range is rarely out of view from anywhere on the island.

Taiwan's modest size accentuates the dominance of its mountains. The island is only 245 miles (394 km) long and 89.5 miles (144 km) across at its widest point, making it just 14,015 square miles (36,300 sq km) in total area, including offshore islands. It straddles the Tropic of Cancer and is the only good-size island in a swath of Pacific Ocean between the Philippines 221 miles (356 km) to the south and Japan's Okinawa island 370 miles (595 km) to the northeast.

The island's mountains are the result of a collision of monumental proportions. Taiwan sits about 80 miles (130 km) from the Chinese mainland on the westernmost edge of the Ring of Fire, the term given to the perimeter of the vast Pacific Ocean, where ocean tectonic plates are in constant conflict with continental tectonic plates. Twelve million years ago, the Philippine plate collided with the Eurasian landmass, buckling the Earth's crust. Land heaved upward, then folded and twisted to form Taiwan's chains of mountains.

This geologic stress deep inside the Earth builds volcanoes around the Ring of Fire, and the continuous friction and grinding between the plates causes frequent and violent earthquakes. The Ring of Fire is in fact the most volcanically active and earthquake-prone region in the world. Although Taiwan has no active volcanoes, it has its fair share of earthquakes. Many fault lines crisscross the island. As the Eurasian and Philippine plates continue to collide, enormous pressure builds. When released, this pressure rocks the Earth's surface.

> **Although Taiwan has no active volcanoes, it has its fair share of earthquakes. Many fault lines crisscross the island.**

Taiwan has had 19 earthquakes measuring more than 7 on the Richter scale since the beginning of the 20th century. A magnitude 7.1 earthquake killed more than 3,250 people in 1935, and a magnitude 6.8 quake on November 14, 1986, killed 15 and injured 44. In the early hours of September 21, 1999, the island was shaken awake by one of its most devastating quakes. It measured 7.3 on the Richter scale and was so violent it buckled buildings in Taipei, 93 miles (150 km) away from its epicenter near the resort area of Sun Moon Lake. It killed 2,415 people and injured 11,305. Around 30,000 buildings were destroyed and 25,000 damaged. The worst-hit area was the central west, where just about every city, town, and village suffered damage.

Regions

On the island's relatively isolated east coast, the eastern flank of the Coastal Mountain Range rises dramatically from the Pacific Ocean, climbing to over 5,000 feet

Qingshui Cliff on Taiwan's east coast typifies the island's spectacular coastal scenery.

(1,500 m), before dropping down to the rich alluvial plains and bucolic scenery of the East Rift Valley—a fault that cuts through the mountains for 100 miles (160 km) between the east coast cities of Hualien and Taitung.

On the western side of the valley, mountains again rise steeply to form the Central Mountain Range. On the range's southeastern flank, the highest of Yushan's jagged and exposed peaks reaches 12,966 feet (3,952 m). Erosion has carved spectacular gorges and left expansive valleys throughout these mountains.

To the west and northwest the mountains yield to foothills cut through by narrow valleys laced with rocky gullies and tablelands. From the base of the hills and tablelands, broad, fertile plains fed by convoluted rivers and streams stretch to the west coast. These rich alluvial plains account for most of Taiwan's agricultural output. Wide tidal flats, swamps, sandy spits, and lagoons characterize the island's west coast. These coastal areas are heavily industrialized and densely populated. Cities, towns, and factories merge to form an almost unbroken string of urban sprawl. Fringing coral reefs with an abundance of marine life line Taiwan's south coast, where coastal land areas are marked by uplifted coral outcroppings.

Hot Springs

While Taiwan has no active volcanoes, it does have plenty of bubbling geothermal activity in the form of hot springs. Around a hundred hot-springs resorts around the island give weary citizens the opportunity for revitalizing soaks. As rain falls in the

Fall leaves splash color along the Qijiawan River in Alishan, the heart of Taiwan's central mountains.

mountains, it seeps into porous sedimentary rock, picking up the rock's minerals along the way. Water seeping deeper beneath the Earth's surface is warmed by the Earth's heat. When it eventually encounters a large fault, the hot, pressurized water rises to the surface within the fault line until it bubbles into a hot-springs pool. Over time, sediment on the walls of the fault lines dissolves under pressure from the rising water, enlarging them. The escaping water also wears the surface opening of the fault lines wider. This creates a type of pipeline for water to run to the Earth's surface quickly and efficiently.

Flora & Fauna

With much of Taiwan industrialized, urbanized, or cultivated, the sparsely inhabited mountain regions are a sanctuary for the island's wildlife. Areas above 6,560 feet (2,000 m) are home to the Formosan black bear, the largest land mammal on the island, distinguished by a white V-shaped mark on it chest and long curved claws that help it dig for food. The slopes of Taiwan's highest mountain, Yushan—in Yushan National Park—harbor 28 species of mammals, 125 species of birds, and 17 species of reptiles, including possibly the largest selection of rare and endangered wildlife on the island. Although there is a good chance of spotting Formosan macaques on the forested slopes of Yushan, sightings of Formosan sambar (a type of deer), Chinese pangolin, and Formosan wild boar are less common. Rare and beautiful, the Formosan clouded leopard may have its last refuge in the Central Mountain Range south of the Tropic of Cancer. The lack of recent sightings leaves conservationists unsure whether the mammal still exists in the wild.

Taiwan's extensive network of estuaries, coastal marshlands, and sheltered areas along the coast and in the mountains make it an appealing stopover for migratory birds. About 480 local and migratory bird species have been identified on the island.

The island was once almost totally carpeted with forest. These days, forested areas take up about 7,336 square miles (19,000 sq km). Hardwoods, conifers, and bamboo are common in the hills and lower reaches of the mountains, giving way to temperate and subalpine coniferous forests at altitudes of between about 8,200 feet and 11,450 feet (2,500 m and 3,500 m). At higher altitudes forests are virgin. On gravelly slopes beyond the tree line—above 11,450 feet (3,500 m)—brushwood and herbaceous vegetation dominate. In the south of the island, varieties of palm and other tropical plant species are common. Kenting National Park, at the southern tip of the island, contains small pockets of protected primal tropical forest. ■

EXPERIENCE:
Blue Highway Cruises

Martial law imposed for 40 years by the Kuomintang was lifted in 1987. Even afterward, however, coastal sailing/cruising was long forbidden. Rules have now been eased, and Blue Highway cruises, offered by the government, have become popular. Landlubbers at last can to set off from Taipei to view their homeland from sea and river. The best launch-point for details and contact information is the Tourism Bureau website (www.taiwan.net.tw).

There are cruises on the **Danshui River** up to Danshui port, then out of Danshui's harbor to blue waters and the wetlands of Guandu Nature Park with the grand Yanmingshan massif as backdrop. On a **Kaohsiung-Liuqiu** tour, you slide past the rugged southwest coast and head to an old fishing port on Liuqiu island. Cruising is also popular in the **Penghu islands.**

A Year of Festivals

Taiwanese festivals, which have their origins in Taoism, Buddhism, and folk religion, are colorful affairs rich in costume, action, and symbolism. They are celebrated according to the lunar calendar, so dates vary from year to year. It is worth planning your visit to Taiwan to coincide with a festival; some of the major ones are outlined below.

During the Divine Palanquin Crossing the Fire, a Lantern Festival ritual, men dash into fierce flames.

Chinese New Year (January/February):
First day of the first moon (lunar month). Celebrations officially run to the 5th day, but traditional holidays run to the 15th. This is Taiwan's most important holiday, the time to get rid of the old and welcome the new, so debts are cleared, houses cleaned, and feuds ended. Many people take time off during the holiday to travel, and most shops and offices close. It is best to avoid Taiwan at this time, as transport and hotels are fully booked in advance. Dates: Feb. 3, 2011; Jan. 23, 2012; Feb. 10, 2013; Jan. 31, 2014.

Lantern Festival (February): Fifteenth day of the first lunar month. This is one of Taiwan's most colorful and popular festivals, celebrated to mark the end of Chinese New Year. Temples, homes, shops, and restaurants display traditional lanterns. Enormous lanterns displayed at Taipei City Hall, a carnival in Kaohsiung, and other large-scale official celebrations also mark the festivities. Dates: Feb. 17, 2011; Feb. 6, 2012; Feb. 24, 2013; Feb. 14, 2014.

Birthday of Mazu (April/May):
Twenty-third day of the third lunar month. The goddess of the sea is one of Taiwan's favorites. On her birthday, noisy celebrations erupt at the more than 500 temples devoted to Mazu. Expect fireworks, dragon dances,

and images paraded on sedan chairs. Dates: April 25, 2011; April 13, 2012; May 2, 2013; April 22, 2014.

Dragon Boat Festival (June, some years late May):
Fifth day of the fifth lunar month. This festival celebrates the life of Quyuan, a hero from ancient times. Dragon boats manned by rowers plow though waterways in a series of competitive events. Dates: June 6, 2011; June 23, 2012; June 12, 2013; June 2, 2014.

Ghost Month (July/August):
First to 29th day of seventh lunar month. The time of year when the gates of the netherworld are open and restless spirits wander the Earth. Devotees appease the ghosts through rituals such as offering food and burning wads of "hell money." People tend to be cautious during this period, so traveling and celebrations are curtailed. Visit a Taoist temple if you would like to see the appeasement rituals. Dates: July 31, 2011; Aug. 17, 2012; Aug. 7, 2013; July 27, 2014.

Mid-Autumn Festival (September/October):
Fifteenth day of the eighth lunar month. Also known as the Moon Festival, it is a celebration of the harvest moon. Disc-shaped moon cakes—symbolizing family unity—appear in bakeries. This is a time of family get-togethers, evening strolls, and moon-gazing. Dates: Sept. 12, 2011; Sept. 30, 2012; Sept. 19, 2013; Sept. 8, 2014.

Aboriginal Festivals

Taiwan's indigenous minorities celebrate their cultures in a number of annual festivals. Most are open to the public, but ask permission to join activities or to take photographs; be on the lookout for and avoid certain no-go areas.

Dahwu Flying Fish Festival (generally March/April):
The Dahwu (Yami) live on Orchid Island off Taiwan's southeast coast. For the long festival, they build traditional fishing canoes, launching them amid blessings and ceremonies.

Bunun Festival (April/May):
Held between the end of April and the start of May, this festival honors farming and hunting.

Ami Harvest Festival (July/August):
This is when Taiwan's largest indigenous group welcomes, feeds, and says farewell to the spirits in thanks for a bountiful harvest.

Saisiat Sacrifice to the Short Spirits (October/November):
Held biannually around the 15th day of the tenth lunar month. The Saisiat honor the spirits of a fabled neighboring tribe of short people who befriended the Saisiat tribe.

Puyuma Annual Festival (late December):
The festival, in which boys are set a number of trials, revolves around the passage from boyhood to manhood.

Know Your Gods

Deities are year-round objects of worship and devotion. Taipei's Xingtian Temple houses an icon of the important god of war, Guan Gong, a famous general, a superb tactician, and expert in controlling finances. He is now the patron saint for businessmen. An extremely busy minor deity is Old Man Under the Moon, the Chinese Cupid, with unusually effective icons at Taipei's Xiahai City God Temple and Longshan Temple. Devotees offer sacrifices, then take a red thread from his clothing and carry it, assuring their true love will enter through their lives. Busloads of young Japanese tourists regularly show up to pay tribute.

The Arts

With a few exceptions, to talk of Taiwanese heritage is to talk of Chinese cultural traditions in art and theater. In fact, Taiwan, with its stunning wealth of Chinese art and antiquities, is probably the best and most convenient place to enjoy these expressions of China's long history of religion, tradition, and art.

The National Palace Museum in Taipei houses the largest and most magnificent collection of Chinese art and antiquities in the world. Taipei's National Museum of History also holds a rich repository of Chinese artifacts. To see the development of contemporary Taiwanese artistic styles, visit the Taipei Fine Arts Museum and the Museum of Contemporary Art. Traditional performance art, such as Chinese

Elaborate costumes, heavy makeup, and stylized gestures characterize Chinese opera.

opera, is popular in Taiwan, especially the Beijing and homegrown versions. Other arts, such as cinema, have evolved into something uniquely Taiwanese.

Chinese Opera

To the Western ear, traditional Chinese opera can take a bit of getting used to. The voices of the performers are shrill; banging gongs and drums are loud and erratic; string instruments twang; and wind instruments screech. But amid the cacophony is a dazzling visual feast of elaborate and colorful costumes, symbolic makeup, absorbing pantomime, and exciting acrobatics and martial arts.

Chinese opera has its origins in the third century, when simple plays were performed for court entertainment.

Chinese opera has its origins in the third century, when simple plays were performed for court entertainment. The form went through transformations over the centuries, gradually gaining popularity. In 1790, an Anhui opera troupe performed before the Qing royal family at the Forbidden Palace. The troupe used themes and techniques co-opted from other opera styles, giving birth to Beijing opera. Performances evolved between 1840 and 1860, and Beijing opera took on its own identity, eventually becoming the most popular form of theater in China.

More than 350 forms of Chinese opera exist in mainland China. Most are named after the area in which they originated and remain obscure. One exception is Cantonese opera, which is popular in the southern province of Guangzhou and neighboring Hong Kong. Like the Cantonese themselves, this opera has a more rough-and-ready nature than the refined Beijing opera.

Taiwanese opera shares popularity with Beijing opera in Taiwan. Taiwan's version is generally performed outdoors on makeshift stages in marketplaces and at festivals. Performers use the Taiwanese dialect, stages are elaborately decorated, and facial makeup is restrained.

Chinese opera depicts action and emotions through widely understood symbols embodied in the actors' gestures, costumes, and makeup. Themes are mainly epic (such as good triumphing over evil), drawn from ancient legends familiar to the audience.

When the hands and body tremble, a character is angry. A curt flick of the sleeve indicates disgust. A hand thrown in the air and sleeves flicked back symbolize surprise. To portray embarrassment, the face hides behind a sleeve. A performer rubbing his or her hands together for a few moments is enacting worry. A chair on the stage is a chair, but when placed on a table it's a mountain, and when used as a seat after being placed on a table is a throne. Opening doors, climbing steps, riding in carriages, rowing boats, eating, and so on are all symbolized by stylized movements.

Color and design in both costumes and makeup indicate social status and temperament. Red makeup shows loyalty and honesty, while white means cunning. A student usually wears a blue gown, while an emperor is decked out in a "dragon," or imperial yellow, robe.

Performances can last for hours, and the audience doesn't always remain rapt. People chat among themselves, eat and drink, come and go, snooze, and generally cause a good deal of clatter. Attention reverts to the stage during popular and exciting scenes.

Bronzework

Some of the earliest examples of China's rich artistic heritage are found in its ancient works of bronze, mainly created between the Shang (ca 1766–1122 B.C.) and Han dynasties (206 B.C.–A.D. 220). Artists typically cast bronze into ritual and utilitarian vessels, musical instruments, and weapons. Many were inscribed with Chinese characters honoring the ancestors of royalty and highly placed officials.

The most famous piece of ancient Chinese bronzework is the "Mao Gong Ding" tripod vessel, on display at the National Palace Museum in Taipei. The inscription on the inside of the bowl has characters, the longest ancient Chinese bronzework inscription unearthed so far. Decorative elements changed with the times. Three-dimensional designs gradually replaced engraved lines and embossed patterns. Later advances included inlays using gold, silver, copper, and turquoise. Fierce-looking *tao tie*, or beast of gluttony, became the most prominent element during the Shang period. During the Western Zhou period (ca 1122–771 B.C.), animal motifs came into vogue. Later, chain-link patterns became popular. The Eastern Zhou period (ca 771–256 B.C.) introduced vertically interlocking designs.

Besides relics found in Taiwan's museums, superb bronzework can be spotted in many temples. These include large incense burners, doors, and, sometimes, dragon columns.

Calligraphy

Calligraphy is regarded as one of China's highest art forms. It was once a pursuit of the literati and privileged classes—the only ones who could afford the time to master it. Those seeking admission into the mandarin class needed to be skilled

---

EXPERIENCE: Watching Traditional Performance Arts in English

Much of Taiwan's traditional-style artistic expression, such as opera and puppet theater, is performed on temporary stages at temples and on closed-off streets during special celebrations. Travelers on short trips thus rarely have an opportunity to experience them. A special package created specifically for visitors is **Taipei EYE** (tel 2568-2677, www .taipeieye.com), a heritage-building stage venue in Taipei where each Friday and Saturday night shows ($) are staged, demonstrating opera, puppet theater, lion dancing, traditional music, and other local forms of performance art.

Actors come off stage in performing and nonperforming roles to mingle with the audience, and you can also visit makeup areas. During shows, a full English translation is provided.

A craftsman puts finishing touches on a boldly colorful and detailed lantern.

in calligraphy. The art demands careful planning and confident execution, qualities admired in administrators and executives.

Calligraphy developed as the Chinese written language became more sophisticated. It was both a means of communication and a form of artistic expression; calligraphers chose a style that would best express a passage of text, often adding imagination and beauty to practical government laws and decrees.

The earliest examples of calligraphy come from rubbings taken from bronzes and other metalwork. The National Palace Museum in Taipei has a treasure trove of calligraphic art, the earliest being Shang-period inscriptions. *Lu Chang*, an 11th-century biography of calligraphers of the Five Dynasties (907–960) and Northern Song periods (960–1127), describes the methods used to achieve the best calligraphic results:

"To display brushstroke power with good brushwork control; To possess sturdy simplicity with refinement of true talent; To possess delicacy of skill with vigor of execution; To exhibit originality, even to the point of eccentricity, without violating the *li* [the principles or essence] of things; In rendering space by leaving the silk or paper untouched, to be able nevertheless to convey nuances of tone."

The Song dynasty (960–1279) produced a number of noted calligraphers. The Yuan period (1279–1368) also had its share of masters. But it was during the Ming (1368–1644) and especially the Qing periods (1644–1911) that calligraphy truly flourished.

Ceramics

Pottery in China dates back to the Neolithic period, but it wasn't until the development of kiln firing during the Han dynasty that ceramics were widely produced.

Improved glazing techniques during the Jin period (265–420) and the Northern and Southern dynastic periods (386–589) allowed for more detail. Tang dynasty (616–906) potters took the craft a step further by developing tricolor glazes in green, yellow, and brown. These ceramics, most often horses, camels, and tomb guards, are among the most famous of Chinese porcelains. The Song dynasty saw the introduction of monochrome ceramics, which became renowned for their technical detail. The familiar underglaze cobalt-on-white painting was the signature of Ming dynasty ceramics. Initially, the quality was poor, but as techniques improved the pieces achieved remarkable delicacy. Five-color, wares of the mid-to-late Ming period were enlivened with colorful motifs.

Quality and production of ceramics reached their peaks in the early decades of the Qing dynasty, aided by a string of technical breakthroughs that allowed for more creativity in shaping and vibrancy in color. Vases became reticulated, oversize, and painted with detailed landscape scenes. Breakthrough *fencai*, or powdery color, enamel for decorating porcelain appeared during this period. Subsequent improvements in the technique resulted in highly detailed compositions of plants, humans, and animals. The Qing era also introduced "tea dust," an opaque glaze finely speckled with green, yellow, and brown.

The height of technical perfection was reached during the Qianlong period (r. 736–1795) of the Qing dynasty. Subsequently, the craft fell into decline as the popularity of porcelain waned and political upheaval took hold. By the time the second Sino-Japanese War erupted in 1937, all kilns were closed and most of the artisans who were left headed to the south of China to make a living.

China reestablished its pottery industry after World War II, and it slowly gained momentum. Leaps in technology over the past few decades mean that excellent porcelains can be had for affordable prices in Taiwan. The town of Yingge, just south of Taipei, is Taiwan's pottery capital. Hundreds of factories turn out porcelains and other ceramics.

> The town of Yingge, just south of Taipei, is Taiwan's pottery capital. Hundreds of factories turn out porcelains and other ceramics.

Cloisonné

Cloisonné is the technique of applying enamel in various colors to the surface of metal objects. It came to China from Persia in the eighth century but was then all but forgotten until around the 1200s. The Chinese, already masters of firing techniques for ceramics, glass, and metals, refined the technique, and by the mid-15th century cloisonné products had reached new levels of quality.

The cloisonné technique involves first soldering brass wire to the surface of a metal object to form a pattern or illustration. The craftsperson then fills in the patterns with colored enamel paste (made by crushing enamel pieces into powder and mixing them with water) and fires the piece in a kiln. After firing, the enamel surface is smoothed and the exposed brass wire and metal gilded. Popular cloisonné pieces include screens, tables and chairs, boxes, chopsticks, earrings, and smoking accessories.

Jade

Even though found in relative abundance, jade is highly prized in China for its soft sheen and subtle hues. Jade sculpture from the Qing dynasty to the present day is perhaps the most sumptuous form of Chinese art.

Ancients believed that wearing jade would increase longevity, allowing them to live as long as the gods. Many people in Taiwan today wear jade jewelry for good luck.

Some simple jadestone artifacts in China date back 12,000 years. Discoveries of small disks, likely used for personal decoration, date back more than 7,000 years, while finely crafted jade objects 4,000 years old point to the stone being used in ritual.

Rendering jade into more sophisticated forms began in the Shang dynasty, and the craft continued to be refined until the start of the first millennium before waning in popularity. The craft was revived during the Ming dynasty, and many skilled craftsmen emerged. Creative technique peaked during the Qing dynasty.

Fake jadeware is prevalent throughout Asia; to the untrained eye it is impossible to distinguish from the real thing. Get professional assistance if you plan to buy.

EXPERIENCE:
Shopping for Jade

The island's most popular spot for finding the perfect piece is **Taipei Holiday Jade Market** (*Renai & Jianguo Rds. under Jianguo Expressway, closed Mon.–Fri.*), right next door to the Taipei Flower Market.

There are 850 stalls, with jade pieces at every price point. Intense colors are desirable, with green the most popular. The more expensive stones have a darker green hue. Semitransparent to translucent jade is more valuable than opaque jade. Avoid jade with numerous cracks or other visible flaws.

Jade comes in three grades: A, B, and C. The finest and most expensive is A. If a seller can't guarantee Type A jade in writing or with a certificate issued by an authorized institute, most likely it isn't Type A jade.

Lacquerware

Lacquer comes from the sap of the lacquer tree (*Rhus verniciflua*). Its use dates to the fifth millennium B.C., when it was used on eating utensils and ritual objects.

Once exposed to air, sap from the lacquer tree turns brown and solidifies. It is then refined and either applied to objects ready for carving or embellishment, or molded into forms. After the base coat is applied to an object, many thinner coats are added to form layers. When the lacquer is dry, it is smoothed and polished to its trademark sheen. For producing forms, fabric or paper is saturated in lacquer and then jammed into a mold. Once the form has set, it is removed and more layers of lacquer are applied.

Lacquerware carving—which began during the Tang dynasty—reached its creative height during the Ming and Qing dynasties. This method involves coating a core of wood or tin with layers of lacquer. When the outer coat has dried, the artist carves decorations into the lacquer. The core is left untouched, serving as the background for the relief.

The use of lacquer was widespread by the first millennium A.D., when the substance coated musical instruments, eating and drinking utensils, weaponry, furniture, and funerary objects. During the Tang dynasty, artists found that iron filings soaked with vinegar would make lacquer sap turn black, instead of brown, as it dried. Adding cinnabar to the sap turned it red. These two colors became the standard for lacquerware.

Painting

Chinese painting is divided into two major schools. *Gongbi* is a meticulous style with strict rules of composition, close attention to detail, and very fine brushwork. *Xieyi* is a more relaxed freehand style that uses a richer brushwork and ink technique.

Although Chinese painting dates back to the Neolithic period with painted pottery, other media such as silk and paper hanging scrolls, fans, and albums appeared much later during the Tang dynasty. Traditionally, figures, landscapes, and flower-and-bird combinations have formed the subject matter of Chinese paintings. Landscapes are not restricted to a single focal point.

Most traditional Chinese painters have also been poets and calligraphers. To the Chinese, artists needed to incorporate "painting in poetry and poetry in painting." Inscriptions, seals, and poetic words helped to explain the painter's sentiments as well as add to a painting's beauty. Color in Chinese painting is added after the basic brushwork. Brushwork in shades of black ink creates the images, which are enriched by subtle, harmonious shades.

Taipei has a thriving arts scene, with many private galleries displaying and selling the work of Taiwanese artists.

Contemporary Art

The Japanese influenced Taiwanese art in the period immediately before World War II. The Japanese were keenly interested in European art, and Taiwanese artists traveling to Japan to study art picked up European techniques. The Taiwanese then applied these techniques to homegrown subjects and themes, and a new style of Taiwanese art began to evolve.

After the Japanese were defeated and the Chinese Nationalist government moved to the island, this style fell away in favor of traditional Chinese artistic themes and techniques. The Nationalists offered encouragement through competitions and other events.

Styles swung back toward the Western again in the late 1950s and '60s as a new generation of Taiwanese artists embraced abstract and pop art. During the 1970s, after the country lost its seat in the United Nations, artists (poets, novelists, and painters) began to explore Taiwan's identity through their work and started to emulate the work of artists during the Japanese occupation, with modern European style and technique.

After the lifting of martial law in 1987, artists began to reflect Taiwan's newfound sense of freedom and identity in their artwork. The Taipei Fine Arts Museum is the best place to go for an introduction to Taiwanese contemporary art. Taipei has a thriving arts scene, with many private galleries displaying and selling the work of Taiwanese artists.

Cinema

The early development of cinema in Taiwan coincided with the Japanese occupation (1895–1945), although early feature films and documentaries shot on the island were made without Taiwanese actors. The first true Taiwanese film using local funding and local actors was *Whose Fault Is It?* (1925). Nonetheless, the Japanese, as expected, tightly controlled the content and subject matter of this and subsequent Taiwanese movies.

The outbreak of the Sino-Japanese War in 1937 put the industry on hold. A number of Shanghai filmmakers followed Nationalist leader Chiang Kai-shek from the mainland at the end of China's civil war in 1949, forming the nucleus of a revived film industry on Taiwan in the 1950s. Government funding helped support the fledgling industry, but only for films in Mandarin. Early attempts at making films in the Taiwanese language were discouraged by the government, received no funding, and petered out.

As Taiwan began its surge toward modernization in the 1960s, the government's Central Motion Picture Corporation introduced a quasi-propaganda genre called "health realism." These films were an attempt to persuade citizens to come to terms with all the fast-paced changes in Taiwanese society by using traditional Chinese values to solve modern social problems.

Toward the end of the 1970s, a low budget sub-genre called "social realism" emerged, featuring the winning formula of sex, violence, and gang subculture. Repetitious themes and plots and over-the-top violence soon led to these films losing their appeal.

By the late 1970s, Taiwanese moviegoers were growing tired of all this moral malaise and escapism. Combined with the emergence of slicker films from Hong Kong and cheap pirated videos of Hong Kong and Western movies, Taiwanese cinema was in trouble and screaming for a change in direction.

The government began to support new, young directors. The groundbreaking film *In Our Time*—a social look at Taiwan since the takeover by the Nationalists in 1945—came out in 1982. It became the model for what was dubbed the New Cinema Movement. *The Sandwich Man* (1983) was directed by three young filmmakers, including one who later became Taiwan's most famous director, Hou Hsiao-hsien. The movie, which depicts U.S. economic aid to Taiwan during the darker days of the Cold War, is regarded as the

Taiwanese director Ang Lee has won Oscars for *Crouching Tiger, Hidden Dragon* and *Brokeback Mountain*.

foremost creative effort of the New Cinema Movement. It enjoyed both critical acclaim and commercial success. New Cinema films generally portray rural people in Taiwan coming to terms with changes in society. Techniques of deep focus, long takes, a nonlinear narrative, and a discontinuity of editing give New Cinema films a decidedly documentary feel.

While most New Cinema directors chose rural settings for their films, others, like Edward Yang, explored urban themes. His movies, including *Taipei Story* (1985), concern the social and personal problems that confront women, disaffected youth, the middle class, and the urban elite. The most famous of the New Cinema films is Hou Hsiao-hsien's *City of Sadness* (1989), which picked up a Golden Lion award at the Venice Film Festival. The film explores the relationship between the Taiwanese and the oppressive Nationalist troops during the early years of the Nationalist government's iron-fisted rule.

The brooding and dour imagery of New Cinema began to lose its appeal in the 1990s, and a second generation of creative filmmakers started to arrive on the scene. Movie themes tended to be more exploratory and less menacing. Tsai Ming-liang's *Vive L'Amour* took the 1994 Golden Lion in Venice. Ang Lee, who has achieved fame in the United States with his Hollywood productions *Crouching Tiger, Hidden Dragon; Brokeback Mountain;* and *Taking Woodstock*, first took on the sensitive subject of homosexuality in *The Wedding Banquet* (1993) and explored the Chinese obsession with food in *Eat Drink Man Woman* (1994).

With a few exceptions—and despite its acclaim—New Cinema never was popular with mainstream audiences. Taiwan's film market continues to be dominated by Hong Kong films, with their crowd-pleasing action, melodrama, slapstick comedy, and beloved stars. ■

Pop Music Scene

Slick numbers sung in Mandarin, collectively known as Mando pop, dominate Taiwan's popular music scene. Artists from Hong Kong, who now record their songs in both Cantonese (Canto pop) and Mandarin, share the limelight with local entertainers. As in most pop music, substance is eschewed for simple lyrics and catchy tunes. Popular themes revolve around the causes of teen angst: love, lost love, and unrequited love. Performers are invariably good-looking and wholesomely sexy. Music and video production is polished and appealing.

Like Hong Kong's Canto pop, Taiwanese Mando pop has a big following among Chinese communities in other countries in East and Southeast Asia, as well as among people in mainland China.

The diva of Mando pop was the much loved Teresa Deng, who enjoyed sweeping pan-Asian appeal. She sang lyrics in Mandarin, Taiwanese, Japanese, and English. Deng's untimely death in 1995, at the age of 43, was mourned throughout the region, and the late singer has since attained legendary status.

The Taiwan music scene also has some vibrant alternatives. Folk and rock tunes, with lyrics attuned to social problems, have earned a number of artists commercial success. Taiwan's alternative music scene has a big following, a somewhat unusual phenomenon in an Asian music scene largely dominated by saccharin banality. It kicked off around 1994 and has grown into a thriving industry. Alternative bands crank it out at crowded pubs and clubs all over Taipei, mostly on weekend nights.

Island capital and nexus of Taiwan's remarkable transformation into a modern, democratic, and vibrant society in just a few decades

Taipei

A uniformed guard lowers the flag in front of Chiang Kai-shek Memorial Hall.

Taipei

As recently as the 1960s, Taipei was little more than a sleepy backwater with few paved roads and a handful of cars. But from the 1970s on, the city began to grow in the unbridled fashion that characterized many Asian cities during the period. Taipei is now a bustling city, home to about three million people.

In 1709 three farmers from Fujian Province established a farm on the banks of the Danshui River in what is now Taipei. More immigrants followed, settling around the Danshui. One settlement became known as Manka, today's Wanhua and the most historic area in the city.

Because of their location on the bustling Danshui River, Manka and the nearby area of Dadaocheng emerged as the most important areas of the city. In 1875 prominent Qing dynasty official Shen Bao-zhen applied to establish the prefecture of Taipei in what is the present-day Zhongzheng District. Today Taipei is the island's largest city and its administrative, economic, and cultural center.

In the four-plus decades since the early 1970s, Taipei has developed the same problems as many Asian cities, where economic growth has taken priority over the environment and

quality of life. But in the 1990s, city fathers took stock. Horrendous traffic jams led to the construction of an extensive mass rapid transit system, the MRT, considered the best in Asia.

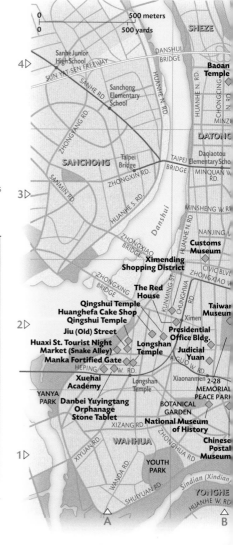

NOT TO BE MISSED:

The classical majesty of the Chiang Kai-shek Memorial **60–61**

Old-style goods shopping on heritage Dihua Street **65**

Snacking adventures at the Shilin Night Market **67**

A spin through Nanmen Market **67**

Joining the devotee throngs at Longshan Temple **68–71**

Chinese artistic genius on display at the National Palace Museum **80–85**

Seeing authentic puppetry at Lin Liu-hsin Puppet Theatre Museum **89**

Bus lanes along widened city streets encouraged people to leave cars at home, and the city's notorious taxi drivers were made to clean up their act—and their cabs. New parks gave the city's population some breathing space.

Taipei's streets are laid out in grid fashion and signposted in English as well as Chinese. But confusion can arise. Streets are divided into sections according to compass direction; alleys are numbered and named according to the major streets they branch off of. Major north–south arteries are also numbered in English as boulevards, east–west arteries as avenues. A typical address, for example, could read No. 24, Lane 18, Zhongshan North Road, Section 2. When heading out have someone write your destination in Chinese. Your hotel will supply you with a card for the hotel written in Chinese so you can find your way back.

Taipei locals are friendly to visitors, but most do not speak English. For English-language directions, check with a hotel or police station. ■

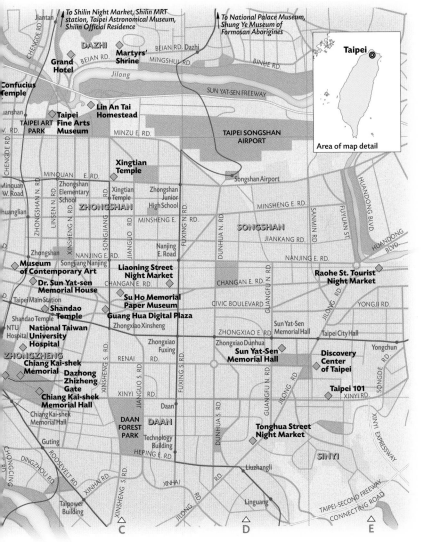

2-28 Memorial Peace Park & Around

In 1996, the name of Taipei New Park was changed to 2-28 Memorial Peace Park in honor of the thousands of Taiwanese who were killed in an uprising against Chinese Nationalist misrule that began on February 28, 1947 (see sidebar p. 59). The park's grounds are interesting for their memorial, museums, and some quirky contents. The park is lively in the morning, when residents take walks and do *tai ji quan* exercises.

Floors 1 through 13 of the Shin Kong Life Tower hold Taipei's largest of its three Mitsukoshi department stores.

Just inside the park's east gate is the **2-28 Memorial,** a rather ungainly postmodernist structure constructed of huge concrete cubes supporting a steel spire. Beyond the structure, the **2-28 Memorial Museum** informs visitors about some of the unsavory aspects of the Kuomintang's early years in power, illustrating them with unsettling photographs and artifacts. The park also houses an open-air theater, along with oddities that include old cannon, two European-built steam locomotives dating back to the late 19th century, and memorial archways.

At the northern end of the park is the **National Taiwan Museum.** Built in 1915 in an eye-catching Greek Revival style, the museum houses exhibits on the island's natural history and a collection of aboriginal artifacts.

The **Presidential Office Building** *(122 Chongqing Rd., Sec. 1, www .president.gov.tw)* is just to the west of the park at the end of wide Ketagalan Boulevard. The Japanese constructed the bold redbrick building, finished in 1919, in the neo-Renaissance style they favored then. Its central tower was long the tallest structure in Taipei. In fact,

The White Terror

On February 27, 1947, the beating and arrest of a vendor for illegally peddling cigarettes ignited large-scale public protests the next day against government repression and corruption that had existed since the Japanese surrendered in 1945. Chinese leader Chiang Kai-shek sent thousands of troops from the mainland to quell the protests. The army showed no mercy, rounding up and executing lawyers, academics, doctors, students, and local leaders. Reports of soldiers knocking on doors and shooting the person who answered were common. Between 18,000 and 28,000 people were murdered and thousands more imprisoned over the next decade in what has become known as the White Terror (white being the color of death for the Chinese). Some remained in prison until the 1980s. It took a new government in 1996 to finally acknowledge these horrors and memorialize those who died, at 2-28 Memorial Peace Park.

in order to keep an eye on things, the Japanese ordered that no building in the city could be higher than the tower.

Next door is the **Judicial Yuan building** (124 Chongqing Rd., Sec. 1). Built in 1934, its design—again, highlighted by a broad brick facade, archway entrance, central tower, and carved ornaments— almost mirrors the design of the Presidential Office Building.

Back in front of the National Taiwan Museum, head north along Guanqian Road toward Taipei Main Station and the 51-story, 804-foot (245 m) **Shin Kong Life Tower** (66 Zhongxiao West Rd., Sec. 1, tel 2389-5858). Once Taipei's tallest building (supplanted by Taipei 101; see p. 87), it houses an upscale department store. From the 46th-floor viewing deck you get sweeping views of the city and mountains beyond.

Cross Zhongxiao West Road to Taipei Main Station and the **Taipei City Mall,** a collection of retail outlets that runs for 650 yards (600 m) to Zhongshan MRT station on the Danshui line, linking

INSIDER TIP:

Shin Kong Life Tower is a favorite gathering spot. On weekends there are concerts and other shows on the large streetside plaza.

—RICK CHARETTE
National Geographic contributor

the commercial areas around Taipei Main Station and Nanjing West Road. While the shops sell nothing out of the ordinary—computers, clothing, souvenirs, books, and magazines—the place is certainly remarkable for its sheer length.

When you emerge from the mall at Zhongshan MRT station, head to the **Museum of Contemporary Art** (39 Changan West Rd., tel 02/2552-3720, www.mocataipei .org.tw), in part of another architectural legacy of Japanese occupation. This former city hall has been caringly renovated. Inside the building, numerous galleries house temporary exhibits. ∎

2-28 Memorial Peace Park
- 56 B2
- MRT: National Taiwan University Hospital station

National Taiwan Museum
- 56 B2
- 2 Xiangyang Rd.
- 02/2382-2699
- $
- MRT: National Taiwan University Hospital station

www.ntm.gov.tw

Chiang Kai-shek Memorial

The massive Chiang Kai-shek Memorial Hall and surrounding park were built to memorialize the Nationalist leader and longtime president of the Republic of China. Work on the 250-foot (76 m) marble-clad edifice began in 1977, two years after the Generalissimo (as he liked to be called) died. It opened to the public in 1980, on the fifth anniversary of his demise. The massive monument was, in its early years, a place of pilgrimage for many Taiwanese.

The graceful National Concert Hall hosts hundreds of cultural performances every year.

These days, as Chiang's aura fades, the surrounding gardens, pavilions, and expansive plaza are still crowded, but more often with people enjoying the sense of open space in a busy city, rather than with visitors paying their respects to the late leader.

Although the memorial may have lost most of its relevance, you cannot help being impressed by its size and grand architectural style. The striking **Memorial Hall** is clad in gleaming white marble, with an octagonal step-pitched twin-eave roof of brilliant blue-glazed tiles topped with a golden dome. It sits amid 62 acres (25 ha) of immaculately tended gardens, hedges, carp ponds, and pavilions. Whitewashed walls topped with blue tiles form a long colonnade that wraps around the complex. Windows on the outer wall are shaped in Chinese motifs, such as plum flowers and open books.

The main entrance to the park is marked by the magnificent 98-foot (30 m) five-arched Ming-dynasty-style **Dazhong Zhizheng Gate** (Gate of Great Centrality and Perfect Uprightness), on Zhongshan South Road. The marble facade and 11 roofs of blue-glazed tiles atop the gate reflect those of the main hall. The huge gate faces southwest toward the Kunlun Mountains in China, symbolizing Chiang's dream of one day retaking the mainland.

Beyond the gate, the complex opens to a vast paved plaza that runs 220 yards (200 m) to the Memorial Hall. Flanking the plaza are the National Theater on the right and the National Concert Hall at left. These are the buildings that make up the National Chiang

Kai-shek Cultural Center.

The plaza narrows to become the **Path of Reverence,** flanked by beds of blazing red flowers, and continues on to the marble steps of the Memorial Hall. To gain entrance, you climb the steps—guarded by auspicious white stone lions—to a towering 46-foot (16 m) archway and mighty bronze doors, beyond which a bronze seated statue of Chiang gazes proudly over the plaza. Inscriptions on the wall behind and to the left and right of the statue are Chiang's descriptions of Sun Yat-sen's "Three Principles of the People" philosophy of ethics, democracy, and science. From there you descend into the bowels of the hall on one of two staircases, each with 89 steps, representing the age of Chiang when he died.

Inside the lower level are an audiovisual room, library, lecture hall, study center, and two small art galleries—the **Chiang Kai-shek Art Gallery** and the **Hua En Art Gallery**—which hold temporary exhibitions of local and international artists.

Much of the area is given over to the enormous 21,500-square-foot (2,000 sq m) **Exhibition Hall,** which traces Chiang's life and achievements through documents, photographs, paintings, and memorabilia. The highlights of the exhibition are two gleaming black bulletproof limousines once used by the late president. The **Chiang Kai-shek Memorial Office** contains the original 1950s furnishings from the Generalissimo's office, including his pens, writing brushes, desk, and cabinets. After visiting the memorial, take some time to stroll around the park and its beautifully tended gardens.

National Chiang Kai-shek Cultural Center

Contrasting with the solemnity of the memorial hall are the two almost identical buildings—the **National Theater** and the **National Concert Hall**—that face each other across the plaza.

These exquisite buildings, both important centers for the performing arts in Taiwan, are rendered in grand Chinese

INSIDER TIP:

For snacks and people-watching, go to the National Concert Hall's Spring Water Pavilion Culture Teahouse.

—DAISANN McLANE
National Geographic Traveler
magazine columnist

palace style. Positioned on white concrete bases, their thick red columns support bright multicolored eaves and furled bright yellow glazed-tile roofs.

More than 800 performances—from opera to modern dance—are held in these two world-class performing-arts venues annually. If you'd like to attend, you can purchase tickets for the day's show at the reception desk on the first floor of the National Theater. ∎

Chiang Kai-shek Memorial
- 56 B2
- 21 Zhongshan South Rd.
- 02/2343-1100
- MRT: Chiang Kai-shek Memorial Hall station

www.cksmh.gov.tw

National Chiang Kai-shek Cultural Center
- 56 B2
- 21 Zhongshan South Rd.
- 02/3393-9888
- MRT: Chiang Kai-shek Memorial Hall station

www.ntch.edu.tw

National Museum of History & Botanical Garden

Although it is overshadowed by the larger National Palace Museum (see pp. 80–85), the National Museum of History is still an important repository of historical Chinese artifacts. The adjacent Botanical Garden makes for a pleasant amble after visiting the museum.

Edged by a lotus pond and paths, the National Museum of History houses world-class antiquities.

National Museum of History

🗺 56 B1
✉ 49 Nanhai Rd.
☎ 02/2361-0270
🕐 Closed Mon.
🚇 MRT: Chiang Kai-shek Memorial Hall station

www.nmh.gov.tw

Most of the museum's 10,000 artifacts were brought in from mainland China or donated by private organizations, adding up to an impressive collection of bronzes, jades, pottery, porcelain, lacquerware, textiles, inscriptions, coins, carvings, paintings, and calligraphy—most without captions in English. The museum offers tours in Mandarin/English at 3 p.m. daily. Free wireless guide facilities are also available.

Just inside the entrance is a corridor running the width of the museum with a collection of stone stelae and carvings of Buddhist iconography from early Chinese dynasties. These include a magnificent four-sided thousand-Buddha column from the Northern Qi dynasty (550–577) and, the centerpiece of the collection, a 5-foot-high (1.5 m) Buddha tower from the Northern Wei dynasty (386–534). This complex pagoda-style stone carving incorporates depictions of hundreds of monks and nuns in acts of devotion.

The elevator to the **second floor** opens to a corridor of traditional Chinese landscape paintings and calligraphy. At the end of the corridor is a gallery housing temporary exhibitions. The remaining galleries on the floor are given over to a large collection of Tang dynasty (618–907) tricolor ceramics that typify the elegance of the period.

Objects in the first part of the collection include utilitarian items, such as tripod jars, incense burners, and glazed ornamental figures in the shape of oxen, hens, and other symbolic animals. You can also see horses and riders involved in the imperial pursuit of polo, a sport that was introduced from Persia during the Tang dynasty. The collection then moves on to more glazed figures of horses, this time without their mounts. These expressive figures, which were used as funerary objects, are magnificently crafted. After horses come camels, also funerary objects. All these saddled animals have similar expressions, heads held high and mouths agape. The final phase of the collection presents figurines from the Tang dynasty: ladies of the imperial court, military and civil officers, and fierce-looking chimeras (celestial guardians).

On the **third floor** is the "General History of Chinese Cultural Artifacts" exhibition, a superb display of relics from various dynasties. Among the treasures are ceramic pillows and gold Buddha images.

The **fourth-floor gallery** has displays of finely woven badges worn during the Qing dynasty (1644–1911) by military and civil officers to indicate rank. The floor also has an exhibition of traditional drinking vessels, including tiny wine cups. Along a corridor off the gallery is a traditional teahouse with timber floors,

wooden tables and chairs, and views of the Botanical Garden.

Botanical Garden

Next to the National Museum of History, 20 acres (8 ha) are divided into 17 sections of plant families, interlaced with shady paths, boardwalks, and ponds. The major attraction is the **Lotus Pond,** where, in summer, water lilies burst into brilliant red, white, and yellow. The prettiest entrance to the Botanical Garden is on Heping West Road. A small plaza inside has a map. Head along the path on the right to reach the Lotus Pond.

Other park highlights include a **Herbarium** (take the path straight ahead from the entrance plaza); a **Palm Garden** alongside the path to the Lotus Pond; and a **Fern Garden** tucked into the northwestern corner of the gardens, where a boardwalk takes visitors through a *Jurassic Park*–like display of thick green foliage. ■

Botanical Garden

- ▲ 56 B1
- ✉ 53 Nanhai Rd.
- ☎ 02/2303-9978
- 🚇 MRT: Chiang Kai-shek Memorial station

http://tpbg.tfri .gov.tw

Consider a Guided Tour

There's no better way to get to get below the surface than via a tour with a knowledgeable local who can deliver facts and insights in English. Taipei's **Community Services Center** (tel 02/2836-8134, www .community.com.tw) offers regularly scheduled cultural and sightseeing tours to some of the most interesting spots in Taipei and the surrounding region. Most tours last four to five hours, include transportation if outside the city, involve a fair amount of walking, and may well include lunch too. Outings generally cost NT$1,000 to NT$1,500 (U.S.$31 to U.S.$47). Your guide will be an expatriate or fluent local.

Chinese Traditional Medicine

Chinese traditional medicine is rooted in the ancient concept of yin and yang, or the balance of contrasting elements in nature, and in the belief in qi, or vital energy. Chinese traditional doctors attempt to manipulate the balance using herbs, minerals, animal parts, acupuncture, massage, and other methods. By attempting to establish harmony among the organs and systems, physicians believe they can keep their patients in good health.

Certain streets in Taipei are lined with shops dispensing traditional medicines. Their exotic ingredients, tucked in row after row of drawers and displayed in jars on shelves, often resemble a small museum of natural history rather than a dispensary. Among the curiosities are cinnabar and amber to relax the nerves; peach pits and safflower to improve circulation; and ginseng to strengthen the heart. Snakes and lizards are often seen floating in large jars.

Throughout much of China's turbulent history, acupuncture and herbs were the primary health treatments. By the 20th century,

A traditional-medicine shop may contain hundreds of ingredients, ready to be measured and mixed.

EXPERIENCE:
Shopping on Dihua Street

Dihua Street, in Taipei's Datong District, is perhaps the single most important heritage street on the island. It is very much a living museum. Lined with shophouses, many a century or more old, this has been the island's most important hub for traditional dried foods, herbs, medicines, and all sorts of other goods since the 1860s. The street is always busy with local shoppers, but the best time for the overseas traveler to visit is in the two weeks before Chinese New Year (usually late Jan. or early Feb.), when the street is closed to vehicles, filled with kiosks, and festooned with decorative lights, with vendors sticking around until midnight. Crowds stream through, hawkers use loudspeakers to be heard above the din, and samples are liberally doled out. Many New Year's comestibles are friendly to the Western palate; some, such as congealed pig's blood, will make you a true cultural adventurer. The easiest way to get here is from Zhongshan MRT station; you then walk west along Minsheng West Road for 10–15 minutes.

Chinese doctors had mapped out 350 precise acupuncture points, grouped into systems of channels that were said to conduct vital energy, or qi, through the body. Modern practitioners insert stainless-steel needles into these points, twisting and moving the needles to achieve the desired effect. Scientists believe acupuncture may release endorphins, which block pain and cause mild euphoria.

More than 2,000 traditional remedies have been documented in Chinese literature, although only about 150 are commonly used these days. The Taiwanese have a high regard for traditional medicine, and millions swear by its efficacy, although most will visit both traditional practitioners and doctors trained in Western medicine to treat their health problems. Western visitors should exercise extreme caution when it comes to trying traditional medicines; some herbal mixtures can be quite powerful or even dangerous.

The use of mixtures to treat ailments is the bedrock of Chinese traditional herbal prescriptions. On a visit to the doctor, the patient will answer questions about his or her state of health. After the diagnosis, and frequently after a traditional physical examination, the doctor will generally select, measure, and cut about four or five ingredients. The patient then takes the ingredients home to boil them with water into a thick brew. Adherents believe such curative blends can reduce fevers, cure diarrhea, eliminate headache, and in general promote good health.

Massage is another common traditional treatment. By restoring qi, or unblocking clogged-up qi channels, it is supposed to cure problems such as stiffness, back pain, fever, or painful joints. The massage can be strenuous, often breaking blood vessels and leading to bruises, which are said to appear where the imbalances existed.

Related to this is the practice of using glass or bamboo suction cups, thought to draw out evil energy and cure arthritis. The cups are heated with a wad of flaming, alcohol-soaked cotton to create a vacuum, and then placed on a vital point, where the flesh swells into the cup. Like massage, it also leaves marks: It is common to see round circular bruises on the backs and legs of sunbathers in Taiwan.

Chinese traditional medicine is gaining popularity in the West. While adherents believe it shows some promise in treating chronic diseases, serious testing still needs to be done to prove its safety and efficacy.

Taipei's Night Markets

The city has a profusion of lively nighttime markets. Some serve up a familiar menu of snack foods, clothes, and knickknacks, while others offer more exotic fare, from fortune- tellers to snake dinners. Markets usually open about 6 p.m. and close around midnight.

From snacks to laptops, Taipei's after-dark markets, such as this one in Wanhua, teem with goods.

Taipei's Night Markets

🅼 56–57

Guang Hua Digital Plaza Market

Taiwan is the world's biggest manufacturer of notebook computers, and it seems most of them are for sale in and around Guang Hua Digital Plaza. Hundreds of retailers sell laptop, notebook, and desktop computers, software and peripherals, digital cameras, mobile phones, and other electronic goods. Many of the polite shop attendants speak a little English, and there is no hard sell. It is perfectly acceptable to go from retailer to retailer comparing prices. Take the MRT to Zhongxiao-Xinsheng station.

Huaxi Street Tourist Night Market

The market—more famously known as **Snake Alley**—has been sanitized by the city fathers. Once notorious for its snake restaurants, brothels, shady fortune-tellers, and assorted tricksters, the market has been transformed from a city embarrassment to a spot promoted by tourism authorities. A few snake restaurants still remain in this covered market street, and they are the main attraction for many visitors, who enjoy the entertaining, but sometimes cruel, antics of the snake handlers in front of these restaurants. Besides the snake restaurants, there are more conventional Chinese eateries that offer pancake soup, salty rice pudding, freshwater turtle, and other seafood. You'll also find shops selling luggage, books, clothes, fruit, and souvenirs. To reach the market, take the MRT to Longshan Temple station.

Raohe Street Tourist Night Market

This market (www.raohe.com.tw), in the area northeast of Bade Road, Section 4, and Fuyuan Street, is introduced by an archway and strings of hanging lamps. About 140 street vendors and 400 storefront stalls line the 1,970 feet (600 m) of narrow Raohe

Street. Traditional Chinese opera and other performances are frequently held at the market. To get there, go to Taipei City Hall MRT station and transfer to the Blue 7 or Blue 12 bus to Raohe Street.

Shilin Night Market

Shilin, home to the largest night market in Taipei, and is a great place to try delicious Taiwanese snack foods. The new multilevel structure that houses the sprawling market has 380 vendors offering plenty of mouthwatering fare (try the oyster omelets). The atmosphere is enlivened with lots of hubbub, blinking neon lights, and workers walking around with signs that advertise specials at their food stalls.

Crowds throng the aisles and streets until late at night. Kids (and adults) shoot pellet guns at balloons to win prizes and fortune-tellers do brisk business. Vendors sell the usual market goods: cheap clothing, shoes, CDs, bags, and toys. Take the MRT to Jiantan station; the market lies just northwest, near Yangming Theater on Wenlin Road.

Tonghua Street Night Market

West of Jilong Road between Xinyi Road, Section 4, and Heping East Road, Section 2, this is one of Taipei's smaller night markets. But what it lacks in size it makes up for in bustle. The market connects with the Linjiang Street Night Market, which offers snacks ranging from sausages and stuffed buns to steamed rice cakes. ∎

EXPERIENCE: Day Markets Beckon, Too

Nanmen Market, located in the lower floors of a multistory building at 8 Roosevelt Road, Section 1 *(tel 02/2321-8069)*, is Taipei's biggest and best known day market. Open daily 7 a.m. to 8 p.m., it has been operating for over a century. Nanmen Market started up in the Japanese colonial era as a vegetable distribution center.

House moms stream through at all hours for the day's foods, and office workers pop in for hot breakfasts, lunches, and take-home dinners. An outing here means exposure to the quintessential Chinese day-market shopping experience. Goods are brought in from all around Taiwan, and the market is also a key Taipei source for Jiangzhe (China's Jiangsu and Zhejiang Provinces) produce. Before Chinese New Year the place really gets hopping, for here are found such popular holiday foods as sausages, preserved hams, and steamed mincemeat-stuffed buns. **Yi-chang Yufang** (Yi-chang's Imperial Workshop), declared top cooked-food vendor at the 2008 Taipei Traditional Market Festival, specializes in Jiangzhe cuisine, with over 100 choices. Beside this is **Junwenshan Meishi Fang** (Junwenshan Fine Foods Workshop), known for the freshest handmade egg dumplings—an auspicious food. The **Shanghai Wanyouqian** (Shanghai All Things Offered) shop sells classic Jinhua ham, smoked over sugarcane skins eight full months. The beancurd sausage is also popular. **Dalian Shipin** (Dalian Foods) is known for its classic "gold and silver ham," another auspicious food: fatty pork stuffed within thinly sliced, steamed pork liver.

Longshan Temple

Longshan (Dragon Mountain) Temple, one of Taiwan's oldest, has survived its share of disasters. Built in 1738, the temple was leveled by an earthquake in 1815, rebuilt, and damaged by a typhoon in 1867. It was fully reconstructed between 1919 and 1924, only to fall victim to a wayward Allied bomb in 1945, which destroyed its main hall but left the statue of the temple's main deity, Guanyin, the goddess of mercy, undamaged. The temple was restored again in 1957.

Dozens of deities are worshiped to varying degrees at Longshan Temple.

Immigrants from three counties in China's Fujian Province who moved in the 18th century to Manka (now Wanhua), Taipei's oldest district, built the temple. The new arrivals modeled and named it after the sacred Dragon Mountain Temple, where they had previously worshiped in China. It was originally intended to be a Buddhist temple, but has since incorporated many Taoist deities and other temple elements into its elaborate design.

The temple is famous for the exquisite detail of its stone sculptures, woodcarvings, and bronzework. Its guardians employed one of Fujian's finest temple architects and builders, Wang Yi-xun, to oversee its reconstruction in 1919. These days only Taiwan's most skilled temple craftsmen are employed to undertake maintenance and restoration work.

The 12 main support columns of the main hall, with their sculptures of dragons hewn from stone, exemplify the rich design. A more subtle example, at least to the Western eye, are the inscriptions on the temple walls and pillars, exceptional for both their abundance and calligraphic sophistication. People still come to Longshan simply to take rubbings of these beautiful inscriptions.

The temple consists of three halls—front, middle, and rear—separated by courtyards. The main gates of the temple are open only during festivals or for the visits of important personages. Temple lore holds that you should enter through the small gate to the right of the main gate and exit through the small gate to the left. The stone-framed window to the left of the main entrance is carved with scenes from the classic Chinese novel *Romance of the*

Three Kingdoms. To the right of the entrance is an octagonal bamboo window on which is carved the Chinese characters for "firecrackers announce that all is well."

In the **courtyard** in front of the main hall, people take turns standing under a huge yellow lantern, holding joss sticks and bowing in prayer.

The small **front hall** is notable for its patterned bas-relief granite walls, inscribed pillars, and pair of dragon columns cast in bronze, the only two such columns in Taiwan. To get to the **first courtyard** you can go through one of the passageways on either side of the front hall. The eastern one leads

Longshan Temple

🏛 56 A2
✉ 211 Guangzhou St.
☎ 02/2302-5162
🚇 MRT: Longshan Temple station

Good Vibrations in Wanhua District

The power and popularity of a Chinese temple come, first and foremost, from the ability of the godly images housed within to answer the specific requests of visiting devotees. The most powerful temples also have miraculous stories circulating about them that "prove" the potency and capabilities of the resident immortals. The aura of Wanhua's Longshan Temple and its ability to protect residents in the district—and much farther afield—are known to all locals.

The temple was originally built, legend has it, after a local merchant hung his incense pouch from Longshan Temple in Fujian Province on a tree while he was relieving himself. The pouch began shining brightly, and locals understood there was a miracle involved.

Reports state that when the temple in Wanhua and the surrounding area were devastated in an 1815 earthquake, the guardian deity, goddess of mercy Guanyin, sat serene and safe within. In

1884, when French marines stood ready to attack Taipei (see p. 34), the local militia mounted a successful defense. Their banners carried an image of Longshan Temple, seat of the area's religious, judicial, social, and commercial affairs.

During World War II, Allied bombers hit the temple (the Japanese commonly billeted troops and stored armaments in such places), and though bombs and fire razed the main hall and melted the iron railings surrounding her, Guanyin was singed and nothing more.

The most memorable way to see Longshan Temple is with an English-speaking guide. Quality tours are regularly conducted by a number of tour outfits that have been vetted by the Taiwan Tourism Bureau (www.taiwantourbus.com .tw). Taipei's Community Services Center (www.community.com.tw), run by Westerners, occasionally offers excellent history and culture tours to Wanhua District and Longshan Temple.

to the **bell tower;** the one on the west side takes you through the **drum tower.**

Guanyin is enshrined in the center of the **main hall** amid a riot of ornate decoration. The goddess of mercy is attended by the bodhisattvas Manjursi to her left and Samantabhadra to the right, while images of 18 lesser attendants cluster around her.

Taiwanese merchants built the **rear hall** at the end of the 18th century as the area grew in stature as a trading port. They enshrined the popular

West Side Room

Drum Tower

Exit (Tiger)

Front Hall

Entrance (Dragon)

Taoist deity of the sea, Mazu—(see sidebar p. 169)— here. The walls are embellished with carvings and pillars. Two of the pillars here are unusual in that their carvings depict human figures.

The temple is almost always bustling with worshipers and tourists; the best time to visit is in the early evening when it is at its busiest and most colorful. ■

Rear Hall

Main Hall

East Side Room

Bell Tower

Longshan Temple

Built in 1738, often hailed as Taiwan's Forbidden City, the temple is the best preserved of its kind in Taiwan. What sets it apart is the exquisite detail of its stone sculptures, woodcarvings, and bronzework. The main hall is for worship of the host deity, Guanyin, the Buddhist goddess of mercy; the rear hall is dedicated to Mazu, the Taoist goddess of the sea. Throughout you'll find altars devoted to a panoply of lesser deities from various religions.

A Walk Around Wanhua District

The first settlement in Taipei city, Wanhua by the early 19th century had become Taiwan's third largest city, thanks to booming trade with the mainland. Its decline began with the settlement of the Danshui River downstream. Many remnants of Wanhua's colorful past still remain, and strolling the busy streets brings its share of entertainment. Evenings are the best time for a walk: The temples and alleys come to life after dark.

The streets around Longshan Temple make up part of Taipei's oldest district.

Start at **Qingshui Temple ❶** (81 Kangding Rd., tel 02/2371-1517), which honors Song dynasty Taoist monk Chen Chao-ying, revered for providing medical care to the poor. Dragons, other mythical creatures, and fine patterned carvings enliven its roof and walls.

Exit the temple from the front and go straight, or west, down Guiyang Street, Section 2, for about 300 yards (270 m). Cross Xiyuan Road and, after 10 more yards (10 m), on your left you'll spot **Qingshan Temple ❷** (218 Guiyang St., Sec. 2), wedged between two buildings. The narrow temple has magnificently carved beams and murals. The deity enshrined in the main hall is King Qingshan, who can dispel pestilence and dispense justice.

Backtrack to Xiyuan Road and turn right, or south, for another 22 yards (20 m), until you come to **Yadong Tianbula ❸** (56 Xiyuan Rd.,

NOT TO BE MISSED:

Qingshui Temple • Longshan Temple • Herb Lane

Sec. 1), a clean, air-conditioned restaurant specializing in Taiwanese snack food. Try a bowl of *mian xian*—vermicelli soup with oysters.

Continue in the same direction on Xiyuan Road and turn right, or west, on Guilin Street. In 110 yards (100 m) beckons the entrance to **Snake Alley ❹**, also called Huaxi Street (see p. 66). Wander past seafood restaurants, antiques shops, and foot massage parlors—as well as the famous snake restaurants. It is not everyone's cup of tea, but it does open a window to an older China, where snake is believed to have magical properties.

INSIDER TIP:

With a green, grassy aroma, Herb Lane is the place to sip minty or bitter tea—a comfort for body and spirit.

—IVY CHENG

Taipei's Community Services Center cooking teacher

Exit Snake Alley at Guangzhou Street and turn left, or east. Walk 110 yards (100 m) and cross Xiyuan Road. On the left is **Longshan Temple ❺** (see pp. 68–71), one of Taipei's most important places of worship. Alongside the outer eastern wall of the temple, **Herb (Qingcao) Lane ❻** is a covered alleyway piled with canvas sacks and boxes of teas and herbs. Goods have been sold here since 1738.

Return to Guangzhou Street, turn right, go back across Xiyuan Road, and continue west the way you came from Snake Alley. In about 100 yards (91 m), on the left side of Guangzhou Street, is **Danbei Yuyingtang Orphanage Stone Tablet ❼** (*243 Guangzhou St.*), in front of Renqi Hospital. Inscriptions tell of the orphanage established by Wanhua residents in 1870.

Continue west along Guangzhou Street for 200 yards (183 m) to where it intersects with Huanhe South Road, Section 2, and turn right. Continue for 330 yards (300 m), across Guiyang Road, to a huge store, **Jia Zhen ❽** (*183 Huanhe Rd.*), on your right. This is the place to pick up useful items and interesting souvenir gifts, including traditional cookware.

🗺	See area map pp. 56–57
▶	Qingshui Temple
🕒	3 hours
↔	0.8 mile (1.25 km)
▶	Jia Zhen store

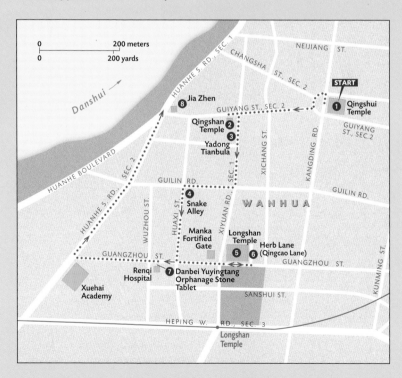

Lin An Tai Homestead

This homestead, built between 1783 and 1785, is the oldest residential building in the city of Taipei. (Its side-wing buildings were added between 1822 and 1823.) It was originally constructed in Taipei's Daan District, a mile (1.6 km) or so southeast of its present location. But under threat from urban development, it was dismantled brick by brick in 1978, warehoused, and rebuilt at its present site in 1983.

A Lin An Tai bedroom reflects the serene outdoors and the skills of 18th-century wood artisans.

Lin An Tai Homestead

- 57 C4
- 5 Binjiang St.
- 02/2598-1572
- Closed Mon.
- $
- MRT: Yuanshan station

The homestead is an outstandingly preserved example of the southern Fujian style seen during the Ming (1368–1644) and Qing (1644–1911) dynasties. It sits at the far end of a substantial spread of lawn and hedges behind a small **crescent pond.** As well as being a concession to feng shui, the pond provided water for breeding fish as well as fighting fires.

Carvings of fruits and vases decorate the alcove main doors to the homestead and surrounding panels and eaves. Family seals and banners on the right-hand side of the door symbolize learning and power.

Just beyond the main doors, the gate hall has more carvings and adornments. On the ceiling, carvings of fruits denote longevity, many generations, and luck. Mythical figures decorate the columns that support the ceiling.

From the gate hall you pass into the **inner court,** where you gain access to the inner buildings and main hall. The wooden doors of the inner rooms have patterned carvings topping delicate latticework.

The **main hall,** the most ornate of all the rooms, contains the wooden ancestral altar. The altar is carved with a legion of legendary figures and flanked by delicately

INSIDER TIP:

Exquisite Fujian-style gardens were specially created here for the 2010 International Flora Expo.

—RICK CHARETTE
National Geographic contributor

crafted wooden latticework shaped into flowers and window frames fashioned with dragons.

Covered corridors connect the maze of inner and outer rooms, 34 in all, some of which have been given over to a small museum displaying imperial-era clothing, weapons, and other artifacts. ■

Confucius & Baoan Temples

These two neighboring temples offer a fascinating contrast in architectural style, from the subtle craft of the buildings and sweeping roofs of the Confucius Temple to the gaudy tribute to the god of medicine at the Baoan Temple. The architecture of the Confucius Temple is in harmony with its meditative nature, while the ornate Baoan Temple reflects Taiwan's devotion to its plethora of deities.

Inside and outside the structures of Taipei's **Confucius Temple** are bamboo groves and sculpted gardens, potted bonsai plants, ponds, and arching miniature bridges. Its temple buildings, while rich with detail, nonetheless hold back on ornamentation to a large degree, which is typical of most Confucius temples in Taiwan.

The annual celebrations on September 28, Confucius' birthday, (also celebrated as Teachers' Day), are held at the temple's **Dacheng Hall,** where the tablet of Confucius is placed. The hall is a stunning example of temple architecture without the usual ornamental gloss. Its distinctive double-eave swallowtail roof is topped by a ship-prow ridge, on the center of which sits a pagoda to ward off evil. At each end of the prow are two cigar-shaped objects, replicas of bamboo cylinders once used to preserve manuscripts. Carved stone dragon columns support the lower-eave roof, while the heavy wooden doors feature superb latticework.

Inside the hall, look up toward the ceiling cavity at the intricate web of support beams and brackets. No nails were used in the construction of the hall.

The **Baoan Temple,** over 200 years old, features dragon carvings on its support columns, as well as roof ridges that seem to groan under the weight of its many porcelain mythological figurines. The interior of the temple is crowded with gilded images of a multitude of deities, including an image of its main god—Baosheng Dadi, the god of medicine—which was brought to Taiwan from Fujian Province in China by immigrants in 1805. ∎

Confucius Temple

- 57 B4
- 275 Dalong St.
- 02/2592-3934
- MRT: Yuanshan station

http://ct.taipei.gov.tw

Baoan Temple

- 56–57 B4

Fairs at the Baoan Temple are as colorful as the temple itself.

Confucianism in Taiwan

Confucius (551–479 B.C.), from a poor but noble family, was the most notable sage of ancient China. His thoughts were official state canon until the end of the Qing dynasty in the early 20th century. Many of his philosophical tenets have endured and remain central to the Taiwanese character.

Confucius' teachings were recorded after his death in a tome that later became required study for Chinese scholars. Confucius believed in harmony, and he taught that true pleasure could not be found in the pursuit of money or sensual delights, but in generosity to friends, frequent social interaction, and obedience to hierarchy. His primary concern was the creation of a moral human who observed and *li*, or ritual, is the practice of following ceremony; rites help guide a person in daily life. *Ren*, or benevolence, is the force that binds people in a web of relationships and obligations.

For Confucius, relationships between people always involved a superior and inferior, such as a ruler and subject, father and son, husband and wife, or older friend and younger friend. Confucius taught that inferiors should always respect and obey their superiors, although those superiors in turn had responsibilities to those below them.

Modern Western thought, which holds that respect must be earned, has eroded the status of traditional Confucian ideals in modern Taiwan. Nonetheless, these ideas have survived and continue to play a central role in Taiwanese society. Hierarchy often determines family relationships and still dominates the Taiwanese educational system.

Family obedience remains strong; fathers rule the home. In Taiwan's political elections, entire families vote as instructed by their fathers. Other family members—mothers, eldest sons—do not hesitate to harangue "inferiors" on all manner of subjects, prescribing tough courses of action spiced with warnings of dire consequences. Many young Taiwanese chafe under this browbeating, even as they do as they are told.

The concept of ren can be seen where relationships are greatly valued, whether at work, at home, or among friends. Ren has also evolved into the modern term *guanxi*, which also deals with relationships and influences, but outside the concentric circles of family and friends. In daily life, many Taiwanese prefer to settle disputes and do business without resorting to outside authorities. It is common in Taipei to see traffic accidents resolved this way: An argument ensues, blame is apportioned, and money changes hands. Only as a last resort are police called in.

Li can be observed in the Taiwanese emphasis on education. The Confucian hierarchy is still in place in schools, and students are strictly

---

EXPERIENCE: Ancient Teachers' Day Rites

In imperial China the official government creed was Confucianism. Each September 28, the birthday of Confucius (Teachers' Day), the ancient rites are conducted at Taiwan's Confucius temples. Those at **Taipei Confucius Temple** are most elaborate and authentic. Government officials attend, pledging diligent and honest service. Ancient music and dance are performed by students decked in period costume, using copies of ancient instruments. Visitors are welcome, though seats limited; tickets for the main and single practice ceremony can be pre-purchased, or bought first come, first serve that day. Call the city's Department of Information and Tourism at 02/2720-8889.

Ritual celebrations each September mark the birthday of Confucius.

ranked based on their test scores, which in turn determine which high schools and universities they attend. The government has moved to relax this educational hierarchy, but progress has been slow.

Confucian ideals will likely continue to loosen in modern Taiwan. As the country continues to modernize and internationalize, it will be increasingly influenced by Western culture and ideals.

Taipei Fine Arts Museum & Environs

The Taipei Fine Arts Museum houses local and international collections of contemporary and modern art in more than 13,000 square yards (11,000 sq m) of exhibition space. It hosts both permanent and temporary exhibitions, including some enthralling electronic media in its catacomb of basement galleries.

Near the Taipei Fine Arts Museum, the Grand Hotel is a grand Taipei landmark.

The museum does its best to exemplify its modern nature in its architecture, with a white-washed chunky design interrupted by full-length windows. Outside, bronze sculptures lead along a plaza to the main glass door of the museum.

Selections of the museum's modest but impressive permanent collection of 3,600 pieces are housed in the second- and third-floor galleries, with exhibitions changing every six to twelve months. The two **second-floor galleries** are given over to highlights from the permanent collection, which present works from numerous Taiwanese artists. The works on display show the development of modern art in Taiwan through a variety of media, including sculpture, watercolor, oils, drawing, calligraphy, and ink painting.

The **third-floor galleries**

present thematic exhibitions that also reflect Taiwan's history through contemporary art. Rotating exhibitions include "Taipei: The Tamsui," "Taipei: Historical Buildings," and "Taipei: The City." The exhibits attempt to present the changing face of Taipei from a fortified city during the Qing dynasty (1644–1911) to a sophisticated, modern metropolis. Paintings depict street scenes, popular temples, restaurants, hot springs, and other elements of Taipei life.

The **basement galleries** serve up works from young and experimental artists who are mainly creating works in electronic media. For the viewer, these pieces often provide wonderfully bizarre encounters with over-the-edge video, film, photography, light, sound, and multimedia expression.

Around the Museum

Just south of the museum is **Taipei Art Park,** a broad expanse of landscaped gardens and modern sculptures, which is worth a stroll after visiting the museum. The park regularly hosts fairs and festivals.

On the north side of the museum is the **Taipei Story House** (181-1 Zhongshan North Rd., tel 02/2587-5565, www.storyhouse.com.tw), long called Yuanshan Villa, an out-of-place, three-story mock-Tudor mansion built of brick and wood in 1914 by a local tea merchant. It houses art and history exhibits and a combination coffee shop/tea room.

Modeled after the imperial style of an ancient Chinese palace,

the 490-room **Grand Hotel** (1 Zhongshan North Rd., Sec. 4, tel 02/2886-8888, www.grand-hotel.org) is a classic Taipei landmark, made even more imposing by its lofty position atop a ridge on the north side of the city. Soaring red columns dominate the hotel's facade, helping to support its sweeping yellow-tile roof—the largest classical Chinese-style roof in the world. Inside, the lobby is pure glamour, with lanterns and more red columns.

A quarter mile (0.4 km) to the east, overlooking the Keelung River, is the **Martyrs' Shrine** (139 Beian Rd., tel 2885-4162). Like the Grand Hotel, the structures here are rendered in the ornate style of the Ming dynasty (1368–1644). The shrine, built in 1969, is dedicated to fallen heroes of the Chinese revolution and the war against Japan (330,000 in all).

INSIDER TIP:

On the museum's fourth floor, a teahouse offers fine teas and splendid views.

—DAISANN McLANE
National Geographic Traveler
magazine columnist

Arched doors at the main gate lead to a vast courtyard; in the main shrine, huge brass-studded doors open to walls inscribed with the names of the heroes along with murals depicting their feats in battle. Of special note is the ceremonial changing of the guard, held like clockwork on the hour. ∎

Taipei Fine Arts Museum
- 57 B4
- 181 Zhongshan North Rd., Sec. 3
- 02/2595-7656
- Closed Mon.
- $
- MRT: Yuanshan station

www.tfam.museum

National Palace Museum

The National Palace Museum holds the world's largest collection of Chinese artifacts, nearly 700,000 items in all. But only a fraction of these, about 15,000, are on display at any one time. The rest of these treasures are stored in thousands of crates in air-conditioned vaults tunneled into the mountain that backs the imposing, Chinese-palace-style building.

The National Palace Museum, with its vast collection of Chinese art and antiquities, is a must-see.

History

This vast collection has its origins in the Song dynasty (960–1279), when Emperor Taizong began gathering treasures from all over China. The ever growing collection shuffled from emperor to emperor and palace to palace over the centuries before finding a permanent home in Beijing's Forbidden City.

The collection expanded considerably during the Qing dynasty (1644–1911), as the dynasty's succession of art-loving emperors scoured China in search of more treasures. While China's 1911 revolution ended China's dynastic rule, the emperor at that time, Puyi, was a hard man to evict. It was when he was finally told to leave in 1924 that the art collection moved to Beijing's Palace Museum, within the Forbidden City.

But this museum had a brief existence. By the time the museum's scholars had painstakingly identified and categorized the vast treasure trove some eight years later, the Japanese had invaded Manchuria and ensconced Puyi as its puppet head of state.

By 1933, with war inevitable, the collection's caretakers feared the collection would fall into the hands of the Japanese, so they packed it up and hauled it by train to Nanjing. A month later it was transferred to a warehouse in Shanghai—until it was threatened again by the Japanese.

Over the ensuing years, the collection was divided up and crates spirited to different parts of China ahead of the advancing Japanese army. After the war, the collection returned to Nanjing, but it did not remain there for long. By fall 1948, Chiang Kai-shek's Nationalists were facing certain defeat by Mao Zedong's Communists. It was decided to begin shipping the most precious artifacts to Taiwan.

Because the Nationalists intended eventually to retake mainland China, they made no plans to establish a museum to display this wealth of treasures. A bomb-shelter warehouse was built in the west coast city of Taichung, and the collection was stored there.

As the years wore on and a triumphant return to the mainland looked less and less likely, the Taiwan government finally built the "temporary" National Palace Museum in Taipei. The museum opened in 1965.

From 2002 through 2006, the National Palace Museum underwent extensive renovations. In addition to new exhibition formats, a multimedia room, interactive displays, and exploratory exhibits were introduced.

Only a fraction of the museum's vast collection is on display at any given time, presented in long-term and special exhibitions throughout the museum's 35 galleries. At the information desk

in the lobby you can rent handheld audio equipment on specific exhibitions to help you make your way through a self-guided tour. Free English-language tours begin at 10 a.m. and 3 p.m.

Long-term Exhibitions

Displayed primarily according to chronology, in some galleries by thematic context, individual pieces within a long-term exhibition may be withdrawn and added at certain periods. The long-term exhibitions feature relics, artifacts, and statuary: bronzes, jades, porcelains, and carvings. Special exhibitions of paintings, calligraphy, books, documents, and embroidery are

National Palace Museum

- 56 B1
- 221 Zhishan Rd., Sec. 2
- 02/2881-2021
- $$
- MRT: Shilin station, then bus 255, 304, minibus 18 and 19 and Red 30; Dazhi station, then Brown 13 bus

www.npm.gov.tw

Google View

Get a visual preview of Taiwan's museums and more before touching down on the island via Google's online Street View service, which uploaded the island in late 2009. Major cities including Taipei and Kaohsiung are covered, as well as many highways and major roads. Within cities, however, views along narrow networks of lanes and alleys are not given. Go to the Google Map service, find the area to be explored, then drag the icon of a human found in the upper-left corner to the map. When the still pictures appear, you can look up, down, and around 360 degrees, and also zoom in for detailed inspection.

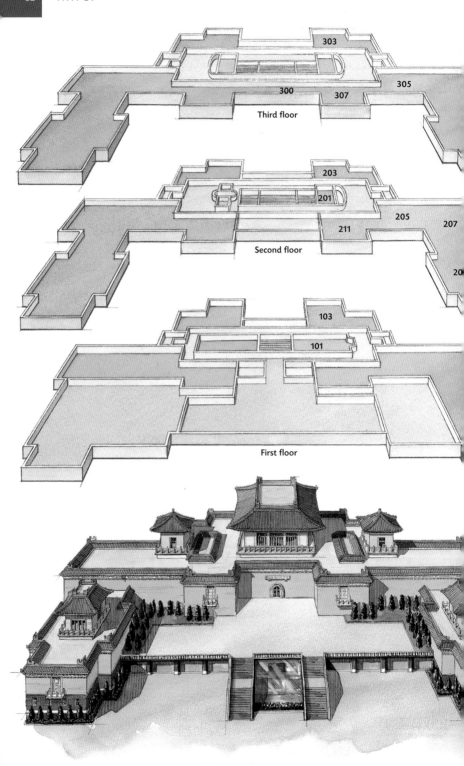

303

300   307   305

Third floor

203

201

205   207

211   20

Second floor

103

101

First floor

Main Exhibition Building

Spread over three floors, the museum's galleries contain priceless collections of bronzes, ceramics, jades, paintings, calligraphy, and rare books, among other artworks and antiquities.

Long-term Exhibitions

101 Compassion and Wisdom: Religious Sculptural Arts

103 Gems in the Rare Books Collection and Early Dwellers of Taiwan

201, 205, 207, 209, 211 The Magic of Kneaded Clay: A History of Chinese Ceramics

203 Prototypes of Modern Styles (960–1360)

300 The Mystery of Bronze

303 The Neolithic Age: The Beginning of Civilization (pre-1600 B.C.E.)

305 Classical Civilization: The Bronze Age (1600–221 B.C.E.)

307 From Classic to Tradition: Ch'in and Han Dynasties (221 B.C.E.–220 C.E.)

short term due to the fragility of the pieces.

First-floor Galleries: A good place to start is **Gallery 101,** with the exhibit on "Compassion and Wisdom: Religious Sculptural Arts." Through exquisite pieces of Buddhist sculpture one explores here both the revelation of Buddhism's religious ideals and also the changing worldly concepts of beauty manifest through the imperial epochs.

The expansive **Gallery 103** is home to two cultural explorations, "Rare Books and Secret Archives" and "Early Dwellers of Taiwan: Illustrated Historical Documents in the Collections of the NPM." The gems of the former are from the museum's priceless collection of 200,000 rare books and nearly 400,000 historical documents, many inherited from leading Qing-dynasty imperial households. The artwork and the materials are windows into Chinese life. The development of book-production technology is unveiled. The gems of the latter are painting scrolls, maps, ancient books, documents, and block prints that give insight into the culture, practices, and belief systems of Taiwan's aboriginal peoples in the 18th and 19th centuries.

Second-floor Galleries: "The Magic of Kneaded Clay: A History of Chinese Ceramics" is a recent undertaking that unfolds in **Galleries 201, 205, 207, 209, and 211.** Emperors, officials, potters, and users of ceramics have all been contributors to the formation of China's various period styles, and this exhibition uses magnificent treasures to illustrate the evolution. It is divided into five sections.

INSIDER TIP:

The world's best collections of Chinese culture are at the National Palace Museum. A recent face lift makes the museum a pleasure to visit.

—YUNGSHIH LEE
National Geographic *magazine*
Taiwan edition former editor

"Pottery and Porcelain" is the introductory exhibit, exploring materials encountered in everyday living and demonstrating how glazes evolved at various kilns and time periods, as well as how official models of decoration formed over time.

"Neolithic Age to the Five Dynasties" (6000 B.C.E.–960 C.E.) represents a long period of evolution that saw ceramics move from primitive beginnings to a more sophisticated stage.

Using the perspective of daily aesthetics, "Song to Yuan Dynasties" (960–1359) explores the decorations and beauty of various sorts of wares.

The "Ming Dynasty" (1368–1644) section deals with the establishment of the famed Jingdezhen imperial kilns, as porcelain production became a state affair and local civilian kilns

competed for market share.

The "Qing Dynasty" (1644–1911) section shows how three emperors, Kangxi, Yongzheng, and Qianlong, personally controlled the pottery work undertaken at the imperial kilns. As the late Qing imperial wares demonstrate, folk-art themes started to creep into the pieces as the dynasty started to decline.

In **Gallery 203** is "Prototypes of Modern Styles (960–1360)," concentrated on the brilliant artistic heights achieved in the Song dynasty (960–1279). This, an age of cultural openness and experimentation, had as its base an appreciation of frugal esthetics in both high art and daily living. This was also an age of scientific innovation, with craftsmen using sophisticated techniques in making daily-use wares of high artistic merit—simple lines and natural grace emphasized. This preference continued during the Yuan dynasty (1271–1368).

Third-floor Galleries:

In **Gallery 303** the visitor enters "The Neolithic Age: The Beginning of Civilization (pre-1600 B.C.E.)." Found jade objects have been key guideposts to the spiritual culture of China's ancient denizens; here, the brilliant works are approached in terms of use in religious worship and indicators of regional styles in East Asia, an area which had developed superior jadework craftsmanship by the late Neolithic era compared to the rest of the Eurasian continent. These pieces also mark the distribution of influence of the three great clans that appear to have dominated China during this era.

In "Classical Civilization: The Bronze Age (1600-221 B.C.E.)," housed in **Gallery 305,** are inscribed bronze vessels created at the peak of this artform, during the Shang (ca 1766-1122 B.C.E.), Zhou—Western Zhou (ca 1122–771 B.C.E.), and Eastern Zhou (ca 770–256 B.C.E.) dynasties. Pieces are wrought in fine detail, and inscriptions demonstrate some of the earliest examples of calligraphy. One of the most treasured pieces is the Mao Gong Ding tripod cauldron. Its 500-character inscription is the most unrestrained example of ancient calligraphy yet found.

The technological mysteries of Shang and Zhou bronze production are unveiled in **Gallery 300** via modern multimedia technology in "The Mystery of Bronze." The knowledge of the ancients is brought to life with virtual-reality and other digital animation.

Moving on in chronological order, **Gallery 307** houses "From Classic to Tradition: Ch'in and Han Dynasties (221 B.C.E.–220 C.E.)." This era marked the end of feudalism and the establishment of imperial rule. The use of bronzeware in ritual tapered off, with artistic creation now brought to everyday objects, in a range of materials.

Other Collections

Calligraphy: Calligraphic works created during the Tang, Ming (1368–1644), and Qing (1644–1911) dynasties are regularly exhibited in special short-term exhibitions. Watch for "Clearing After Snowfall" and "Sending Regards to a Friend," both by Yuan Huan Tieh, and "Three Passages of Calligraphy," by Ping An, Ho Ju, and Feng Chu Tieh.

Paintings: "Early Spring" by Kou Shi Hang—ink and color on silk mountain scenes on scroll—and the similar but more landscape-expansive scenes of "Travelers Amid Mountains and Streams" by Fan Kuan are two Song dynasty masterpieces exhibited at the museum from time to time. Also keep an eye out for the classic "Bamboo" by Wen Tung, one of the most important pieces of calligraphic art. The museum's special exhibitions of Ming and Qing paintings are crowd favorites for their grand and highly decorative landscapes. ■

A gilded bronze Buddha image cast by an unidentified Qing dynasty artist in 1782 is among the museum's treasures.

Sun Yat-sen Memorial Hall & Around

The Sun Yat-sen Memorial Hall is a graceful tribute to the founder of modern China, a man revered in both China and Taiwan as the "National Father." Taipei residents come here to honor the man who helped to end China's dynasties, visit the memorial's exhibits and art galleries, fly kites, exercise, and relax in the plaza and gardens that surround the hall.

The Sun Yat-sen Memorial Hall houses pieces of the revered revolutionary leader's past.

Sun Yat-sen Memorial Hall

- 🅰 Map p. 57 D2
- ✉ 505 Renai Rd., Sec. 4
- ☎ 02/2758-8008
- 🚇 MRT: Sun Yat-sen Memorial Hall station

www.yatsen.gov.tw

The massive memorial hall, with its roof of yellow-glazed tiles, sits at the end of an expansive plaza awash with flowers bordered by hedges. A bronze 20-foot (6 m) statue of a seated Sun dominates the grand entrance gallery. On each side of the statue, on small pedestals, are two immaculately uniformed guards, bearing arms and standing so still they could be mistaken for statues themselves.

To the right of Sun's statue is a gift shop selling Sun-related souvenirs. Beyond it is a gallery with photographs and paintings of Sun over the years, his books, and narrations of the many uprisings he led against the Qing dynasty (1644–1911) rulers in China. Photographs of revolutionary "martyrs" cover the gallery walls, and Sun memorabilia, including his watches, clothes, and walking sticks, fills glass cases. There are no captions in English. Next to the gallery is a public library with 300,000 volumes pertaining to Sun's political philosophy. The hall also contains art galleries given over to Chinese art. The excellent artworks have no English captions.

The **Zhongshan National Gallery** on the second floor holds significant foreign and domestic exhibitions; the third-floor **Yat-sen Gallery** displays Chinese paintings and calligraphy, while the **Deming Gallery** is given over to the works of Taiwanese artists.

Taipei 101

Looming beyond the Sun Yat-sen Memorial to the southwest on Songzhi Road, the new 101-floor Taipei 101 is the tallest building in Taipei. The building's design is meant to symbolize the growth of bamboo, with each shoot unfolding from the one below. The effect—eight tapered tiers emerging from a pyramid base and topped with a circular column and radio tower—is eye-catching, to say the least. The building's spectacular 140-foot-high (42 m) glass-domed enclosure covers an indoor plaza 31,000 square feet (2,865 sq m) in size. Elevators shoot visitors to observation decks on the 89th and 91st floors. Views from these decks are outstanding.

Discovery Center of Taipei

This is one of the city's newest museums, showing different stages of Taipei's development through four floors of artifacts, scale models, photographs, topographical maps, and video displays. Many of the displays are interactive. One of the more interesting exhibits is an interactive topographical map of Taipei, which has a touch screen that highlights different areas of the city and their development.

In another exhibit, you can breathe in old Taipei by sniffing lemongrass, tea, and camphor, once among the major exports carried on the Taipei Basin's Danshui River.

The center's first floor incorporates scenes of modern Taipei and records people's impressions of the changing city. The second floor features temporary exhibitions, while the third-floor gallery contains exhibits about Taipei's modern era, including the rapid transformation of the Xinyi District from a rural area of rice paddies into the city's bustling commercial district. The fourth floor explores the old walled city, with scale models and cutaways. If you are in a group, ask in advance for an English-speaking guide; a self-guided text tour is also available for a deposit. ■

Taipei 101 (Taipei Financial Center)
- 🅰 57 E2
- ✉ 8 Songzhi Rd., Xinyi District
- ☎ 02/8101-8899 (Observatory reservations)

www.tapei-101 .com.tw

Discovery Center of Taipei
- 🅰 57 E2
- ✉ Taipei City Hall, 1 Shifu Rd.
- ☎ 02/2757-4547
- 🕐 Closed Mon. & national holidays

www.discovery .taipei.gov.tw

In the Words of a Revolutionary

"With the invention of modern machines, the phenomenon of uneven distribution of wealth in the West has become all the more marked. . . . After comparing various schools of economic thought I have come to the realization that the principle of state ownership is most profound, reliable and practical. Moreover, it will forestall in China difficulties which have already caused much anxiety in the West. I have therefore decided to enforce the principle of the people's livelihood simultaneously with the principles of nationalism and democracy, with the hope to achieve our political objective and nip economic unrest in the bud."
—*Fundamentals of National Reconstruction*, Sun Yat-sen, 1923

More Places to Visit in Taipei

Chinese Postal Museum

With its staggering collection of more than 500,000 Chinese and foreign postage stamps, 20,000 postal-related items, 6,000 documents, and 20,000 books related to postal systems, this museum rates as one of the largest museums of its type in the world. During the weekends, vendors sell postage stamps outside the museum, catering to the area's sizable community of avid philatelists. 🅐 57 B1 ✉ 45 Chongqing South Rd., Sec. 2 ☎ 02/2394-5185, ext. 851 🕐 Closed Mon. 💲 $ 🚌 Bus: 3, 243, 248, 262, 268, 304

The Taipei Astronomical Museum transports visitors via a tour of stargazing history.

Customs Museum

The most outstanding feature of this museum is its Preventative Operation Section, which contains displays of contraband nabbed from smugglers over the years. In addition, you can't miss the 10-foot-high (3 m) ivory pagoda carved in astonishing detail. There are also exhibits on the not-so-foolproof methods drug traffickers use to try to conceal illegal goods; among the most interesting: phony incense sticks. http://museum.customs.gov.tw 🅐 56 B3 ✉ Directorate General of Customs Building, 13 Dacheng St. ☎ 02/2550-5500, ext. 2212-2214 🕐 Closed Sat.–Sun., reservations required 🚌 Bus: 9, 12, 52, 206, 223, 250, 274, 304, 601

Sun Yat-sen Historic Events Memorial Hall

This lovely Japanese-style complex with gardens of bonsai, carp ponds, and arching bridges was once a luxury inn where Sun stayed in 1913. There is a modest collection of Sun memorabilia, including photographs and documents. 🅐 57 B2 ✉ 46 Zhongshan North Rd., Sec. 1 ☎ 02/2381-3359 🕐 Closed Mon. 🚇 MRT: Taipei Main station

National Taiwan University Hospital

Opposite the Gongyuan Road entrance to 2-28 Memorial Peace Park stands a striking neo-Renaissance–style building, one of two that make up the city's old hospital. Built in 1916, it forms the larger component of what was once the biggest hospital complex in the Far East. Its pilaster, supported by four sets of Roman columns, and generous windows surrounded by plasterwork enliven its red-brick facade. The other hospital (1907) has a more muted appearance, but its first-floor entrances, colonnaded second-floor veranda, and double-pitched roof lend a classical look. 🅐 57 B2 ✉ 1 Changde St. 🚇 MRT: NTU Hospital station

EXPERIENCE: Enjoy Taiwanese Puppet Theater

Traditional glove-puppet theater was brought over to Taiwan from south China hundreds of years ago by settlers moving across the Taiwan Strait. It was long a primary form of local entertainment, with troupes traveling the island and giving shows at temporary stages at temples and other community gathering places. The advent of television almost killed the art, but interest has been renewed in keeping with the Taiwan "native soil" movement, the yearning to learn more of their own traditions after decades of force-fed learning about China

under martial law. Two fine venues to take in performances in Taipei are at the **Lin Liu-hsin Puppet Theatre Museum** (*www.taipeipuppet.com*) and the **Puppetry Art Center of Taipei** (*www.pact.org.tw*). Note that the former provides more English-language support. For both, try to go to weekend performances, when kids make up the majority of the audience. However, though on surface level a children's attraction, puppet theater has the history and sophistication of traditional opera, and in fact incorporates myriad elements.

The Red House

The octagonal building was constructed in 1908 as a market (it still serves this function, see p. 19) and became a theater for Beijing opera, then movies, after the Japanese occupation. Renovated in 1999, the two-story building includes a second-floor theater that hosts performances of puppetry and children's theater under a domed ceiling. There is a café and artist workshops. *www.redhouse.org.tw* 🅰 56 B2 ✉ 10 Chengdu Rd. ☎ 02/2311-9380 🕐 Closed Mon. 🚇 MRT: Ximen station

Shandao Temple

This is one of seven major temples built by Japanese Buddhists during Japan's occupation. Constructed in 1933, it little resembles other Buddhist temples in Taiwan; from a distance it looks like an apartment building with a four-columned entrance gate. The nine-floor temple has a museum with a fine collection of Buddhist art. The most outstanding relic is an exquisitely carved wooden image of Guanyin from the Song dynasty (960–1279). 🅰 57 B2 ✉ 23 Zhongxiao East Rd., Sec. 1 ☎ 02/2341-5758 🕐 Closed Mon. 🚇 MRT: Shandao Temple station

Shilin Official Residence

This expansive estate of former President Chiang Kai-shek was turned into a park and opened to the public in 1996. After entering via the very long entrance driveway, you can follow park pathways past a number of gardens, pagodas, pavilions, and an experimental greenhouse. You'll encounter a fountain in a garden full of statues; a lovely orchid pavilion with classically sculpted wooden walls and decorated eaves; and a Chinese garden with winding pathways and carp ponds. 🅰 57 C4 ✉ 60 Fuiln Rd. ☎ 02/2881-2512 🚇 MRT: Shilin station

Shung Ye Museum of Formosan Aborigines

Five floors of exhibits describe Taiwan's recognized aboriginal groups. A topographical map of Taiwan in the lobby shows the territories and villages of the tribes, and each tribe has a section of the museum devoted to its history and culture. Exhibits include arts and crafts, scale models of dwellings, weapons, utensils, farming and fishing implements, costumes, and ornaments. The spiritual side of the cultures is explored through funerary objects and items used for sacrifice, divination, and exorcism. *www.museum .org.tw* ▲ 57 D4 ✉ 282 Zhishan Rd., Sec. 2. ☎ 02/2841-2611 🕐 Closed Mon. & Jan. 20–Feb. 20 Ⓢ $ 🚇 MRT: Shilin station, then bus 213, 255, 304, minibus 18, 19, Red 30

Su Ho Memorial Paper Museum

The first floor of this delightful museum has displays of handmade paper from all over the world; create your own pieces of paper using the museum's equipment *($)*. The second-floor exhibit takes you through the history, materials, and process of paper manufacture; the third floor has exhibits tracing the history of paper manufacture in Taiwan. On the fourth floor is a mock-up of a handmade-paper factory. Reservations required and all visits guided. *www.suhopaper.org.tw* ▲ 57 C2 ✉ 68 Changan East Rd., Sec. 2 ☎ 02/2507-5539 🕐 Closed Sun. & major festival days Ⓢ $ 🚇 MRT: Zhongxiao-Xinsheng station

Taipei Astronomical Museum

This museum's four floors of exhibition halls take you through the themes of ancient astronomy, planet Earth, space science and technology, stars and galaxies, and the universe, using models, images, photographs, computer animation, and video. The museum has telescopes for closer looks at the heavens *(3-day advance reservations)*. The IMAX Dome Theater has spectacular hourly shows from 9 a.m. to 4 p.m. (extra shows on weekends), featuring space exploration, while the Iwerks 3D Theater gives viewers a different experience with the aid of polarized glasses. *www.tam.gov.tw* ▲ 56 D4 ✉ 363 Jihe Rd. ☎ 02/2831-4551 🕐 Closed Mon. Ⓢ $, $ for IMAX & Iwerks shows 🚇 MRT: Shilin station, then the Red 12 or Red 19 bus

Ximending Shopping District

This trendy area is Taipei's answer to Tokyo's Shinjuku District. The department stores, cinemas, pedestrian malls, boutiques, second-hand clothing stores, and restaurants attract throngs of young people during the evenings and on weekends, when a number of local streets are closed to vehicles. It's an entertaining display of youth fashion and attitude. ▲ 56 2A 🚇 MRT: Ximen station

Xingtian Temple

This bustling temple is dedicated to Guangong, the red-faced, black-bearded god of war and patron saint of merchants. It is an outstanding example of Taoist temple architecture, which eschews much of the over-the-top ornateness of other temples. Multilevel roofs have carved ship-prow ridges and are adorned with large colorful dragons. A huge brass incense pot with a gilded dragon handle sits in front of the main hall. Here, nuns and priests in blue robes bless people with incense sticks as part of the practice of touching various places on their bodies to invite back souls who have received a fright and left the body. In the covered courtyard near the main hall—notable for its carved dragon columns—rows of tables groan under the weight of offerings. The temple differs from many others in that it has no donation box, prohibits the burning of paper money, and discourages raucous ceremonies. It also runs a charitable foundation. *www.ht.org.tw* ▲ Map 57 C3 ✉ 109 Minquan East Rd., Sec. 2 ☎ 02/2502-7924 🚇 MRT: Minquan West Rd. station, then Red 32, 63 9shuttle) or 225 (shuttle) bus

Colorful gold-mining towns, spectacular coastal scenery, hill-perched cities, and Taiwanese tea culture—just a short distance from Taipei

Around Taipei & the North

Tea and all its lovely trappings form an intrinsic element of Taiwan's north.

Around Taipei & the North

Taipei can be used as a base from which to explore areas around the city as well as the island's north. Most attractions are within easy reach—not much more than an hour's drive away—making for quick excursions from the sometimes hectic capital. Because they are close to the capital, however, many of these destinations get crowded on weekends.

Using bottle tops, board-gamers compete in Wenchang Park, Taoyuan City.

To the city's north, just 40 minutes from central Taipei, the mountains of Yangmingshan National Park offer a delightful escape from Taipei. Within the park's boundaries, roads and hiking trails climb to some truly spectacular vistas of the Taipei Basin and northern Taiwan, while the park's hot springs, fumaroles, lakes, and mountain meadows provide scenic diversity.

To the west of Yangmingshan, and easily accessible by MRT from Taipei, is the rustic hot springs resort of Beitou, Taiwan's oldest. Here you can stay in a tranquil Japanese-style inn for a taste of hot-springs bathing in your own room. You can also reach another historic town, Danshui, by MRT from Taipei. Here you can take in remnants of the island's European colonial history, along with the story of one of its most famous foreign residents, Canadian missionary and benefactor George Leslie

Mackay (1844–1901). Most of the compact town's attractions are close together, making it ideal for a walking tour.

A more rambunctious side to Taiwan's recent history is found at Jiufen, which grew from a tiny mountainside settlement to a raucous town of prospectors, merchants, and prostitutes after the discovery of gold in the 1890s. The town's laddered streets and charming old buildings bedecked with balconied teahouses draw visitors from the city.

From Danshui, the North Coast Highway follows a weathered coastline of cliffs and rock formations east to Keelung, Taiwan's second biggest port. Just to the southeast of that city, the Northeast Coast & Yilan Coast National Scenic Area hugs the narrow corridor between the mountains and Pacific Ocean. Travelers along this route are treated to rugged scenery, sandy beaches, and ocean vistas.

The east end of the Northern Cross Island Highway begins in Yilan County and cuts through the mountains and some beautiful scenery.

Guanyi

15

Zhubei   1

1   Hsinchu

1

Toufen   3

Zhunan

61   1   Shitoushan

Houlong

1   6

Miaoli   3

Shitan

3   6   MIAOLI

1

Sanyi   Dahu

Huoyanshan
(Fire Mountain)   3
Nature Reserve   Shengxing

Houli   Station

△   CENTRAL
A   WEST
p. 207

Southwest of Taipei, you will find the town of Yingge, famed for its pottery factories and shops. Sanxia Zushi Temple in nearby Sanxia is recognized as an outstanding example of a traditional temple exquisitely restored using modern techniques.

West and southwest of Taipei in the counties of Taoyuan and Hsinchu, attractions are more of the man-made variety, with a number of theme parks, including the quirky Window on China, with its miniature replicas of famous destinations, including the Forbidden City, the Sphinx, and the Eiffel Tower. ■

NOT TO BE MISSED:

Savoring tea in Muzha 94–95

Hiking in Yangmingshan National Park 98–101

Beitou's hot springs and its folk art museum 102–103

Exploring imperial history in old Danshui port 104–105

Strolling the former gold-rush town of Jiufen 108–109

Aboriginal life in Wulai gorge 120

The art of pottery in Yingge 121

Muzha's Teahouses

Tea plantations cling to the hills above the narrow, 2-mile-long (3.2 km) Maokong (Cat's Hollow) Valley in the southeast section of Taipei. The area is a favorite among city dwellers, who head here in the cool of the evening to drink tea at one of the numerous hillside teahouses while enjoying views of twinkling lights below. A daytime trip to the teahouses in the valley, named for the cat's-paw-shaped hollows in the rocks along Zhinan Stream, is just as rewarding.

Northern Taiwan's high altitudes and mild climate create ideal conditions for growing tea.

**Muzha Tea
Plantation
circular route**

  93 C3

🚌 Bus: 236, 237,
282 to Chengchi
University, then
minibus 10 from
the university

The teahouses are found along Zhinan Road, Section 3, a 4-mile-long (6 km) loop that heads south for 2 miles (3 km) from Chengchi (Political) University to the head of the valley. The road heads west across Zhinan Stream and then north again, twisting for 1.5 miles though Lane 40, Lane 38, and Lane 34 to a junction one-half mile (1 km) above Chengchi University.

The road meanders through idyllic plantations before reaching a cluster of picturesque hillside teahouses, where you can sip tea and watch farmers at work.

About 350 yards (320 m) north of the Zhinan Stream along Lane 40, the **Yaoyue (Inviting the Moon) Teahouse** sits amid wooden pavilions and topiary gardens. You can drink tea and take in splendid views of the teahouses and temples on the other side of the valley. The teahouse is encircled by forest, with sections cleared to allow for daytime panoramas and views of the distant lights of Muzha in the evening.

About 400 yards (365 m) north on Lane 40 is the **Taipei Tea Promotion Center,** a handsome two-story redbrick building with white trim. The inside, housing artifacts related to tea farming and brewing, is awash with light streaming in through latticed floor-to-ceiling windows.

Displays show how teas are classified and include free tastings and lessons on brewing. The center also has displays of machinery used in the fermentation and curing process and pottery tea sets with information on how they are made. Spectacular views of downtown Taipei can be enjoyed from the experimental tea plantation situated on the slopes behind the center; the acrid but appealing smell of maturing tea

INSIDER TIP:

Head up the signposted trail behind the Taipei Tea Promotion Center to the area's highest point and best views of Taipei Basin.

—RICK CHARETTE
National Geographic contributor

leaves adds to the atmosphere. English-language tours *($)* of the center and plantation need to be arranged by phone at least three days in advance.

On Lane 38, about 300 yards from the display center, **Big Teapot Teahouse** juts out on pillars over the tiered plantation slopes. The building is covered in bright red bricks, while dark latticed railings stand between patrons and the hillside plantation. The interior is lined with dark lacquered wood in imperial style. Views sweep across hillside plantations down to Taipei city.

The Big Teapot Teahouse is one of the best places in Muzha to try "tea cuisine." Most local teahouses serve up dishes using locally raised free-range chicken. The Big Teapot's Three Cup Range Chicken *(San Bei Yeji),* a traditional rural recipe, is delicious and a superb match for the plantation's Iron Goddess and Baozhong teas. A cable-car service glides visitors from Taipei Zoo to Zhinan Temple and on to the tea plantations *($).* ■

Renting a Car

The best places to pick up an auto: major airports and downtown locations. Some car rental companies allow a customer to return a car to a location other than the pick-up spot, although a surcharge may apply. Full insurance coverage may not be included in the cost. Make sure you ask; opt for a plan that is comprehensive. To drive, you must have a valid international driver's license. Rental firms used to dealing with foreigners advertise in the three English daily newspapers. The Tourism Bureau also has useful information on its website (*www.taiwan.net.tw;* go to "Links").

Yaoyue Teahouse
- ✉ 6 Lane 40, Zhinan Rd., Sec. 3
- ☎ 02/2939-2025

Taipei Tea Promotion Center
- ✉ 8-2 Lane 40, Zhinan Rd., Sec. 3
- ☎ 02/2939-1473
- 🕐 Closed Mon.; experimental plantation open 10 a.m.–11:30 a.m. & 2 p.m.–3 p.m.

Big Teapot Teahouse
- ✉ 37-1 Lane 38, Zhinan Rd., Sec. 3
- ☎ 02/2939-5615

Taiwanese Tea Culture

With its high mountain slopes, Taiwan is ideal for growing tea, and it produces some of the world's best brews. Differences in flavors depend on the type of plant, the altitude at which it is grown, the climatic conditions in the area, the timing of the harvest, and the methods used to cure the leaves.

After tea pickers finish their work, the leaves undergo a traditional curing process.

Probably the most famous tea in Taiwan is Dongding Oolong, which comes from around the town of Lugu in Nantou County. This region of high foothills bordering the Central Mountain Range is home to some of the best tea in the country. Tea was first planted in Nantou about 150 years ago, and the moist hills, cool climate, and leached soil have turned out to be perfect for the growing of tea.

Like all quality teas, Dongding Oolong undergoes lengthy curing. The leaves are softened in the sun for two hours, then rolled for 20 minutes. This bruises them and brings the juice to the surface. The juice oxidizes when it makes contact with the air, a process known as fermentation. This lasts three hours, after

which the leaves are heated again to stop the fermentation. It is this partial fermentation that distinguishes Oolong tea from green tea, which is not fermented, and black tea, which is fully fermented.

Next, farmers pack the leaves into bags and roll them vigorously until they are pressed into hard little kernels. The kernels dry overnight and are then cooked over a charcoal fire for 40 minutes. This imparts a smoky aftertaste that is one of the tea's hallmarks.

A more curious type of tea is Dongfang Mei Ren, or Oriental Beauty, from the border region of Hsinchu and Miaoli Counties. This is no ordinary brew; its flavor derives from insects that live and breed on the tea leaves. The bugs deposit their egg sacks in a sticky paste, which is harvested and brewed with the leaves. The tea picks up an unusual scented flavor, like an Earl Grey, but earthier and more robust. All Oriental Beauty is organically grown—otherwise the insects would die and the unique tea would lose its signature flavor.

Oriental Beauty is famous and costly—100 U.S. dollars for 600 grams (21 oz)—but it is not Taiwan's most expensive tea. That title belongs to Lishan Oolong, which can cost more than 200 U.S. dollars for 600 grams (21 oz). Lishan Oolong grows on the slopes of Lishan (Pear Mountain) at altitudes above 7,200 feet (2,200 m). At that height, a sudden mountain freeze can wipe out an entire crop. Lishan tea is picked just twice a year, compared with five harvests for Dongding Oolong, and the growing time makes for flavor that is so con-centrated that the leaves can be brewed up to ten times. It is one of the world's finest teas, a pale gold liquid that is subtle and refined.

Many other varieties of tea are grown in Taiwan, notably the lightly fermented Baozhong and the more heavily fermented Iron Goddess or Tieguanyin tea (sometimes also called Iron Buddha), which has a slightly sweet aftertaste. The tea one chooses to drink depends on the time of day, the guests being served, and one's general mood.

All Taiwan teas are brewed full leaf; no tea bags are used. The preparation of tea follows a standard ritual. Allow freshly boiled water to cool slightly, then pour it over the leaves in the pot to wash them. Swirl this water around, pour it into the assorted mugs and cups, and then drain them. For the second brew—the best—steep the leaves for a few seconds, then pour the brew into a pitcher to stop contact with the leaves. Serve it to guests in small cups. Subsequent steepings take more time, and the better the quality of the tea leaves, the more times they can be brewed.

EXPERIENCE: Have a Sip and See

Can tea really taste that good? Even the most uncompromising coffee drinker could be converted to the delights of Taiwanese teas—surprisingly little known outside the country—during a visit to the island. Taiwan was long one of the world's great tea exporters, before the British began cultivating their own in South Asia.

Taiwanese restaurants automatically provide tea with meals, and convenience stores offer a large variety of refreshing iced teas. But to get the best out of the tea-drinking experience, sit down to *he cha* (literally, "drink tea") at one of the island's numerous delightful teahouses or at one of the many teasellers' shops.

In Taipei, top-rate tea-tasting tours, mixed with visits to the city's old tea-processing area in Dadaocheng (Datong District) and the history-display facilities of the Taipei Tea Merchants Associa-tion, are given by local experts through the **Community Services Center** *(tel 02/2836-8134, www.community.com.tw)*. Learn how to choose the best tea, how to brew it, and how to taste it. Each three-hour outing is NT$600 (U.S. $19). The **Taipei Tea Merchants Association** *(6F, 24 Gangu St., Datong District, tel 02/2555-7598)* runs its own half-day **Dadaocheng Tea Search Fun** history walking tour with tea sampling along the way. A week's notice is required for English tours.

In business since 1890, **Wang's Tea** *(26 Lane 64, Sec. 2, Chongqing North Rd., Datong District, tel 02/2555-9164)* occu-pies the firm's original factory site, where the traditional charcoal-roast method is still used. Free English-language tours are given with advance notice. On Saturdays you can also enjoy free performances of *nanguan* music, an old style imported from China that is associated with such cultured pursuits as tea drinking.

Yangmingshan National Park

From Taipei's Shilin District, Yangde Boulevard winds high into the mountains on the north side of the city to the entrance of Yangmingshan National Park. Along the way its passes the luxury villas of Taipei's moneyed classes, who prefer the area's cooler climes, cleaner air, and panoramas. In the park, trails lead hikers up the mountainsides. You can also drive along roads leading closer to the summits, following well-marked signs to the park's main attractions.

Yangmingshan's azaleas light up hillsides each year.

It is best to visit Yangmingshan during the week. On weekends and holidays, the park can become intolerably crowded. Private vehicle access is strictly controlled at these times to encourage use of buses.

The crowds come to Yangmingshan National Park for the varied landscape, ranging from craggy cliff faces, sulfur-ravaged mountainsides, and steamy hot springs to tranquil lakes and expansive alpine meadows. The **Yangmingshan National Park Headquarters and Visitor Center** is located within the park, right beside the main road. Here you'll find displays on the park's geology, flora, and fauna. You can also pick up maps and other information.

Just before the visitor center, along hilly and winding pathways, **Yangming Park** (*$*) presents a pleasant collection of landscaped gardens with ponds, grottoes, waterfalls, stands of forests, and various artifices, including its famous flower clock. The park is an easy and relaxing place to spend a few hours. It blazes with color from the middle of February to the end of March, when cherry blossoms open and gardens of rhododendrons and azaleas splash the park with color. Wildflowers also bloom in other areas of the national park.

This is a particularly beautiful but busy time of year in Yangmingshan, as people head up from Taipei to enjoy the park's springtime colors and atmosphere.

By car, you can backtrack 1 mile (1.6 km) along Yangde Boulevard, then turn east (left) onto Jingshan Road and follow signs to the park's sights. Along this road you'll come across a particularly fine example of the weird workings of Mother Nature at **Lengshuikeng Fumarole Nature Preserve,** where sulfurous clouds billow out of a bowl-shaped fumarole (vent) to waft above thick bamboo groves. Here you will also find **Milk Lake,** surrounded by rocks covered in thick foliage and named for the yellowish white color of its water. The water's unusual pallor comes from its high sulfur content. Elsewhere in the park at Dayoukeng, Macao, and Sihuangping, you can find similar hollows belching steam and corrosive gases. These have caved in the Earth's surface and turned the surrounding areas into a lunar landscape of yellow sulfur and crumbling rocks.

Yangmingshan was first used for growing wet rice and grazing water buffalo during the late Qing period, and a number of pasturelands atop plateaus can still be found in the park. Some, including **Qingtiangang** (*$ per car on access road)*—a luxuriant meadow covered by a blanket of deep green grass at the end of an access road just to the east of Lengshuikeng—even have a small herd of cattle grazing contentedly. Qingtiangang is popular for family picnics, boisterous student outings, and kite flying.

Go back and continue along Jingshan Road. You'll soon come to the entry point for **Menghuan Pond** on the left. The pond's waters are blanketed by a layer of plants, mostly Taiwan *isoetes,* a rare type of water fern native to Yangmingshan. A scenic trail encircles the pond.

Continue north along Jingshan Road until it meets a T-junction and follow the signs west to the **Xiaoyoukeng Recreation Area** (*$*) along the northern saddle of Qixingshan (Seven Stars Mountain)—Yangmingshan's highest peak, which rises to 3,739 feet (1,120 m). This takes you to one of the park's major geological sites. Here, strong acidic hot springs and sulfur gases rising through the Xiaoyoukeng fault have eroded the rock face, causing it to crumble and collapse. The result is a huge,

Yangmingshan National Park

 Map p. 93

✉ 1-20 Zhuzihu Rd., Yangmingshan, Taipei

☎ 02/861-8744

 Bus: 230, 260 to Yangming Park, 15-minute walk up pathway to visitor center

www.ymsnp.gov.tw

Guided Taipei-Area Nature Hikes & Walks

Taiwan is over two-thirds mountain. In traditional Chinese culture, hiking was frowned upon, with heavy sweating seen as unhealthy and strenuous exercise viewed as something unavoidable for the working class. But healthy hiking is now much in vogue. Trails and associations are springing up everywhere.

Guides with Taipei's Community Services Center (tel 02/2836-8134, www .community.com.tw) **lead regularly scheduled hikes and walks—usually half-day outings—for a fee, and the Chinese Taipei Mountaineering Sport Association** (tel 02/2239-1669, www.mtnrgsport.org.tw) **welcomes foreigners on its regular Sunday morning Taipei-area hikes.**

EXPERIENCE:
Sampling Yangmingshan Produce at the Source

The Yangmingshan slopes are dotted with farms open to visitors, where you can pick your own in-season fruits. On weekends local city folk flock to these places, especially families, for a taste of rural living and big mountain views. Most farms also provide barbecue facilities for all-day picnics. The strawberry season is November through April, during which most farms will also have other fruits ripening, such as passion fruit, pomelo, and pitayas. Many farms are located along Bishan Road; try **Eastern Forest Farm** (43-10 Bishan Rd., tel 02/2790-7252) and **Berry Garden Farm** (38-2 Bishan Rd., tel 02/2790-2492).

of Yangmingshan and Datun Nature Park. The park stands in the shadow of 3,543-foot-high (1,080 m) **Datunshan,** the second highest mountain in Yangmingshan park after nearby Qixingshan. The entrance to Datun Nature Park is opposite the entrance to the Butterfly Corridor. The park opens to a valley locked between towering mountains, where meadows are cut with a meandering pond and crisscrossed by raised wooden walkways.

You can continue toward Datunshan's peak along Bailaka Highway or climb the trail from Datun Nature Park. The trail takes you through stands of bamboo and pampas grass on the way to the summit. The views from the

INSIDER TIP:

Datun Nature Park is an easy, green escape from Taipei's hustle, especially in the spring when the azaleas are out in force.

—JULIA ROSS
Travel writer and former Fulbright scholar in Taiwan

steaming, barren scar shoveled out of the side of the mountain, one of Yangmingshan's more unusual sites. A terrace above the visitor center at Xiaoyoukeng offers startling views of the phenomenon. Inside the center is a scale model of the mountain and surrounding area, with lots of geological information to help put it all into perspective.

You can climb **Qixingshan** from **Xiaoyoukeng Visitor Center** (69 Zhuzihu Rd., tel 02/2861-7024, closed Mon.). The assent covers about 1 mile (1.6 km) and takes about 40 minutes—time and energy well spent. From the top of Qixingshan the 360-degree views are breathtaking.

Datun Nature Park

From just south of Xiaoyoukeng, turn west (left) on Bailaka Highway (County Route 101A) to the northwestern section

observation pavilion on the mountain's windswept peak are magnificent. You see startling panoramas of mountains and rivers, Taipei's urban sprawl, and the Pacific Ocean dotted with large ships and fishing boats. To the west, you can see the Danshui River, whose wide mouth can turn a brilliant orange in the late afternoon sun. In the south, mountains fade into the distance.

Under the layer of haze that fills the Taipei Basin, Taipei and its suburbs are in full view in the early morning from Datun. During the day, this urban panorama is impressive for its sheer size, but after dark it becomes beautiful, changing into a vast sea of twinkling lights. At each observation platform along the trail is a map with the names of the peaks in front of you. Qixingshan is among the most impressive of the lot, with one slope dominated by a smoldering crater.

Trails

May is when Yangmingshan's 151 species of butterflies are at their population peak on the mountaintops (keep an eye out for the blue-spotted monarch), but at other times of the year you will still be able to spot plenty of the elegant flyers, especially along the shady **Butterfly Corridor,** an easy 1.8-mile (3 km) trail that winds from the eastern slopes of Datunshan to the Erziping area. At this elevation are an abundance of nectar-bearing wildflowers. You can pick up the popular trail opposite the entrance to Datun Nature Park; it takes about two hours (one way) to walk.

From Erziping, you can join up with the forested **Bird-Watching Trail,** where you may spot up to 20 different species of birds, including the Taiwan blue magpie and the colorful Muller's barbet, with its emerald green chest. To spot the birds at their most active, it is best to go at dawn or dusk. The trail ends at Qixingshan camping area, near the administrative offices of Yangmingshan National Park. ■

Birding is popular at Yangmingshan, where black-capped kingfishers are among the visual rewards.

Beitou

The Japanese opened the first hot-springs hotel here in 1896, making Beitou Taiwan's oldest such resort. Beitou reached its peak during World War II, when it became popular with Japanese troops on R&R. Locals say that kamikaze pilots used to spend their last few days at the resort, "marrying" Beitou girls before flying off to meet their fate.

Beitou
🅜 93 C4

Beitou Hot Springs Museum
✉ 2 Zhongshan Rd.
☎ 02/2893-9981
🕐 Closed Mon.
🚇 MRT: Xinbeitou station, or taxi

Taiwan Folk Arts Museum
✉ 32 Youya Rd.
☎ 02/2891-2318
🕐 Closed Mon.
💲 $
🚇 MRT: Xinbeitou station, then taxi or bus 230

In the ensuing years, Beitou's popularity gradually waned. But a hot-springs boom and the arrival of an MRT line in the late 1990s revived the town. Beitou is now the most convenient place in which to experience hot springs (see pp. 42–43) close to Taipei.

A snapshot of Beitou's history and Taiwan's hot-springs culture can be found at the **Beitou Hot Springs Museum,** a 5-minute walk up Zhongshan Road from the Xinbeitou MRT station. The Victorian-style brick-and-wood building, originally built by the Japanese in 1913, once served as a public bathhouse. The 50-by-20-foot (15 by 6 m) Romanesque **indoor bathing pool** on the first floor gives some idea of how seriously the Japanese took hot-springs bathing. Columns supporting a recessed ceiling frame the pool; motifs of swans, sailboats, and snowcapped mountains are embossed on stained-glass windows.

The beautifully restored **Tatami Room,** enclosed by sliding rice-paper screen doors, dominates the second floor. Other rooms in the museum are given over to exhibits on such subjects as hot-springs geology and the history of the area. The **Hollywood of Taiwan Film Gallery** traces the flourishing local filmmaking industry of the 1950s and '60s, when many films

were shot in and around the area.

A little farther east along Zhongshan Road, the thick clouds of steam hanging over a giant bubbling sulfur pit at **Hell Valley** (tel 02/2893-9981, closed Mon.) evoke the apocalyptic atmosphere that earns the area its name. This haunting natural phenomenon is one of Beitou's most famous attractions.

According to its curators, the **Taiwan Folk Arts Museum** (on Youya Road, farther up hilly Zhongshan Road from Hell Valley) was once a club and inn for kamikaze pilots. The traditional Japanese-style building is now a museum and garden housing a wildly eclectic private collection of artifacts on Taiwanese and aboriginal culture. One of the more interesting and unsettling is an **exhibition on the practice of foot-binding** on the second floor of the main building. It takes you through this traditional process with explanations, photographs, and displays of the tiny slippers worn by the women who suffered this fate.

A loftier, more expansive view of the steamy phenomenon that occurs in Hell Valley can be found at **Longfeng Valley** along Quanyuan Road, where wooden observation decks overlook a former sulfur mine, one of 27 that once existed in Beitou. ■

Beitou Hot Springs Museum (built 1913), the former public bathhouse

Typical volcanic terrain

Steam

Steam rises from heated water.

Mineral deposits collect around the edge of pools.

Water is forced toward the surface through cracks.

Underground water course and reservoir of water, heated by subterranean hot rocks

Heated rocks beneath the Earth's surface

A Walk Around Danshui

You can find evidence of Taiwan's colonial past throughout the historic port town of Danshui, settled in 1629 by the Spanish, who were expelled by the Dutch. The Chinese and British followed. Reminders of the work of respected Canadian Presbyterian missionary George Leslie Mackay are in evidence among the bustling streets along the Danshui River.

From the Danshui MRT station catch Red Bus No. 26 along Zhongzheng Road to the **Aletheia University bus stop,** about 1.25 miles (2 km) from the MRT station. From the bus stop, after paying an entrance fee, walk up a garden path to a hill overlooking the mouth of the Danshui River and the Pacific Ocean. You will find the red concrete fortifications of **Fort San Domingo** ❶ (*1 Lane 28, Zhongzheng Rd., Danshui, tel 02/2623-1001, closed Mon.*). This small, sturdy fort neatly encapsulates much of Taiwan's history. Built by the Spanish in 1629, it was later occupied by the Dutch, Chinese, and British, who turned it into a consulate. After Britain recognized mainland China in 1972, the British vacated the compound and

returned it to the Taiwanese government in 1980. The fort's first floor has four prison cells opening onto a small, high-walled exercise yard, as well as a scale model of the fort and information about its history. On the walls of the two second-floor rooms are replicas of maps from the period and a wonderfully crafted scale model of a 17th-century Dutch warship, the *Prins Willem*.

A footpath runs alongside the fort to the **Former British Consulate** ❷, a redbrick Victorian building constructed in 1871 that provides river views from its wide verandas and bay windows. The rooms are filled with late 19th- and early 20th-century furniture, which tends to clash with such latter-day additions as wall-to-wall carpeting and linoleum. Return to the entrance of the fort and turn right toward **Aletheia University** (formerly known as Oxford University College), passing an imposing neo-Gothic-style church on the left.

Across a spread of lawn and gardens is the original college building, now housing the **Tamsui Oxford Museum** ❸ (*32 Zhenli St., Danshui, tel 02/2621-2121, tours by appt.*). The small museum building, which is also the original Oxford College that Mackay built in 1882, is a delightful amalgam of British colonial design and Chinese architectural flourishes, including a traditional tiled roof crowned with a steeple shaped like a Buddhist *chedi* and topped with a crucifix. The museum is dedicated to missionary Mackay, who was greatly respected in Taiwan for his benevolence. Inside you'll find photos, diaries, historical information, and other memorabilia.

Return to the entrance to the university and head left down narrow Zhenli Street.

Danshui Biking Around the River

Dedicated bike paths line both sides of the Danshui River in Taipei County, stretching on the right bank from **Guandu Wharf to Danshui port** (but not the coast itself) and on the left bank past the river mouth to the **Shihsanhang Museum of Archaeology** (see p. 128). This is perhaps the best riverside biking in the Taipei area, with **Yangmingshan** (see pp. 98–101) on one side and **Guanyinshan** on the other. Cafés and eateries line the path. Bike-rental kiosks are found at **Guandu Wharf** and by both docks of the **Danshui-Bali Ferry** (bikes allowed on board), on the right bank at the base of Danshui Old Street.

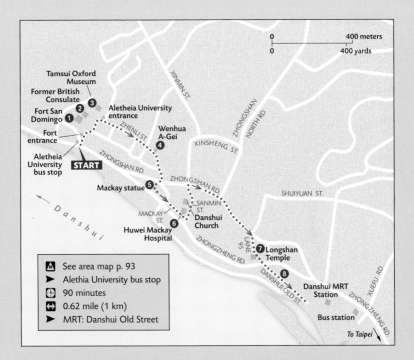

0   400 meters
0   400 yards

Tamsui Oxford Museum
Former British Consulate
Fort San Domingo ❶   ❷ ❸   Aletheia University entrance
Fort entrance   ZHENLI ST.   Wenhua A-Gei ❹
Aletheia University bus stop   XINMIN ST.   XINSHENG ST.
START   ZHONGSHAN RD.
Mackay statue ❺   ZHONGSHAN RD.   ZHONGSHAN NORTH RD.
Danshui   SANMIN ST.   SHUIYUAN ST.
MACKAY ST.   ❻ Danshui Church
Huwei Mackay Hospital   ZHONGZHENG RD.   LANE 95
        ❼ Longshan Temple
        ❽   Danshui MRT Station   XUEFU RD.
        DANSHUI OLD ST.   ZHONGZHENG RD.
        Bus station
        To Taipei

⛰ See area map p. 93
► Alethia University bus stop
🕐 90 minutes
↔ 0.62 mile (1 km)
► MRT: Danshui Old Street

After about 150 yards (140 m), small eateries and food kiosks line the left-hand side of the street. A few doors down on the left is the open-fronted restaurant **Wenhua A-Gei ❹** *(6-1 Zhenli St., tel 02/2621-1785)*; sample some of its famous homemade soy milk and *a-gei*, a Japanese dish of vermicelli noodles inside tofu.

Continue down Zhenli Street toward the river for about 110 yards (100 m) to the intersection at Zhongshan Road. Turn right at the intersection and walk down the hill for 110 yards (100 m). Here, in a tiny park in the middle of the street, is a large **granite bust of Mackay ❺**, whose features have taken on a distinctly Chinese appearance. Directly to the left as you face the statue is a small lane that leads 33 yards (30 m) to the **Huwei Mackay Hospital ❻** *(closed Mon.)*, which now houses a small museum dedicated to the missionary. Built by Mackay, it was the first Western hospital in Taiwan. Next door is **Danshui Church**, also built by Mackay, although there is not much left

NOT TO BE MISSED:

Fort San Domingo • Former British Consulate • Tamsui Oxford Museum • Longshan Temple

of the original structure. Return to Zhongshan Road via Sanmin Street and turn right, or southeast, toward the MRT line. About 275 yards (250 m) along the road is a Bank of Taiwan building at the head of Lane 95. Turn right into this narrow lane, and after 55 yards (50 m) you will come to the **Longshan Temple ❼**, dedicated to the goddess Guanyin. This venerable place of worship was built in 1796 and is among the oldest in Taiwan. Cross Zhongzheng and proceed down Gongming Street, the two collectively known as **Danshui Old Street ❽**, lined with renovated old shop-houses filled with cafés and eateries selling old-style Taiwanese treats.

North Coast

From Danshui, the North Coast Highway (Provincial Highway 2) skirts the coastline east to the port city of Keelung. The area is known for its wide sandy beaches and rocky coastline, which sprouts numerous eye-catching rock formations. The 40-mile (64 km) route can easily be covered in a single day.

Primary beauty: Mushroom-shaped yellow rock formations stand out against a cloud-studded blue sky at the Yeliu GeoPark, along the most dramatic portion of Taiwan's north coast.

About 15 miles (25 km) east of Danshui is one of the most popular beaches along the north coast: **Baisha (White Sand) Bay** (closed dusk–8 a.m., $), a generous sweep of white sand locked between rocky promontories. The beach can get so crowded on summer weekends that it becomes hard to see the sand for all the umbrellas and bodies.

The half-mile (0.8 km) stretch of sandy beach is markedly quieter midweek and during the winter months.

Expansive sea views open up along **Cape Fugui,** where the Taiwan Strait, East China Sea, and Pacific Ocean come together. This portion of the north coast is noted for its rugged rocky outcroppings, lush greenery, and a small fishing port dotted with popular seafood eateries.

About 2 miles (3 km) farther east at **Shimen** (Stone Gate), a massive natural stone arch stands by the coastal side of the highway. You can climb to the top of the 26-foot (8 m) arch, relax on remnants of gun emplacements, and take in the views.

Legend holds that during the Qing dynasty, 17 merchants drowned after their boat sank on a rough crossing of the Taiwan Strait. One merchant's dog vainly attempted to rescue his master before swimming ashore, where it sat on the beach and eventually pined away. The **18 Kings Temple** memorializes these unfortunate souls as well as the dog, whose statue takes pride of place in the main shrine overlooking the ocean just to the east of Shimen.

Worshipers at the temple light cigarettes and place them in censers, just as they would incense, believing the merchants were fond of smoking. You reach the temple via a side road at the highway's 19-mile (31 km) mark.

Just before the town of Jinshan, about 24 miles (39 km) along the highway, a signposted side road heads inland to the **Ju Ming Museum,** which celebrates the works of one of Taiwan's foremost artists. The museum contains about 500 sculptures and 500 paintings by the prolific Ju, with many of his pieces placed outdoors on 26 acres (10.4 ha) of undulating parkland. The grounds also display sculptures created by other artists.

Back on the highway, at Jinbaoli Street in the center of Jinshan, you can see fine examples of Qing dynasty buildings. A viewing platform in the town looks out over the rocky Candlestick Islets, 500 yards (460 m) offshore.

Taiwan's north coast reaches its most dramatic point at the 1-mile-long (1.6 km) promontory at **Yeliu,** about 3 miles (5 km) east of Jinshan. **Yeliu GeoPark** (tel 02/2492-2016, www.ylgeopark.org. tw, $) is where you'll find amazing rock formations in almost recognizable shapes, sprouting from a desolate sandstone landscape. A stone bridge leads over a tidal pool to the tip of the promontory and spectacular views.

INSIDER TIP:

On the north coast, Ju Ming's tai chi series—hulking works of bronze chiseled into graceful poses—is not to be missed.

—EMILY HAILE
Travel Telegraph *blogger and former* National Geographic Traveler *magazine researcher*

Outside the geopark is **Cheng Qing Lake Exotic Marine Life Museum** (tel 02/2492-1111, $$$), worth a stop if you enjoy aquariums and dolphins. The 1-mile (1.6 km) stretch of sand at **Green Bay** has been developed into a resort called Green Bay Seashore Recreation Club ($$), with water sports, paragliding, and camping. ■

North Coast
🅰 93 C4–D4

Visitor Information
✉ North Coast & Guanyinshan National Scenic Area Tourist Center, 33-6 Xiayuankeng, Shimen Township, Taipei County (beside coastal highway)
☎ 02/8635-5100
www.northguan-nsa .gov.tw

Ju Ming Museum
✉ 2 Xishi Lake, Jinshan Township, Taipei County
☎ 02/2498-9940
🕐 Closed Mon. unless a national holiday
💲 $$
www.juming.org.tw

Jiufen

Perched high on a mountain behind Shenao Bay about a 45-minute drive east of Taipei, isolated Jiufen sprang to life in the 1890s with the discovery of gold. Over the years, thousands of prospectors poured into the town to seek their fortunes. At the peak of the gold rush in the 1930s, Jiufen had become so rambunctious it earned the nickname "little Shanghai." After World War II, the gold ran out and the town's gilded prosperity faded.

Once a raffish gold-mining town, Jiufen is a well-visited nostalgic flash from the past.

Jiufen
 93 D3

But good times returned after the release of the Taiwanese film classic *City of Sadness* by director Hou Hsiao-hsien in 1989. The film uses Jiufen as a stand-in for Taipei as it details the period between the end of Japanese occupation and 1949, when Nationalist forces established a government-in-exile.

After the release of *City of Sadness,* the town's narrow streets and antique architecture captured the fancy of Taiwan's artists, who moved there for both inspiration and cheap studio rentals. Visitors, wanting a little of the past on an island bent on progress, followed.

Jiufen has a charm hard to find anywhere else in Taiwan. It's a pleasure, even when the masses arrive on weekends, to wander its laddered streets and narrow alleys, lined with homes and art and souvenir shops, and to relax in teahouses and cafés with stunning views of the mountains and the Pacific Ocean.

Most people come to the village along County Route 102, which becomes Qiche, or Car, Road along Jiufen's eastern edge. The junction of Qiche Road and Jishan Street is a good place to

INSIDER TIP:

Visible from just about everywhere in Jiufen, the crest of Mt. Keelung is worth the short walk for terrific coastal views.

—RICK CHARETTE
National Geographic contributor

start exploring on foot. Most of the attractions are on level ground or downhill from here.

The first section of **Jishan Street** is densely packed with jewelry shops, boutiques, art galleries, and handicraft and souvenir shops, along with numerous small restaurants and cafés. About 110 yards (100 m) along Jishan Street, near its end, is the junction with **Shuqi Road,** a steep, 362-step pathway running north–south. This street provided most of the shooting locations for *City of Sadness.* The old buildings bordering the stone steps are almost all three stories high, with uninterrupted views to the sea. Here you'll find more teahouses, galleries, and restaurants, but with food and decor of a higher caliber than those on Jishan Street.

At the corner of Shuqi and

Qingbian Roads, **Jiufen Folk Art Gallery** has exhibits on local history. A second-floor café offers coffee and tea with great views. Opposite the gallery, also on the corner of Shuqi and Qingbian, is the **City of Sadness restaurant** *(35 Shuqi Rd., tel 02/2496-9917),* where scenes from the movie were filmed.

From the restaurant, turn left and head west along Qingbian Road for about 15 yards (13 m), then turn right at Shibei Alley to the **Jiufen Gold-Mining Museum.** The small museum houses a collection of gold-mining implements, antique lamps and tools, and plenty of rock samples, but it lacks English-language captions and information. However, the curator, who gives demonstrations of gold mining, keeps visitors entertained. ∎

Jiufen Folk Art Gallery
- ✉ 131 Qingbian Rd.
- ☎ 02/2497-9400

Jiufen Gold-Mining Museum
- ✉ 66 Shibei Alley
- ☎ 02/2496-6379
- 💲 $

EXPERIENCE: Homestays

In the 1990s the picturesque little town of Jiufen began filling up with artists and became a popular day-tripper destination after appearing in a well-known television advertisement and movie. Locals began offering rooms and, sometimes, homes to overnighters. The homestay experience in Taiwan has since exploded, notably along the quieter east coast, with some people moving out of busy cities to open facilities. Many organize tours and activities to introduce local-area produce, crafts, and attractions. The **Tourism Bureau** *(http://info.taiwan.net.tw/homestay/english/index.html)* has listings of vetted homestays in all regions, with descriptive detail. A longer list, with more detail, is at *www.taiwan.net.tw;* click on Accommodation and then choose B&B.

Keelung

This city of 390,000, reached by both the North Coast and Northeast Coast Highways, is Taiwan's second biggest seaport. Like the island's other ports, it was a gateway for foreign occupiers, missionaries, traders, and merchants. Although today's Keelung has little to show for this in terms of historical sites, it makes for an interesting stopover along the north and northeastern coastal routes.

Keelung

🗺 93 D4

Visitor Information

✉ Tourist Information Center, Keelung City Govt., 1 Gangxi St., Keelung City

☎ 02/2428-7664

http://tour.klcg.gov.tw

You can start your tour of the city at the huge statue of the goddess of mercy, Guanyin, located on a hill in **Zhongzheng Park**, close to the city center. The 74-foot (22.5 m) statue serenely overlooks the city and its harbor; behind it is a Buddhist temple.

Climb farther up the hill to **Ershawan Fort,** a fortification that once guarded the entrance to Keelung Harbor. All that is left of the original fort, built in 1840, is the renovated medieval-style fortress gate. Once through the gate,

you can amble along shaded paths and view the reproduction cannon that mark the fort's former gun emplacements.

INSIDER TIP:

In terms of variety and vividness, the night market of Keelung is one of Taiwan's best. Try the fish soup, deep-fried tempura, and flavored ice.

—YUNGSHIH LEE
National Geographic *magazine*
Taiwan edition former editor

For views of the odd rock formations that define much of the north coast, head to **Heping (Peace) Island,** an islet protecting the south side of Keelung Harbor. On the 163-acre (66 ha) island's north shore is an old-style amusement park *(tel 02/2462-8714, $)*.

Among local travelers, Keelung is most famous for lively **Miaokou Yeshi** (Temple Mouth Night Market), which runs past Dianji Temple on Rensan Road. This stretch of restaurants and food stalls is a good place to try Taiwanese snack foods and soak up the bustling atmosphere. ∎

Talking to the Gods Via Sky Lantern

The annual 15-day **Pingxi Sky Lantern Festival** usually begins mid-February, in the Pingxi Valley, about 12 miles (20 km) southwest of Keelung and just west of Taipei. On the day of the **Lantern Festival,** about midway into the festival, thousands come to release traditional "sky lanterns," miniature hot-air balloons of delicate bamboo-strip frames covered in rice paper, after dusk. Individuals write their wishes to the gods on the paper lanterns (symbolizing peace and good fortune), then set them aflame before releasing them to the gods on high. Lanterns are sold on-site.

Trains travel up the Pingxi Valley from Ruifang, in turn reached by commuter train from Taipei.

Northeast & Yilan Coast National Scenic Area

The Northeast and Yilan Coast National Scenic Area hugs the narrow corridor between Taiwan's eastern mountains and the Pacific Ocean, running from Nanya, just east of Keelung to the fishing port of Nanfangao, 75 miles (121 km) to the south. Coastal scenery, including sandy beaches and wide-open ocean vistas, characterize the area, which can get crowded on weekends and holidays; if you can, choose a weekday for a calmer visit.

Most of the sights can be reached easily by traveling along the Northeast Coast Highway (Provincial Highway 2), although to get to some attractions you will need to park off the highway and walk a short way. Not all directions to attractions are signposted in English, so it may be best if you take a guide along.

Nanya is the northern gateway to the Northeast and Yilan Coast National Scenic Area. It is known for the sea- and wind-eroded rock formations and outcroppings scattered along the coast. The area's small, picturesque fishing villages set against a backdrop of lush green mountains add to the effect.

Just over a mile (1.6 km) farther at **Bitou Cape,** wind and wave erosion has created an array of cliff and rock formations, including sea caves, platforms, undercuts, bluffs, and knolls. The platforms at the bottom of the cape are weathered into patterns. A trail leads from the Bitou Elementary School onto the cape and to sweeping panoramas. It ends at the towering, brilliantly white **Bitou Lighthouse,** standing 390 feet (120 m) above the crashing surf; the lighthouse itself is 40

A climber takes on Longdong (Dragon Hole) Cape, the northeast coast's most popular rock-scaling destination.

Northeast & Yilan Coast National Scenic Area

🄰 93 D3–D4

✉ Fulong Visitor Center, 6 Xinglong St., Fulong Village, Gongliao Township, Taipei County

☎ 02/2499-1115, ext. 221

www.necoast-nsa .gov.tw

feet high (12.3 m). Coastal views here are spectacular.

The sandstone cliffs rising from the sea at **Longdong (Dragon Hole) Cape** make it the premier rock-climbing destination in Taiwan. The 100-foot (30 m) cliffs are popular for their surface variety, and they are a good place to learn the sport. From the top of the cape, there are stunning views to Bitou Cape to the north and Sandiao Cape to the south.

You can take a trail down to **Longdong Bay Park** (tel 02/2490-9445, $), site of the northeast coast's largest bay. With its surprisingly clear water flush with marine life, it's a popular spot

INSIDER TIP:

At the parks along the coast, you can dip your feet in crystal clear lagoons that the ocean fills with the tide.

—EMILY HAILE
Travel Telegraph *blogger and former* National Geographic Traveler *magazine researcher*

for divers, snorkelers, and fishermen, who cast their lines from the rock platforms at the water's edge.

On the bay's south side is **Longdong South Ocean Park** (tel 02/2490-2112, $), which combines a marina, seawater pools, and marine-ecology exhibitions. The entrance to the park is at the 60-mile (96 km) mark along the highway. Its seawater pools are converted abalone ponds, where

water rises from knee-deep to 10 feet (3 m), depending on the tide. Because the pools are connected to the sea, you can often find yourself swimming among shoals of fish, sea anemones, sea stars, shrimp, and crabs.

Jinshawan (Golden Sand Bay) Beach Park—just south of Longdong—is a pleasant sweep of sandy beaches. Though comparatively small, there is a children's recreation area, beach volleyball courts, windsurfing facilities, trails, and scenic platforms.

In contrast, 200-acre (80 ha) **Yanliao Beach Park** (tel 02/2490-2991, $$) is the largest beachside park on the northeast coast. You'll find it at the 65-mile (104 km) mark of the highway. Its network of walkways and pavilions lends a Chinese character to the area. The park's sandy beach (the longest in Taiwan) stretches south for about 2 miles (3 km). It was the ideal landing spot for the Japanese when they first arrived in 1895. A monument in Taiwan-temple style near the beach honors those who fought against the occupation. The park also incorporates terraced rice fields and rolling hills, where you can catch some ocean panoramas. On the beach you can rent sailing, surfing, and fishing gear or snack at a café. A new gentle-grade coastal bike path stretches south all the way to Fulong. Bike rentals available.

About 2 miles (3 km) south is Taiwan's largest camping area, **Longmen (Dragon Gate) Riverside Camping Resort** (tel 02/2499-1791, $). The campgrounds are found in the

Among the coastal area's attractions are colorful temples. This one is on the Caoling Historic Trail.

national scenic area—a surprisingly picturesque spot given that part of it used to be a quarry. Campers pitch tents in a meadow or on wooden platforms. The area also has log cabins and roofed wooden platforms where camper vans can hook up to power sources. You can hire paddleboats, rowboats, and canoes for jaunts upstream. From the campground, Yanliao Beach Park (see p. 112) can be reached via a suspension bridge.

Near Longmen, **Fulong Beach** (tel 02/2499-1211, $) is another wide, long sweeping stretch of sand. It's the area's most popular, mainly because of the estuary, which makes it ideal for the more sedate water sports. Walkways dotted with shady pavilions take you along the coast and river.

The **Fulong Visitor Center** (tel 02/2499-1115, ext. 221), the official visitor center for the national scenic area, provides plenty of information and has displays of local geology, geography, culture, and flora and fauna. It also has a couple of theaters showing short films about the area. Best of all is the delightful driftwood exhibition, where local artists have created pieces using driftwood washed up along northeast coast beaches during typhoons. A cultural display introduces the lives of local farmers and fishermen, and an art gallery hosts exhibitions of works by local artists.

Maoao Fishing Village, tucked into the north side of Sandiao Cape, is the coast's best example of a traditional fishing village. Three banyan-edged streams run down from the mountainside and through the village, adding an appealing flavor to the many simple, traditional stone houses that dot the village.

At **Sandiao Cape**—the easternmost point of Taiwan—panoramas open to the Pacific Ocean: the rugged coastline north to Bitou Cape and south to Honeymoon Bay. At the tip of the cape you can see the whitewashed **Sandiao Cape Lighthouse** *(tel 02/2499-1300, closed Mon.).*

Two miles (3.2 km) farther south at **Lailai,** anglers balance on slippery stone platforms and brace themselves against the crashing waves. This part of the coast supports a rich growth of plankton and algae, which attracts an abundance of fish and, in turn, anglers.

South from the nearby village of **Dali,** coastal rock formations take the shape of tofu (rock sectioned into squares, similar to bean curd)

Nature as artist: Nanya is famous for its striated, weathered sandstone formations.

and *cuesta* (rocks gently sloping to a peak on one side, with a sheer face on the other), all of which adds up to some splendid scenery.

Behind the town's Tiangong Temple is the southern end of the **Caoling Historic Trail,** which heads north to the small town of Fulong. The trail is the remaining section of a renovated Qing dynasty road, built in the early 19th century as a trade link between the Taipei Basin and the Lanyang Plain and to encourage more settlers to move to the plain. The 6-mile (10 km) historic trail takes you up to some outstanding views of the coast, ending at the Shuangxi River, just to the west of Fulong.

About 3 miles (4 km) south of Dali you'll find the village of Daxi, which faces **Honeymoon Bay.** The bay gets its name from its heart-shaped shoreline, although unromantic viewers might say it more closely resembles a horseshoe. The beach is notable for its wide spread of sand, which at low tide extends about 330 feet (100 m) from the shoreline and reveals legions of tiny scurrying crabs. In the right conditions, waves can reach a formidable 6 feet (2 m), making the bay popular with Taiwan's surfers.

Stone paths interspersed with lookout pavilions and lined with shady banyan trees follow the shoreline at **Beiguan Tidal Park** *(tel 03/978-0727, parking $).* From them you can look out over coastal rock formations (consisting mainly of pointy cuestas and patterned tofu rock) that jut into the Pacific. One such path leads to the top of one of the largest cuestas for wide-ranging ocean and coastal views. ∎

EXPERIENCE: Biking Taiwan

Over the past decade governments at all levels in Taiwan have been active in promoting recreational cycling in their jurisdictions, and new facilities are constantly being built. Two Taiwan firms, Giant and Merida, are in the elite of bicycle manufacturers worldwide, and at the initiative of Giant in particular there is now a concerted effort to make Taiwan what is called a Kingdom of Bicycles, meaning a paradise for those seeking recreational cycling opportunities.

Taiwan's culture grows more and more bike-identified.

In **Taipei** a bicycle-path and riverside-park system encircles practically the entire city, and on weekends locals flood the system's trails for big-vista fun on wheels. Bike-rental kiosks dot the path, notably by **Dadaocheng Wharf, Guandu Wharf,** and **Dajia Wharf,** all stops on the Blue Highway boat-cruise network (bicycles can be brought on board these craft for a rewarding cruise/bike experience). Rentals are cheap, the quality good, and the bikes can be returned to any kiosk. Side paths shoot up small waterways in north Taipei, one toward the **National Palace Museum** (see pp. 80–85), and another, longer, trail (5.25 miles/8.5 km) leads to coastal **Danshui** (see pp. 104–105). Visit the Specialty Tours section of the website *taipeitravel .net* for more information on biking in and around Taipei, including a bike-path map.

In the Taipei area, the **Yangmingshan Cycling Club** (*http://taipeiycc.blog spot.com*) is a group of expatriates that schedules regular road-biking excursions, everyone welcome.

In the **Sun Moon Lake** area (see pp. 220–222), slow excursions along the long loop road that circles the lake are very popular. Bikes can be rented at the Sun Moon Lake Youth Activity Center, right beside the road. Visit *www.sunmoonlake.gov .tw* for details.

The tiny village of **Guanshan** (see pp. 174–175), nestled in the isolated East Rift Valley on Taiwan's east coast, has a long and level dedicated bike path that meanders through farmland by rice paddies and rushing streams. The views are idyllic, evoking the Taiwan of a hundred years ago. Numerous bike-rental facilities crowd the path's starting point, and there are small hotels within walking distance of the path for travelers wishing to stay overnight.

All of Taiwan's offshore islands are sleepy, particularly in comparison to the busy main island, and bicycling on the main roads is both safe and leisurely. Only remote **Matsu** is not bike-friendly, being too hilly.

In general, rental facilities are located in the main town on each island or island group; check with the visitor center of the respective national park or national scenic area that has jurisdiction in that area.

Sanxia Zushi Temple

Sanxia Zushi Temple is an outstanding example of modern restoration techniques applied to traditional Taiwanese temple architecture. Originally built in 1769, the temple has been rebuilt three times, the last time beginning in 1947. Restoration is still under way, and visitors can watch the restoration crew at work. The temple's architecture and adornments represent the highest standards of Taiwanese temple art.

The ornate Sanxia temple is one of Taiwan's finest examples of temple architecture.

Sanxia Zushi Temple
🅰 93 C3
✉ 1 Changfu St., Sanxia, Taipei County
☎ 02/2671-1031
💲 $ (donation)

Each beam in the tiered roofs of the temple's buildings is opulently decorated, and few parts of the interior and exterior walls have escaped painting or carving. The beams that support the temple's roofs are carved with lifelike human figures and gilded. Interior walls have shallow engravings and bas-reliefs illustrating a wealth of Chinese legends. In addition to themes from Chinese mythology, the temple's carvings depict bears, Pekingese dogs, turkeys, squid, and crab—elements rarely seen in Taiwanese religious buildings.

The complex contains an abundance of doors, panels, pillars, and statues cast in bronze. Camphor and cypress, after being carved into mythological characters and scenes, have been covered in gold leaf.

Enter the complex via the first courtyard to Sanchuan Hall through the heavy bronze **Sanchuan doorway.** Walls and window frames flanking the doorway are adorned with stone carvings. Two stone lions, carved boldly to epitomize their vigilance, guard the entrance. The male lion holds a pearl in its mouth, while the lioness plays with a cub.

The ceiling of **Sanchuan Hall** is a superb example of the structural complexity employed in Chinese temple architecture. Layers of stacked brackets climb to the ridges of the roof, using an ancient and ingenious technique that allows them to hold the immense weight of the tiled roof while eliminating the use of nails in construction.

Dragon Door Hall (to the right) and **Tiger Door Hall** flank Sanchuan Hall. Carvings of coiled dragons, lion cubs, and flowers cover the stone drums on each side of the doors. The drums, like the stone lions that guard the Sanchuan doorway, are there to protect against evil spirits.

The two halls take you to the second courtyard in front of the main shrine. Here, three pairs of **stone pillars** are adorned with intricate three-dimensional figures. One of the pairs of columns features flowers and birds; each pillar sports 50 birds—each with its own distinct posture—perching on the branches of plum trees.

A pair of bronze lions guard the steps leading up to the **Main Shrine,** where the icon of the Zushi, or Divine Progenitor, is enshrined on a high altar in the central hall. At the entrance to the hall are extraordinarily detailed stone columns, with decorative figures carved three to four layers deep. The Divine Progenitor sits under a spiraling wooden ceiling embellished with gilded ridges and relief patterns. The carvings that enliven the

roof ridges are cut from Chinese cypress.

The **Drum Tower** (to the left) and the **Bell Tower** flank the main shrine. Each has a hexagonal, three-tiered roof topped by six wildly posing mosaic-tile dragons strung along the ridges.

The sun god presides in the **East Shrine** behind the Bell Tower, while the moon god sits in the **West Shrine,** behind the Drum Tower. These gods are guardian deity images cast from bronze and positioned to maintain a favorable balance of the opposing principles of yin and yang.

INSIDER TIP:

Sanxia's Zushi Temple is a standout for its whimsical stone carvings of courtesans, warriors, and dragons.

—JULIA ROSS
Travel writer and former Fulbright scholar in Taiwan

Li Mei-shu Memorial Gallery

Li Mei-shu is regarded as one of Taiwan's most influential post–World War II artists and is the man responsible for the magnificence of Sanxia Zushi Temple. Li began to restore the then dilapidated temple in 1947, and he was still working on it shortly before his death 36 years later. The memorial gallery houses many of Li's paintings and chronicles his life's work. ∎

Li Mei-shu Memorial Gallery

✉ 10 Lane 43, Zhonghua Rd., Sanxia, Taipei County
☎ 02/2673-2333
🕐 Closed Mon.– Fri.; groups by appt. only
💲 $
www.limeishu.org

Jiaoxi & Yilan County

Jiaoxi in Yilan County is a popular hot-springs town with more than a hundred hotels and inns clustered within a mile (1.2 km) radius of the town's railway station. Bathing at the hot springs dates back to the Qing dynasty, when locals built walls around the pools to protect the modesty of the bathers. After the Japanese occupiers arrived in 1895, they further improved on the situation, constructing bathhouses and inns.

These days water is pumped from the hot springs directly into hotel guest rooms. Most hotels also have outdoor bathing pools for daytime visitors. The water is colorless and odorless; some drink it for its health-giving properties.

About 550 yards (500 m) north of the railway station at

Crowds enjoy Yilan's International Folklore and Folk Game Festival for its wide variety of competitions.

the junction of Zhongshan and Gongyuan Roads is **Jiaoxi Park,** often called Yuanshan Park, a pleasant area of landscaped gardens dotted with carp ponds.

Follow Zhongshan Road south from the railway station for just over half a mile (1 km) to the richly adorned **Xietian Temple** (51 Zhongshan Rd., Sec. 1, tel 03/ 988-2621). The temple, built in 1804, is one the largest in northern Taiwan devoted to the god of war, Guangong.

About 2 miles (3.5 km) west of the railway station along Wufeng Road, **Wufengqi Waterfall** tumbles down from the surrounding mountains. A pathway leads into the hills to this three-tiered spectacle. Climb the trail to the more dramatic second section. The trail then continues to the top of the falls, where you can watch water pour over rocks to pools 330 feet (100 m) below.

South of Jiaoxi in the city of Yilan, the **Taiwan Theater Museum** (101 Fuxing Rd., Sec. 2, Yilan City, tel 03/932-2440, ext. 400, closed Mon. & national holidays, $) has an interesting and colorful collection of Taiwanese opera paraphernalia, musical instruments, and costumes, as well as puppet-theater artifacts. Displays illustrate the evolution of Taiwanese folk

EXPERIENCE: Adventure Sports—Jump Right In

In recent decades the Taiwanese, especially the younger generation, have been leaving traditional forms of exercise such as tai chi and opting for adventure sports with gusto. Now popular are mountain biking, mountain hiking, road cycling, white-water rafting, and rock climbing. A number of quality outdoor-adventure enterprises have arisen that are accustomed to handling travelers from overseas; you can ask to be included in outings as part of a local group or just your own group (generally a minimum of four).

Topping the outfitter list are **Barking Deer** (*www.barking-deer.com*), **FreshTreks** (*www.freshtreks.com*), and **In Motion Asia** (*www.inmotionasia.com*).

---

opera using mock-ups of traditional opera stages. The puppet theater has a collection of brightly clad marionettes along with their tiny, exquisite props.

Forest Recreation Areas

Yilan marks the eastern terminus of the Northern Cross Island Highway (Provincial Highway 7), which cuts across Taiwan's central mountains. Look for the **Qilan Forest Recreation Area** (*6 Taiya Rd., Sec. 4, Taiping Village, Datong Township, Yilan County, tel 03/980-9606, $*) 26.5 miles (38 km) southwest of the city of Yilan on a branch of Highway 7 that leads to Lishan. This beautiful area in the Lanyang Valley, made lush by abundant rainfall, has superb views to the mountains. About 7.5 miles (12 km) inside the recreation area you'll find the **Chinese Historic Men Arboretum,** a haunting primeval forest featuring 51 huge, ancient cypress trees. Each is named after a famous person from Chinese history whose time period supposedly corresponds to the age of the tree. Some 10.5 miles (17 km) west of the town

of Qilan along the Northern Cross Island Highway, the frequently fog-shrouded **Mingchi Lake** nestles amid soaring mountains at the **Mingchi Forest Recreation Area** (*41 Mingchi Ln., Yingshih Village, Datong Township, Yilan County, tel 03/989-4106, $*). A trail dotted with lookout pavilions meanders through the old-growth cypress trees around the lake.

Just south of Qilan, the calcium carbonate–rich waters at **Renze Hot Springs** seep from the earth at a scalding 203°F-plus (95°C). The resort's hotels add cool water to the spring water to make soaking bearable.

From Renze Hot Springs, the road climbs to **Taipingshan National Forest Recreation Area** (*58-1 Taiping Ln., Taiping Village, Datong Township, Yilan County, tel 03/980-9619, http://trail.forest .gov.tw, $*). The area has gardens, a forest park, and a wildlife preserve. A narrow branch road twists another 11 miles (18 km) to the crystal-clear waters of **Cuifeng Lake,** the largest alpine lake on the island. ■

Jiaoxi & Yilan County

▲ 93 C2–D3

Visitor Information

✉ Business and Tourism Dept., Yilan County government, 1 Xianzheng N. Rd., Yilan City

☎ 03/925-1000, ext. 1355

🕐 Closed Sat.–Sun.

http://tourism .e-land.gov.tw

Wulai

The mountain retreat and hot-springs resort of Wulai is within easy reach of Taipei, just 40 minutes south by car or bus. Although Wulai village is little more than a jumble of souvenir shops, hotels, and eateries, the area serves up some spectacular scenery. The Wulai region has a sizable population of Atayal aborigines, who put on shows at various venues.

Wulai
🗺 93 C3

Wulai Aboriginal Culture Village
✉ 31 Pubu Rd., Wulai Township
☎ 02/2661-6635
💲 $

No traffic is allowed into Wulai; vehicles park at the tollgate at the northern end of the town. From there a small bridge crosses the Nanshi River into the village. It only takes about five minutes to walk through Wulai village. Where it stops, another bridge crosses back over the Nanshi. From here you can reach **Wulai Falls,** the area's major scenic attraction. They are a magnificent sight, especially after it rains, which is often. Water plunges

from a cliff face laced with green foliage and pummels the Nanshi River 262 feet (80 m) below.

Just left of the bridge, on the banks of the Nanshi River, people commune with nature at Wulai's **Outdoor Hot Springs.** Pool walls built from riverbank rocks regulate the amount of cool water that mixes with the hot-springs water, creating different temperatures for each of the three pools.

Beyond the bridge, a mini electric railway ($) regularly heads south about 1.25 miles (2 km) to **Wulai Aboriginal Culture Village,** directly across the river from Wulai Falls. You can also reach the falls on foot in about 20 minutes via a paved one-lane road that winds through the gorge alongside the Nanshi River. The Wulai Aboriginal Culture Village is owned and operated by local Atayal residents. The village has handicrafts and Atayal food for sale and holds regular song and dance performances. A ticket to the **Aboriginal Culture Center** includes a show.

From Wulai village, a cable car ($) climbs spectacularly to the top of Wulai Falls. A renovated amusement park, **Yun Hsien Holiday Resort** (tel 02/2661-6386, www.yun-hsien.com.tw, entry with cable car ticket), has nature trails, a swimming pool, paintball, and eco-tours. ∎

Visitors enjoy spectacular views of Wulai Falls after they get off the cable car that climbs steeply up the gorge.

Yingge

Yingge is famed for its wealth of pottery factories and for the shops that produce and sell a wide variety of ceramics—all of which has led tourism authorities to label it the "city of pottery." It's worth a visit to see how lumps of local clay are expertly transformed into fine pieces by the town's legions of artisans.

The **Yingge Ceramics Museum,** a unique building combining curved and linear glass curtains with exposed concrete and steel, is a good place to get an introduction to ceramic techniques.

The front entrance—a large opening in the wall—is connected to the main building by a bridge over a pool; it takes you past cascading water and installation artworks. The ceramics museum is made up of three interlocking buildings. In the north building are the principal display rooms as well as offices. The middle building—the lobby—uses its open spaces and glass walls to allow in natural light. On the south side, the facade of the museum's most striking building is a gently curving wall of glass.

Inside, more than 2,000 pieces of pottery, ancient and contemporary, take center stage in displays based on four themes: "Development & Techniques of Ceramics in Taiwan," "History of Yingge Town," "Prehistoric, Aboriginal, and Taiwanese Works of Ceramics," and "Industrial and High-Tech Ceramics." You will find plenty of background material in English. Audio guides are also available in English. The museum's 250-acre (10 ha) ceramics park has outdoor displays.

Yingge's streets are lined with pottery shops, many with factories

An artisan carefully shapes a clay vessel in Yingge.

on the premises, selling what seems like an endless array of ceramics. They range from toilet bowls and simple earthenware teapots to musical instruments, copies of Ming and Qing dynasty pieces, and exquisite glazed porcelains. The town's historical production core, the main draw, is cobblestoned **Old Pottery Street.** This pedestrians-only section of Jianshanpu Street has 105 shops. English is widely spoken, and overseas shipments handled. ■

Yingge
Ⓜ 93 C3

Yingge Ceramics Museum
✉ 200 Wenhua Rd., Yingge, Taipei County
☎ 02/8677-2727
🕐 Closed Mon.
💲 $

www.ceramics.tpc .gov.tw

Taoyuan & Hsinchu Counties

Most visitors to Taiwan come to Taoyuan County without knowing it when they fly into Taiwan Taoyuan International Airport, about 30 miles (50 km) southwest of downtown Taipei. Taoyuan's easy access from Taipei means that many city dwellers travel there on weekends, so it is wise to avoid those times because of crowds. Farther southwest, the city of Hsinchu is notable for being the birthplace of Taiwan's huge computer and electronics industry.

Kitschy but fun: A replica of the Jefferson Memorial enchants kids at Taoyuan's Window on China.

**Taoyuan &
Hsinchu Counties**
🅜 92–93 B3, C3
Cihu
🅜 93 C3
✉ Daxi Township,
    Taoyuan County
☎ 03/388-3552
💲 $
http://travel-tao
yuan.tycg.gov.tw

At **Cihu,** near the town of Daxi, 30 miles (50 km) southwest of Taipei on Provincial Highway 7, Chiang Kai-shek lies entombed above ground in a granite and marble coffin in one of his former country villas. The gravesite is "temporary," as before his death Chiang had requested his body be returned to his native province of Zhejiang in mainland China. The number of visitors coming to pay their respects has dwindled in recent years as Chiang's myth continues to unravel. But visitors still come to the heavily guarded tomb, bowing before the sarcophagus of the former R.O.C. leader.

Spread over 67.5 acres (25 ha) near the town of Longtan, the quirky, run-down, but nevertheless entertaining **Window on China** theme park presents famous structures on a scale of 1:25. Here you can wander around Beijing's

Forbidden City, the Great Wall of China, and Taipei's Longshan Temple in a lot less time than if you were taking on the real deal. Nor has the rest of the world been forgotten, from the Statue of Liberty to the Leaning Tower of Pisa. The models are meticulously executed. Hundreds of to-scale bonsai trees and human figurines surround the miniature structures. You can go through the park—suitably enough—on a miniature railway and also enjoy rides (see sidebar this page).

The western section of the Northern Cross Island Highway starts in Taoyuan County before climbing into the hills near **Shimen Reservoir Scenic Area,** which contains one of Taiwan's largest lakes. The dam was completed in 1964 and now serves not only as a water storage area and hydroelectric power station, but also as a weekend refuge for harried Taipei residents. The shimmering emerald waters of the lake amid verdant mountainsides make it an engaging spot. You can hire a boat for a paddle or a cruise or follow the trails around the lake.

Farther along the highway, the aboriginal town of **Fuxing** is nestled beautifully amid the Central Mountains. The highway continues to wind its way east–southeast through some of the most spectacular scenery in Taiwan before reaching the city of Yilan near the northeast coast.

Hsinchu

The city of Hsinchu, the capital of Hsinchu County, is known for two things: its wet and windy weather and the Hsinchu Science Park, the center of Taiwan's huge computer and electronics industry (see pp. 124–125). The city does not have a lot to offer visitors aside from bars and clubs.

In the south of Hsinchu County, just south of Window on China, is **Leofoo Village,** a large theme and safari park. The theme park is divided into sections, including the Wild West, Arabian Kingdom, China Town, Fairy Tale Town, and the South Pacific. The park's **Flume Ride** crawls up to the top of a mock-up of a volcano before dropping back down to earth at a hair-raising 45-degree angle. Minibuses haul visitors through the safari park to view lions, giraffes, zebras, and other animals of Africa. ∎

Riding the Water

In addition to its uniquely entertaining miniatures of famous places, the **Window on China** has a theme park that offers a slew of classic rides, from bumper cars to a merry-go-round (the largest in Taiwan, with traditional, colorful wooden horses).

Upping the fun quotient at the amusement park are an indoor roller coaster, bumper boats, and Asia's tallest water flume ride. **Waves of Water Bombers** involves a pyramid and a Nile River canoe that plunges 12 stories, splashing as it goes.

Window on China Theme Park
Ⓜ 92–93 B3
✉ 60-2 Henggangxia, Gaoyuan Village, Longtan Township, Taoyuan County
☎ 03/471-7211
Ⓢ $$$$, parking $
www.woc.com.tw

Shimen Reservoir Scenic Area
Ⓜ 93 B3
✉ 1 Huanhu Rd., Fuxing Village, Daxi Township, Taoyuan County
☎ 03/471-2000
Ⓢ $ per vehicle

Hsinchu
Ⓜ 92 B3

Leofoo Village
Ⓜ 92–93 B3
✉ 60 Gongzigou, Renan Ward, Guanxi Township, Hsinchu County
☎ 03/547-5665
Ⓢ $$$$$
www.leofoo.com.tw/village

Taiwan's Silicon Valley

Taiwan has long been a strong exporting country, but until the 1980s the economy was powered by low-tech, high-volume exports such as toys, T-shirts, shoes, textiles, tennis rackets, and other inexpensive goods. Then, in the 1980s and '90s, producers of these low-cost items began to abandon Taiwan and set up their factories in China, Southeast Asia, and elsewhere, where land was plentiful and labor was cheaper.

Laptop computers rank high in Taiwan's high-tech output. Since the 1980s, hundreds of companies have invested billions of dollars to make Taiwan one of the world's top exporters of electronics.

The exodus left a large hole in the island's industrial heartland, and Taiwan's days of making and exporting cheap goods were gone. In its place, Taiwan has found another kind of commerce: electronics, a potent industry that separates it from Asia's economic also-rans.

The island, quite simply, is a world-beater in electronics. It makes more computer monitors, mouses, motherboards, compact disk drives, digital cameras, and scanners than any other country in the world, and turns out more than one-quarter of the world's desktop computers as well as almost 80 percent of its notebook and laptop computers.

Taiwan also excels in the manufacture of computer chips. Taiwan Semiconductor Manufacturing Corporation and United Microelectronics Corporation are the world's top producers of built-to-order integrated-circuit chips, devices that drive the world's computers, cell phones, and video games.

Taiwan's high-tech success is no accident. The government kick-started the industry in 1980 when it established the Hsinchu Science Park. Companies investing in the Hsinchu park were given tax breaks, research and development money, training, and technical assistance. The science park has been a runaway success, and today much of Taiwan's electronics output comes from Hsinchu, a one-stop high-tech shop 90 minutes south of Taipei by car. Currently, the Hsinchu complex is overflowing; some 400 companies operate there, and dozens are on the waiting list. Total investment is approaching 34 billion dollars (U.S.) and annual revenue generated by the park exceeds 30 billion dollars. More than 80 percent of the companies in Hsinchu are high-tech, producing semiconductors, telecom products, computer components, optoelectronics, and related hardware.

Taiwanese workers turn out a sizable percentage of the world's silicon chips.

Several other Asian countries that have since jumped on the high-tech bandwagon have been unable to reproduce Taiwan's success. Hsinchu's size and organization give it a key competitive advantage over latecomers to the electronics game: When all related companies are near each other, they can work easily together. A producer of integrated circuits, for example, need only look next door to find companies that specialize in complicated tasks like making the masks used to produce the chips, testing the chips, and packaging them.

With the Hsinchu Science Park filled to overflowing, the government opened a second science park near Tainan in 1996, where it offered the same perks as at Hsinchu. The Tainan park enjoyed so much initial success that a third park has been opened near the central city of Taichung.

High-tech products now account for more than half of Taiwan's exports, and the little island has become the world's 16th largest exporting country. Not surprisingly, the people of Taiwan are enthusiastic converts to the world of electronics, and their per capita use of computers, cell phones, and the Internet is among the highest in the world.

Entrepreneurial Spirit: Morris Chang

In Taiwan, where the successful business entrepreneur is a national icon, Morris Chang is a hero. If any single individual is identified with the island's high-tech success and, specifically, the success of Hsinchu Science Park, it's Chang. He founded the powerful Taiwan Semiconductor Manufacturing Company (TSMC) in 1987, the largest chip-maker in the world—headquartered right here.

Born in China at the height of the Chinese Civil War in 1949, he moved to the United States and studied at Harvard, MIT, and Stanford. In 1986 the Taiwan government recruited him to serve as head of the Industrial Technology Research Institute, promoting industrial and technological development. Chang moved back to Taiwan and saw that Western firms might outsource manufacturing to Asia; he founded TSMC.

One of the most influential business figures in the region, he is regularly consulted on business policy by the ROC government. Pressure by Chang and his firm to allow more substantial investment in mainland China has played a significant role in the Taiwan government's decision to open up business ties across the Taiwan Strait.

Miaoli County

Miaoli County extends south from near Hsinchu to the northern border of Taichung County in Taiwan's Central West region. It's a little out of the way if you are using Taipei as a base for travel in northern Taiwan, but if you are traveling from Taipei down the arterial Sun Yat-sen Freeway or Formosa Freeway to Taichung or Kaohsiung, the journey could profitably be punctuated by some stopovers along the way.

Misty forests speak of timeless mystery in Miaoli County.

One of these stopovers should be **Shitoushan** (Lion's Head Mountain), just inside Miaoli's northern border. When viewed from a distance (and with sufficient imagination), 1,627-foot (496 m) Shitoushan does resemble the head of a lion. But more significance lies in the mountain's attachment to Buddhism. Shitoushan's mountainsides are dotted with Buddhist temples, some built into caves and set amid beautiful forest scenery. If you are after a few days of peace and solitude, some of the monasteries have rooms and dormitories and welcome visitors.

From the gate above the visitor center parking lot, stone steps take you toward the mountaintop, passing many temples, shrines, and other attractions along the way. They then descend gently past more of these structures. The last section of the trail, through forest and bamboo groves, is particularly appealing. The hike takes about three hours; along the way are small, traditional eateries, many run by the local Hakka people.

The steps will bring you first to the temple called **Quanhua Hall** (tel 037/782-2020). At Quanhua's main hall, **Kaishan Monastery,** you can see nuns and monks going about their business in serene surroundings. Below the hall, nuns serve vegetarian meals at the temple's cafeteria. The temple provides overnight accommodation.

At the peak of the trail you reach **Wangyue (Viewing the Moon) Pavilion,** where you can linger and enjoy the expansive mountain vistas before heading back down past more temples, cave shrines, and pavilions.

Sanyi

Located beside the Sun Yat-sen Freeway in southern Miaoli, Sanyi is Taiwan's wood carving center. **Zhongsheng Road,** the town's main street, is lined with stores and workshops. On nearby Shuimei Street, you'll find a

INSIDER TIP:

Carved wood treasures for sale in and around Sanyi include miniature bird statues and intricate Buddhist icons.

—LAURA MORELLI
National Geographic Traveler
*magazine Authentic
Shopping Guide editor*

staggering 200 shops selling wood carvings and other wooden items. Follow the signs to **Guangsheng Village,** where wood sculptors have set up workshops and don't mind visitors watching them work.

Also in Guangsheng Village, the **Sanyi Wood Sculpture Museum** houses exhibits of fine

Transformations

Small, forested Sanyi is known for carvings made from the wood of camphor trees, which grow well in the acid clay soil of Sanyi's hillsides. Though still thriving, wood carving here reached its peak in the 1966–1973 period, when 70 percent of the population was involved in the industry. Today, a fair amount of wood used in art pieces comes from stumps of harvested trees.

wood sculptures, along with information on the history, techniques, and styles of wood carving, but unfortunately for Western visitors, mostly in Chinese.

South of Sanyi, tectonic forces, wind, and rain have weathered the mountains at **Huoyanshan (Fire Mountain) Nature Reserve** *(Forestry Bureau, 2 Zhongshan Rd., Hsinchu City, tel 03/522-4163),* creating jagged peaks and rock-strewn slopes. The best views of Huoyanshan are from the south. They are most impressive at sunset, when the mountain gives off a fiery red and orange aura.

A 10-mile (16 km) stretch of railway between Sanyi and Houli to the south will thrill train buffs. Trains twist through tunnels and over bridges straddling deep river gorges into the mountains. The delightfully restored **Shengxing Station** sits at the railway's highest point, 1,320 feet (402 m) above sea level; visitors can walk through an abandoned tunnel. ■

Miaoli County
🅐 92 A1–A2, B2

**Shitoushan
(Lion's Head
Mountain)**
✉ Lion's Head
Mountain
Visitor Center,
60-8 Liuliao,
Qixing Village,
Emei Township,
Hsinchu County
☎ 037/580-9296
**www.trimt-nsa
.gov.tw**

Sanyi
🅐 92 A1 92
Visitor Information
☎ 037/787-2801
(Sanyi Township
Administration)
www.sanyi.gov.

**Sanyi Wood
Sculpture
Museum**
✉ 88 Guangsheng
Village, Sanyi
Township,
Miaoli County
☎ 03/787-6009
🕐 Closed Mon.
💲 $
**http://wood.mic
.gov.tw.gov.tw**

More Places to Visit Around Taipei & the North

Dongshan River Water Park

The park, often called Qingshui Park, is located next to the Dongshan River in Yilan County, east of Luodong. It is full of ponds, pools, spouting fountains, pavilions, and jetties; visitors can wade in the shallow pools or hire boats to row around the deeper areas. Ceramic dragons guard the riverbank, which is lined with colorful mosaics. ◪ 93 D2 ✉ 20-36 Xiehe Rd., Wujie Township, Yilan County ☎ 03/950-2097

Jinbaoshan Cemetery & Teresa Deng's Grave

The grand views to the valley below, the town of Jinshan, and the coast from this manicured cemetery are stunning. But most people come here to pay homage to Taiwan's most famous musical export, Teresa Deng, whose death in 1995 at the age of 43 sent the island into mourning. Deng's pop music—sung in several languages—reached millions throughout Asia. A graveside sound system plays her most famous songs. ◪ 93 C4 ✉ 18 Xishi Lake, Jinshan Township, Taipei County ☎ 02/4498-5900

Shihsanhang Museum of Archaeology

Located west of the mouth of the Danshui River, at the foot of Mount Guanyin across from Danshui port and ferry, this expansive facility was built right over a major archaeological site, which itself is one of the exhibits, that dates back some 500 to 1800 years. The museum was opened in 1998 to showcase the finds here and elsewhere in the area. The Shihsanhang people, unlike other pre-modern Taiwan dwellers, had metalmaking know-how, perhaps acquired from China traders. On display are silver, copperware, gold jewelry, and coins. Visit the Bridge of Time, which enables visitors to travel through the Shihsanhang culture.

Leave time to ride rented bikes along the meandering paths that stretch from the museum upriver to the Bali-Danshui ferry. The pathways go through a mangrove conservation area. Museum tickets ($) can be purchased at the museum itself, both ferry terminals, and the Danshui MRT station; the price includes museum entry, to/from ferry rides, and shuttle-bus to/from the museum. *www.sshm.tpc.gov. tw* ✉ 200 Bowuguan Rd., Bali Township, Taipei County ☎ 02/2619-1313

Visitors can wade through shallow waters in Dongshan River Water Park.

Underdeveloped and unspoiled Taiwan, with great beauty defined by spectacular gorges and coastlines, and bucolic hinterlands

East Coast

Stunning sapphire blue water adds to the magic of a Shakadang (Mystery Valley) Trail walk in Taroko Gorge.

East Coast

Locked between Taiwan's Central Mountain Range and the Pacific Ocean, the largely unspoiled east coast presents the island's most beautiful river and coastal scenery. Steep, towering sea cliffs drop perpendicularly into the sea, and raging rivers cut deep and spectacular chasms into the mountains. Inland, charming hamlets idling on rolling hills, tea plantations, hot springs, and valley views offer respite from the coastline's drama.

Relative isolation gives the east coast a special appeal. Photo-op panoramas abound.

One advantage to touring the east coast is the ease of accessibility to its highlights. Most are laid out before you as you drive down its coastal highway, which for most of the journey between Hualien, the region's biggest city, and Taitung to the south hugs the contours of the coastline.

At Qingshui Cliff, between the port cities of Suao and Hualien, sheer rock walls drop straight into the sea from towering mountains reaching 3,000 feet (1,000 m). The occupying Japanese managed to carve a road along the edge of the cliff face in the 1920s.

An equally surprising engineering feat is the road that runs the length of stunning Taroko Gorge, just to the north of Hualien, and the easternmost section of the Central Cross Island Highway. Taroko is one of Taiwan's

major attractions (avoid weekends unless you like crowds), and the scenery is arguably the best you will find on the island. It was during the construction of the highway between 1956 and 1960 that easy access was gained to the vast marble deposits in the gorge, setting off a mining boom and earning nearby Hualien the moniker of "marble city."

The East Coast National Scenic Area stretches a little over 100 miles (160 km) south of Hualien to Taitung and is well suited to a scenic drive. Green and Orchid Islands, both a boat ride away from Taitung, offer remote tropical splendor with a dash of history and culture, while inland from Taitung toward Hualien, in the East Rift Valley National Scenic Area, the landscapes switch to bucolic. ∎

NOT TO BE MISSED:

Area of map detail

Taipei

THE EAST COAST

0   30 kilometers
0   15 miles

AROUND TAIPEI & THE NORTH
p. 91

TAROKO
NATIONAL
PARK   Swallow
Taroko   Grotto
Dayuling   Gorge   Qingshui Cliff
8   Tianxiang
CENTRAL   Xincheng
CROSS ISLAND   Tunnel of   Xiulin   ◁ 6
HIGHWAY   Nine Turns
Tianchi   Meilun R.   9
14   Jian   Hualien
Dongmen   Ami Cultural Village
Carp L.
Shoufeng
HUALIEN   9
Hualien Farglory Ocean Park
CENTRAL   EAST   Fenglin   11
WEST   16   Wanrong   Fanshuliao   ◁ 5
p. 207   Guangfu
RIFT   11   Fengbin

VALLEY   Ruisui   Qimei
Hot Springs
Ruisui   Dagangkou
9
NATIONAL   11
Zhuoxi   Changbin
SCENIC   Yuli
Antong   ◁ 4
Dongli   Antong
Hot Springs
20   AREA
Chishang
SOUTHERN   PACIFIC
CROSS ISLAND   23   Chenggong   OCEAN
HIGHWAY   TAITUNG
Guanshan
Bunun Village   9   Donghe   ◁ 3
Yanping   11
Hongye Hot Springs   Luye
Chulu   Chulu Pasture
Beinan Cultural Park
THE SOUTH   Beinan   National Museum
p. 157   of Prehistory
Zhiben   Taitung   Green Island
Hot Springs   11   Visitor Center   Gongguan
Green I. Human Rights
24   Zhiben   Memorial Park
Zhiben Forest   Nanliao   Haishenping   ◁ 2
Recreation   Green Island
Area   Taimali   (Ludao)
9
Dawu
9
Orchid Island
(Lanyu)
Langdao   Dongqing
Yeyou   Village   ◁ 1

Central Mountain Range

East Rift Valley

A   B   C   D

Hualien

Known as "marble city" because of large deposits of marble mined from nearby Taroko Gorge, Hualien is the largest city on the east coast. It's a tidy and busy place sitting in the shadow of the Central Mountain Range. The city serves as a jumping-off point for trips to spectacular Taroko Gorge and down the rugged east coast to Taitung, but it is not without its attractions, both within the compact city center and nearby.

The Hualien Aboriginal Dancers perform in Taipei and at the Ami Cultural Village south of Hualien.

Hualien
 131 C5

Carp Lake
 131 C5
✉ Jct. of Provincial Hwy. 14 & Provincial Hwy. 9C, Shoufeng Township, Hualien County

Meilun Riverside Park follows the narrow flow of the Meilun River, which cuts through the city. You can get to the park from a pathway just before a bridge at the northern end of Zhongzheng Road. Follow the park north for about 550 yards (500 m) and cross another bridge to reach Hualien's **Martyrs' Shrine,** built into the hillside of Mount Meilun. The shrine memorializes Chinese heroes important to the history of Taiwan. Steep steps introduce this stately and tranquil place, done in the classical Chinese architectural style of sweeping swallowtail roofs supported by imposing red columns and adorned with colorful eave paintings.

Farther up the hill, the park—which also has a playground and meandering pathways—affords some fine views of Hualien city.

Near the western end of Zhonghua Road, just before it crosses a small canal on the way to Carp Lake, is Hualien's most renowned temple, **Cihuitang,** the Hall of Motherly Love. On the left side of the temple complex is the ornate **Regal Mother of** the West Temple (Wangmu Niangniang Miao).

Extensive use of Hualien's marble is on display next door at the **Palace of the Jade Emperor** (Yuhuang Dadi Dian), a pilgrimage site that holds up to 2,000 devotees in its dormitories. The temple's dormitories are full

INSIDER TIP:

Seven-color jade stones—as well as jade of various other hues—can be found along the riverbanks of Hualien County.

—LAURA MORELLI
National Geographic Traveler
magazine Authentic Shopping editor

during festivals, especially on the 18th day of the second lunar month (about six weeks after the lunar New Year), when pilgrims from all over East Asia arrive here to receive the blessings of priests in an attempt to rid themselves of their chronic ills.

On the outskirts of Hualien, **Carp Lake** (Liyutan), one of Taiwan's largest natural lakes, makes for a pleasant half-day excursion. The lake is set amid pineapple and other tropical fruit plantations in the foothills of the dominant Central Mountain Range. You can take your choice from the hundreds of rowboats and paddleboats clustered on the shoreline and head out onto the lake, or amble around the quiet 3-mile (4 km) path that encircles the lake. *(Bike rentals available.)* A

number of well-marked hiking trails lead from the lake up into nearby hills to some calming views of the lake and surrounding countryside.

Just south of Hualien, the **Ami Cultural Village** celebrates the culture and traditions of the local Ami aboriginal tribe—Taiwan's largest aboriginal ethnic minority, numbering about 150,000—with displays of arts and handicrafts, and regular daily cultural shows.

Six miles (9.6 km) south of the city center on Highway 11, adjacent to the East Coast National Scenic Area Visitor Center (see pp. 140–144), is the world-class **Hualien Farglory Ocean Park.** Spread over 126 acres (51 ha), the park has themed areas that include a dolphin aquarium, a water park, a sea lion and seal habitat park and theater, plus plenty of rides. Hotel shuttle buses will take you there from Hualien. ■

Ami Culture Village

- 🅰 131 C5
- ✉ 93-1 Haibin, Renan Village, Jian Township, Hualien County
- ☎ 03/842-2884
- 💲 $$
- 🚌 Bus: Hualien-Taitung bus (Hualien Bus Co.) from Hualien railway station

Hualien Farglory Ocean Park

- 🅰 131 C5
- ✉ 189 Fude, Yanliao Village, Shoufong Township, Hualien County
- ☎ 03/812-3199
- 💲 $$$$$
- 🚌 Bus: Hualien-Taitung bus (Hualien Bus Co.) from Hualien railway station

Betel Nut Beauties

Along roadsides outside major towns and cities, you are bound to notice young, scantily clad girls perched on stools inside glass booths, most times looking extremely bored. These girls are purveyors of betel nut, or *binlang,* the fruit of the areca palm that gives users a mild stimulating buzz when chewed. It also leaves the teeth and gums with permanent deep-red stains. The betel nut beauties' uniform usually consists of a clinging blouse worn with a miniskirt, often enhanced with side slits—and sometimes less than that. The girls' main customers are truckers and taxi drivers, who, once they pull up in front of the booths, are attended by the girls, who give the drivers titillating views while filling their orders.

Taroko Gorge

Taroko Gorge is simply a spectacular place, a wonderland of natural beauty that would leave even the most jaded traveler impressed. Its deep marble canyons, rushing white water, and towering cliffs put it in league with the world's best scenic attractions. The only route through the gorge, the Central Cross Island Highway—a marvel of engineering in itself—runs along the bottom of the main gorge, taking in much of its splendor along the way.

Sheer beauty: It's no wonder that Taroko, with its gifts of nature, is at the top of Taiwan's scenic attractions list.

Construction of the **Central Cross Island Highway** (see pp. 216–219) through Taroko Gorge was thought near impossible. In 1956 road crews, mainly decommissioned military personnel who had come over from mainland China with the Kuomintang government, started blasting and bulldozing their way through cliffs of solid marble. By 1960, at the cost of more than 450 lives, a 48-mile (78 km) road had been carved, completing the connection between the east and west coasts of the island.

The gorge is part of **Taroko National Park,** which encompasses 92,000 acres (37,000 ha) of the island's Central Mountain Range. The origins of this stunning place lay in the formation of the island of Taiwan some 12 million years ago, when the Philippine tectonic plate collided with the Eurasian landmass, buckling the Earth's crust and heaving land upward—twisting and folding it in the process. Huge slabs of marble emerged; over time they were etched by the Liwu River, eventually forming a boulder-strewn gorge embraced by cliffs of solid marble.

Spectacular views are almost immediate as you follow the Central Cross Island Highway from the national park's entrance up

EXPERIENCE: Riding the Suao to Hualien Highway

This 122-mile (180 km) coastal ride between the port cities of Suao and Hualien serves up truly spectacular scenery. The highway, much of it edging precariously along the cliff faces of the Central Mountain Range, runs across the mouth of Taroko Gorge, dipping and rising roller-coaster fashion to superb views of the Pacific Ocean crashing into sheer cliff faces hundreds of feet below.

The route, carved in 1875 as a trail south, was opened to convoy traffic in 1932. It has been gradually widened to allow vehicles to travel both ways. The highway reaches its dramatic best at **Qingshui Cliff.** Buses from Taipei take this route and offer the best views. A lot of the scenery is missed in the faster, more comfortable, trains from Taipei because of the numerous tunnels.

into the gorge. You snake along a road carved out from the looming cliff side, often disappearing into tunnels and emerging to even more staggering views of the canyon, the rushing Liwu River, and soaring cliffs. These views become ever more dramatic as you climb farther into the gorge toward the main settlement of **Tianxiang,** nestled between green mountains 14 miles (22.5 km) west of the park entrance.

About 100 yards (91 m) east of Tianxiang, you can climb across a suspension bridge to the lofty **Xiangde Temple,** a collection of pagodas, ornate prayer halls, and bodhisattva statues—including a gilded 36-foot (11 m) Avalokitesvara bodhisattva image. Next to the image is the six-level **Heavenly Summit Pagoda.** Climb to the top for even loftier vistas of Tianxiang and the surrounding countryside.

About 1.2 miles (2 km) east of Tianxiang, not far from the Tunnel of Nine Turns, the two-story **Lushui Geological Exhibition Hall** stands beside the highway at the head of the Lushui-Heliu Trail, part of the original Hehuan Old Trail

trade and communications route built by the Atayal tribe over the mountains. There is an information center inside, and two quality exhibits, the first on the peculiar geology of this region and the reasons for the emergence of the gorge, the second on the building of the Central Cross Island Highway. Time should also be left for tea or coffee at the small restaurant, which has an attractive patio featuring green marble tables and chairs; Lushui means "green waters," reference to the rushing Liwu River below.

Cycling or walking along the Central Cross Island Highway from the park entrance to Tianxiang brings you more in touch with Taroko's majesty, but you will need to be on constant lookout for passing traffic. Long sections are barely wide enough for two lanes of cars, with no dedicated bike lanes. If you do cycle or walk, start from Tianxiang and head east to the park entrance—it's downhill all the way. There are several sections, including the **Tunnel of Nine Turns** (see p. 137), that are vehicle-free, perfect for a stroll. Another option might be to get off the road to hike along designated trails (see pp. 138–139). ■

Taroko Gorge

◩ 131 C6

Visitor Information

✉ Taroko National Park Headquarters and Visitor Center, 291 Fushi Village, Xiulin Township, Hualien County

☎ 03/862-1100

🕑 Closed 2nd Mon. of each month

www.taroko.gov.tw

Driving Taroko Gorge

This drive, along the Central Cross Island Highway from the entrance of Taroko National Park to the park's main settlement of Tianxiang, measures only 14 miles (22.5 km), but be sure to allow plenty of time for parking and taking in the sights. The route, which follows the lip of the gorge, twists and turns most of the way.

A waterfall adds to the tableau at Taroko's Eternal Spring (Changchun) Shrine.

On the north side of the Liwu River, opposite the entrance to the national park, is the **Taroko National Park Headquarters and Visitor Center ❶** (tel 03/862-1100). Here you can pick up brochures and maps. Park rangers post notices of weather conditions and areas to avoid.

A signposted side trail leading to the **Eternal Spring (Changchun) Shrine ❷** starts 1.4 miles (2.3 km) west of the entrance. Its mountainous backdrop, classical Chinese design, and 45-foot-high (14 m) waterfall make for a picturesque sight. A steep trail behind the shrine (see p. 139) leads up into the mountains for stunning views of the peaks of the Central Mountain Range.

From the Eternal Spring Shrine the road climbs alongside the steep walls of the gorge for 4.8 miles (7.7 km) to a turnoff to **Buluowan Recreation Area ❸** (tel 03/861-2528, closed 1st & 3rd Mon. of month). A short steep road leads to a local Taroko community that has become a dolled-up tourist

NOT TO BE MISSED:

Swallow Grotto • Yindianren (Indian) Rock • Tunnel of Nine Turns • Liufang Bridge

village. Set in the foothills, enclosed on three sides by mountains, the setting is spectacular.

The recreation area is the best place to take in some of what is left of the historic **Hehuan Old Trail ❹**. Before the opening of the highway, this trail was the main cross-island route, blazed by the Atayal people centuries ago.

Back on the main road, go west for 2.5 miles (3.6 km) to **Swallow Grotto ❺**, a section of the highway where a long tunnel was blasted through the cliff. The lower marble sections on the opposite cliff are pockmarked with hundreds of small grottoes, etched out of the rock by underground streams long dried up. Thousands of swallows once made their nests here, but increasing traffic over the years has scared them off. They may soon start returning, however, as park authorities have closed this dramatic section of the highway (a bypass has been built) to allow pedestrians more time to admire the scenery without worrying about traffic. The grotto continues for 500 yards (457 m) to a café and souvenir shop.

Farther along is Jinheng Bridge and, on the Liwu River's north side, the brooding **Yindianren (Indian) Rock 6**. Weathered into a shape resembling the profile of a Native American chief, this one of Taroko's most famous sights.

Another pedestrians-only section awaits 2.2 miles (3.6 km) on from Yindianren, the twisting **Tunnel of Nine Turns 7** (Jiuqudong), a series of short tunnels cut through sheer marble. The drama of Taroko reaches its peak here. The gorge squeezes between cliffs, and tiered waterfalls

tumble down along the Liwu River, which rages down this narrow section of the gorge. You gain some perspective of the gorge's sheer size near the end of the Tunnel of Nine Turns, where it opens to more extensive vistas. From the viewpoint at **Liufang Bridge 8**, you can see how the tunnel was cut through the mountains.

A mile and a quarter (2 km) farther into the gorge you reach the **Bridge of Motherly Devotion 9** (Cimu Bridge). Stop for a look at the riverbed with its scattering of huge boulders thrown down from the mountains.

Heading west for another 1.25 miles (2 km) brings you to **Tianxiang 10**. This resort town, set on the edge of the gorge and backed by mountains, is where you'll find most of Taroko's accommodations, from guesthouses to a luxury hotel. Just before Tianxiang, a suspension bridge leads over the river to the six-story Heavenly Summit Pagoda: Climb to the top for some outstanding views. The pagoda is part of the lofty Xiangde Temple complex (see p. 135).

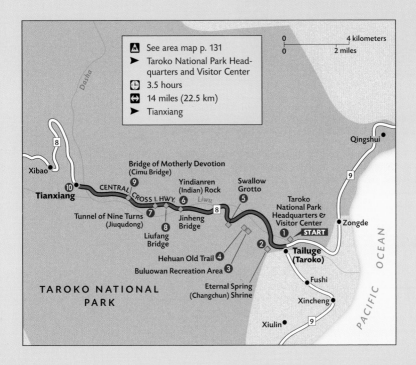

Baiyang Falls & Other Trails

Many of Taroko's trails are hunting and intervillage routes carved by the Atayal aboriginals, who once inhabited much of the gorge. Nearly all of the villages have disappeared, but a number of the trails have been turned into hiking paths. Some are little more than a stroll, others are more difficult. All are spectacular.

Water Curtain Tunnel is but one take-your-breath-away treasure along Taroko's magnificent Baiyang Falls Trail.

Baiyang Falls Trail

This delightful amble along a branch gorge takes in the most awesome scenery of all of Taroko's trails. The trailhead is a 1,000-foot-long (300 m) tunnel, half a mile (1 km) north of Tianxiang on the Central Cross Island Highway. The end of the tunnel opens to cliff faces and a narrow gorge formed by the fast-flowing Liwu River.

Here you'll find a map board (in Chinese) and a viewing platform.

You then cross a small bridge, which hugs the contours of the gorge for most of the way. Initially, the trail rises gradually to another lookout with views down to the gorge's rapids, before leveling out and winding along the side of the gorge and through numerous tunnels to reach the thundering **Baiyang Falls.** Here, water pours between huge bleached boulders and crashes into an emerald lagoon.

The best views of the 50-foot-high (15 m) waterfall and the patterned-marble face of the gorge can be had by crossing a wood-planked suspension bridge to a lookout.

Cross back over the suspension bridge and follow the trail another 220 yards (200 m) to **Water Curtain Tunnel** (Shuiliandong). Park authorities closed the tunnel after the September 21, 1999, earthquake (see sidebar p. 218), declaring it too dangerous to enter. But if you shine a flashlight past the padlocked gate, you see the "water curtain" formed by water pouring through the roof of the cave. You return along the same route. The 1.3-mile trail (2.1 km) takes 90 minutes to walk. Bring a flashlight because of the tunnels; there are a grand total of eight, some quite long.

Eternal Spring (Changchun) Shrine Trail

Climbers of the short but strenuous Eternal Spring Shrine Trail are rewarded with vistas of the Central Mountain Range. The trailhead begins a few hundred yards off the Central Cross Island Highway, 1.4 miles (2.3 km) west of the entrance to Taroko National Park. From the temple, you begin a steep climb as the trail zigzags up to stunning views of the peaks of the Central Mountain Range.

A **bell tower** and the nearby **Guanyin cave temple** mark the trail's highest point. Another trail then drops back down to the Central Cross Island Highway, about 2 miles (3 km) east of the temple. The 0.85-mile (1.35 km) trail takes about 25 minutes to walk.

Lotus Pond Trail

This 4-mile (6.4 km) trail climbs to Lotus Lake, which, at 4,000 feet (1,200 m) above sea level, is Taroko's highest natural body of water. The trail begins at Huitouwan, about 4 miles (6.4 km) west of Tianxiang, at a hairpin turn on the Central Cross Island Highway.

The first section, which runs for 1.6 miles (2.5 km), is not much more than a leisurely stroll, taking about 30 minutes. But then the going gets tough. After crossing a rickety suspension bridge to the right, the trail zigzags its way up the mountain, climbing 1,640 feet in 2.7 miles (500 m in 4.3 km) before reaching Lotus Lake. The second section of the hike takes about two hours and can be grueling. You return via the same route. There is a small hostel at the lake.

Mystery Valley (Shakadang) Trail

Following a hunting trail originally blazed by aborigines, you follow the **Shakadang River**—a tributary of the Liwu River—for 2.75 miles (4.4 km), passing through forest areas thick with giant ferns and by crystal-clear ponds, huge white boulders, and layered marble cliffs. Begin at Shakadang Bridge just beyond the national park headquarters near the park's eastern entrance. Cross the bridge and

INSIDER TIP:

To hike Taroko's trails is to enter an intricate Chinese landscape painting. The land, layered with trees, rocks, and water, draws lots of weekend walkers.

—MARILYN TERRELL
National Geographic Traveler
magazine chief researcher

head left down the iron stairway to the trail. The trail, noted for its numerous feet-wetting river crossings, continuously opens to stunning views of the gorge and surrounding mountain peaks. Timber-decked lookouts are placed along the trail to enhance the vistas. You return the way you came; the round-trip takes about four hours. ∎

Baiyang Falls & other trails

- Taroko Gorge: 131 C6
- See Taroko National Park Headquarters and Visitor Center, p. 135.

Driving Down the East Coast

This Pacific Ocean journey begins in the city of Hualien and hugs the isolated and relatively unspoiled eastern coastline before reaching Taitung, 106 miles (170 km) south. The drive takes you through the East Coast National Scenic Area.

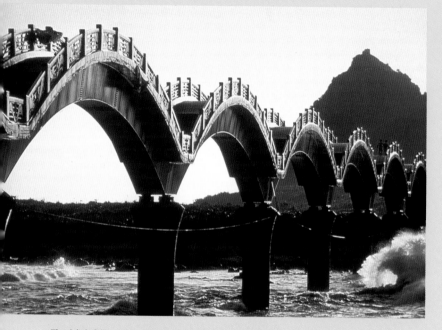

The delightfully scalloped footbridge at Sanxiantai was built to resemble a dragon. It reaches to a rocky islet with an encircling timber-decked walkway.

Begin at the **Hualien Visitor Center ❶** *(tel 03/867-1326)*, located on Highway 11 about 11 miles (18 km) south of Hualien's city center, at the entrance to the East Coast National Scenic Area. The staff will provide you with area maps and brochures. The center also has an exhibition hall with environmental displays and aboriginal handicrafts. Along the sides of the exhibit room is a scale model of the coastline. Push the button on the wall and a funky model of a VW Kombi van appears and slowly rumbles along the route.

Three miles (5 km) farther on is the **Henan Temple ❷**, with its 50-foot (15 m) honey-colored statue of the goddess of mercy,

Guanyin, standing on the side of a hill and overlooking the Pacific Ocean.

From Henan Temple, the highway narrows to two lanes and climbs higher along the base of the mountains that line the Coastal Mountain Range, offering broad ocean vistas. It then briefly turns inland, serving up a rustic feel of rolling hills, farmhouses, and rice fields at Shuilian, until you reach a bridge at **Fanshuliao ❸**, 9 miles (14 km) on from Henan Temple. Once you drive over the bridge—which spans the Fanshuliao River—park, cross the highway, and walk a short distance to the old, abandoned bridge that sits adjacent to the one you have just crossed. From here, you can get stunning views if you peer over the precipice down the narrow, deep gorge that cuts through the mountains to the nearby Pacific Ocean.

Local legend has it that the Ami aborigines who lived in the area so revered courage that anyone who could vault across the gorge—which measured a good 40 feet (12 m) wide—using bamboo poles would become their leader. The bamboo groves in the 200-foot-deep (60 m) gorge are said to have flourished from the poles that the young men used in their attempts.

Highway 11 climbs farther up the side of the mountains to even more lofty ocean views, before dropping to **Baqi Recreation Area** ❹, which lies 3 miles (5 km) farther on. From the lookout are sweeping vistas of the gray-black sands at **Jiqi Bay,** and the mountains running strung out along the coast and jutting into the Pacific Ocean.

The highway then winds down to the bay and the graceful 1.5-mile (2.5 km) sweep of **Jiqi Seaside Resort** ❺ *(visitor center, tel 03/871-1251),* which lies locked between verdant headlands and backed by steep foothills. The beach here is popular with locals despite the unappealing color of its sand. At the northern end of the beach, 3 miles (5 km) from the Baqi lookout, you can park near the visitor center and have a stroll.

Highway 11 begins to follow the contours of what has now become a rugged coastline as the verdant mountains of the Coastal Mountain Range clash with the Pacific, offering some of the drive's very best scenery. Next, the highway loops inland for a brief stretch and winds through the town of **Fengbin** before turning back to the coast for more ocean and mountain vistas.

NOT TO BE MISSED:

Fanshuliao • JOKI • Sanxiantai • Donghe Bridge

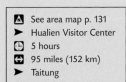

🗺 See area map p. 131
► Hualien Visitor Center
🕒 5 hours
↔ 95 miles (152 km)
► Taitung

Then it's onto the rocky coastline at Shimen, 15.5 miles (25 km) south of Jiqi Bay. Just beyond a "tourist" sign announcing your arrival in **Shimen,** park at the first building on the coastal side (the left) of the highway. The two-level, open-concept building here is **JOKI** ❻ *(3 Shimen, Gangkou Village, Fengbin Township, Hualien County, tel 03/878-1616)*. Worth a visit is the fascinating coffee shop and art gallery that overlook the rocky coast. Featured here are some wildly imaginative furniture and sculptures made from timber, steel piping, and smooth rocks with vein patterns collected from the shore.

Just over a mile (2 km) farther down Highway 11, a road to the left leads to **Shitiping** ❼ (Stone Steps Terrace), named for the volcanic rock that has been worn into terraced slabs along the coast for about half a mile (1 km). The visitor center *(tel 03/878-1452)* displays illustrations and explanations of the local topography, marine life, and vegetation, but the information is written only in Chinese. The Shitiping area has been landscaped into a park, and a wood-plank walkway leads the way to observation decks that are great for viewing the breakers thumping into this unusual coastline.

The **Xiuguluan River** (see p. 145) empties into the Pacific Ocean at the 68-kilometer mark of Highway 11. The river is spanned by the graceful, 131-yard-long (120 m) **Changhong (Rainbow) Bridge,** offering commanding views of the Coastal Mountain Range and the river's exit into the Pacific. About 100 yards (91 m) beyond the bridge a sleek, tall obelisk marks the Tropic of Cancer. You are now officially in the tropics.

Six miles (10 km) farther along the highway, you come to the **Baxian Caves** ❽ (Caves of the Eight Immortals, see sidebar this page). Evidence of human habitation during the Paleolithic Age has been discovered in these caves, and the visitor center *(tel 089/881-418)*—which has been fashioned to resemble the inside of a cave—carries out this subterranean theme, displaying some stone relics dating from the period, geological information, and life-size figures of the first inhabitants spearing deer and cooking fish; little of the information is in English.

Behind the Baxian Caves visitor center are pathways leading to a dozen small caves, which are now crammed with gilded Buddha and bodhisattva images, worshippers, and sightseeing travelers; gift stalls here do a brisk business selling religious paraphernalia.

Eight Immortals

Frequently featured in Chinese art, the Eight Immortals lived during the Tang and Song dynasties. They all attained immortality through chance. After an out-of-body experience, mystic Li Tie Guai found his body had been cremated, so he moved into a lame beggar's body; he carries a crutch and is a patron of the disabled. Alchemist Zhong Li Quan found a container holding the elixir of life; he carries a fan and is the patron of the military. Musician Lan Cai He nursed beggar Li back to health, carries a flower basket, and is a patron of florists. Senior citizen Zhang Guo Lao, who refused to die, is seen with a donkey and is a patron of old men. He Xian Gu ground a magical stone and drank it with water; depicted with a flower basket, she is a patron of housekeepers. Lu Dong Bin dreamed his violent death before turning to Taoism and befriending immortal Zhong; he carries a fly-whisker and is a patron of barbers. Flautist Han Xiang Zih grabbed a sacred tree branch; he carries a flute and is the patron of musicians. Fed up with a corrupt royal court, Cao Guo Jiu was meditating on a mountain when he chanced upon the other immortals; he is the patron of actors.

Buddha images enshrined in the Baxian Caves are magnets for travelers.

After the Baxian Caves, the coastal plain widens and the Coastal Mountain Range becomes more distant, but no less imposing. **Shiyusan,** or Stone Umbrella, is a narrow though very large spit of rock that projects about 1,000 yards (914 m) into the sea at the 106-kilometer mark of Highway 11; it's worth a brief stop to check out its rock formations and some splendid views.

Four miles (6.4 km) south, veer left off Highway 11 for 1.5 miles (2 km) to reach **Sanxiantai** ❾ Platform of the Three Immortals (*visitor center, tel 089/850-785*), where a neck of land reaches out to a small island, connected by a lovely scalloped footbridge designed to resemble a dragon (see p. 140). Wood-plank pathways wind around the windswept island, which is crowned by three huge black-faced rocks said to resemble the three immortals, Chinese legendary figures who visited the area centuries ago. The walk takes about 90 minutes. The wave-bashed beach at Sanxiantai, made up of smooth black pebbles, attracts a lot of interest from travelers.

Backtrack to Highway 11 and continue south for 15 miles (24 km) through the town of **Chenggong** to the **East Coast National Scenic Area Visitor Center** (tel 089/841-520, ext. 1800). While the center has displays of aboriginal artifacts, illustrations, and models of east coast topography, flora, and fauna, plus a section devoted to outdoor activities, little is labeled in English. There are good views of the Pacific and **Green Island** (see pp. 152–153) from the plaza in front of the center. The adjacent **Ami Folk Center** (tel 089/841-751), set against a generous sweep of landscaping, features traditional aboriginal dwellings and ceremonial houses.

Turn right just before the **Donghe Bridge** ❿—at the 140-kilometer mark—and head west for about 200 yards (182 m) to a parking lot, where you can look down to spectacular views of the **Mawuku River.** The river's water rushes through a deep gorge littered with giant white boulders, set against a stunning mountain backdrop. Head back to the bridge and cross it to the small fishing village of **Jinzun.** Just before the village, on the left, is a small coffee shop (no Chinese or English name). Here you can relax in a convivial atmosphere while enjoying lofty hilltop

INSIDER TIP:

The ocean is so invitingly blue here that all you want to do is take a dip, but steep dropoffs occur a few feet from shore and the current can be strong.

—EMILY HAILE
Travel Telegraph *blogger and former* National Geographic Traveler *magazine researcher*

views of black-sand beaches and rolling surf from its terrace. A trail from the coffee shop leads to the beach.

Six miles (10 km) farther south, just past the town of **Dulan,** the scenery opens to long beaches and palm groves. Just over a mile (1.6 km) past town you come to an intriguing tourist road sign: **Water Flowing Upwards** ⓫. Turn right just past the sign, drive past the souvenir shops immediately on the left, then park and check out the wide irrigation channel next to the road where the water appears to run uphill—at least when there is water, after heavier rainfalls. No detailed scientific explanation needed, however; it's an optical illusion.

The last stop before Taitung, 7.5 miles (12 km) past Water Flowing Upwards, is **Xiaoyeliu** ⓬. Behind the visitor center (tel 089/281-530)—which features some tropical fish tanks and geographical information about the area—is a lovely garden of lawn, palms, and pathways winding down to the coastline. Here sandstone rock formations, different from the volcanic rock that defines much of the east coast, inspire names such as honeycomb rock and fungus rock.

EXPERIENCE:
Spotting Dolphins & Whales

Taiwan's waters have 29 of the 60 cetacean (whale and dolphin) species found worldwide. The Kuroshio (Japan Current) slides by south to north, bringing migrating whales that are believed to breed in the coastal waters. About 70 percent of whale tours out of Yilan County report sightings; out of Hualien County, about 90 percent. **SeaWhale** (www.seawhale.com), which operates out of Hualien City, with morning and afternoon trips, is recommended by the Taiwan Cetacean Society because of its eco-friendly philosophy; too many operators chase and harass. Details on tours are found at www.eastcoast-nsa .gov.tw. Tours are generally two to three hours; many operators offer educational commentary—in Chinese only.

Xiuguluan River

Emerging from its source at an altitude of 10,200 feet (3,200 m) in the Central Mountain Range, the Xiuguluan River—the east coast's longest—snakes downstream for 67 miles (108 km) before emptying into the Pacific Ocean midway between Hualien and Taitung.

Fierce white water and spectacular scenery account for the Xiuguluan River's popularity.

The river's lower section initially slices through high cliffs near Ruisui before reaching Qimei, about 6 miles (10 km) from the coast. It then gushes through a steep-walled gorge, flows under Changhong (Rainbow) Bridge near Dagangkou, and opens up broadly to the sea. In all, there are 23 sets of rapids from start to finish.

The premier way to enjoy this spectacular course is, of course, by raft; indeed, the river draws some 100,000 people every year. The trip takes three to four hours and can vary from leisurely to downright invigorating. The best times are during the April to October monsoon season.

You can join a group for a white-water-rafting trip at Ruisui. For more information and to book a trip, visit the Ruisui Rafting Service Center *(215 Zhongshan Rd., Sec. 3, Ruisui Township, tel 03/ 887-5400)*; you can also arrange a trip through your hotel in Hualien. All gear is provided, but bring a change of clothing, as you will likely get soaked. If you make your own way to Ruisui, get there before noon, as few, if any, rafts leave after that time.

You can also drive 18 miles along the lower river via the Ruigang Highway, which begins near Dagangkou at the 68-kilometer mark of Highway 11. This is also an ideal cycling route for accomplished bicyclists, featuring challenging cliff-hangers and some steep grades.

In June the river comes alive with 200 six-person rafts in a world-class race that draws spectators all along its banks. ∎

Xiuguluan River
⚑ 131 C4
Visitor Information
☎ -East Rift Valley Scenic Area Visitor Center, 03/887-5306
www.erv-nsa.gov.tw

East Rift Valley

The sleepy seaside city of Taitung is the springboard for a trip into the nearby East Rift Valley. Splicing the Coastal Mountain Range from just below Hualien in the north to Taitung in the south, this area provides a rural respite from the drama of Taroko Gorge and the ruggedness of the east coast. Highway 9 follows the valley floor past rolling hills, pasturelands, tea farms, forest recreation areas, hot springs, and plantations embraced by towering mountains.

Gentle breezes and lofty launch pads make the East Rift Valley one of Taiwan's top parasailing areas.

East Rift Valley

🅜 131 B3–B4, C4–C5

Visitor Information

✉ East Rift Valley National Scenic Area Visitor Center, 215 Zhongshan Rd., Sec. 3, Ruiliang Village, Ruisui Township, Hualien County

☎ 03/887-5306

www.erv-nsa.gov.tw

A web of side roads and lack of English road signs can make exploration difficult without some local knowledge. The best way to tour the area is to have your hotel arrange a private driver or contact a qualified local travel agency.

Although a dairy farm would seem like an unusual tourist attraction, locals flock to **Chulu Pasture** (*1 Muchang, Mingfeng Village, Beinan Township, Taitung County, tel 089/571-002, $ per vehicle*) to check out cows wandering in lush meadows and being milked in sheds. They pose for photographs in front of fiberglass bovines and gulp down the farm's famous milk in its snack bar/souvenir shop. Most tourist buses arrive in the afternoon to watch the herds being milked and then led out to pasture.

Leaving Chulu, Highway 9 winds through some lovely valley scenery to the **Bunun Village** (*tel 089/561-211*), one of the few self-sufficient aboriginal communities in Taiwan. The community is home to 165 people who have successfully turned their hand to tourism while maintaining their communal culture. The well-run cooperative has an arts and handicrafts center, stores, a restaurant serving up Bunun food, accommodations for visitors, and a theater with cultural programs twice daily. The shows are non-commercial and nonexploitative.

Also in Yanping Township, in tiny Hongye Village, is Taiwan's own "Field of Dreams" at Hongye Primary School (1 Honggu Rd., tel 089/561-015). Students of the school, mainly Bunun aborigines, became the unlikely heroes of Taiwan in 1968, when they beat a powerful Japanese Little League all-star team while the latter team was on a goodwill tour of Taiwan (see pp. 148–149). The school's modest main hall has been turned into the intriguing **Little League Memorial Hall** with pictures and paraphernalia of the school's proud baseball past, including photographs of the joyous, victorious 1968 team.

Nearby **Hongye Hot Spring Resort** (120 Honggu Rd., tel 089/551-637 ext. 101, $) is an open-air complex of hot-springs pools owned and operated by the Bunun tribe. The resort's numerous circular and free-form pools and Jacuzzis sit under thatched shelters. A timber-decked, open-air restaurant overlooks the hot-springs scene, while the surrounding mountains add to the peaceful nature of the place.

Highway 9 continues to wind north through the valley over a series of bright red steel-arched bridges fronting river gorges, past plantations of pineapple and palm trees, and through hamlets nestled on mountainsides.

Climb up Luye Scenic Drive through tea plantations to **Luye Tea Farm,** on Luye Plateau. Its two-story pavilion and teahouse offer startling views down into the valley formed by the Beinan River. Pastures and pineapple and palm plantations form patchworks in the valley across to the Dulan Mountain. The teahouse has an open-air gallery on its second floor. Downstairs you can sample the variety of teas and sweets on sale here.

On a more sporting note, the tea farm is a favorite among parasail pilots, who launch themselves from the plateau using one of the two ramps in front of the teahouse. ∎

Cool Tea

Local folks closely follow the rules of yin and yang in their diets. All foods are either yin or yang. Yin foods cool you down, yang foods warm you up. It doesn't matter if the food is actually heated up or refrigerated. Kucha is a popular summertime cooling drink. Consumed by the bowl, it's also said to ameliorate such "hot" ailments as sore throat and high blood pressure, caused by too much heat stored up in the body.

Bunun Village
🄰 131 B3
✉ 191 Ward 11, Taoyuan Village, Yanping Township, Taitung County
☎ 089/561-211
www.bunun.org.tw

Luye Tea Farm
✉ 145 Lane 42, Gaotai Rd., Yongan Village, Luye Township, Taitung County
☎ 089/550-152

Baseball in Taiwan

On a calm summer evening in Xinzhuang, a suburb of Taipei, kites fly in the blue sky, children play, and smoke rises from barbecues. But inside Xinzhuang Baseball Stadium, it's more like a madhouse. Attention is riveted on the field, where the yellow-clad Brother Elephants are losing 6 to 0 to the Sinon Bulls. It doesn't look good.

Pregame streamers greet players. Baseball was introduced to Taiwan by Japanese colonists.

Soon the Elephants score two runs, and two innings later, in a flurry of base hits, they score five more times, sending their fans into a deafening crescendo of flag-waving, drum-pounding, trumpet-blowing support. The Elephants beat the Bulls 8 to 6. It's a dramatic comeback for the Elephants, and their fans walk happily away into the night. The presence of so many supporters, sitting in a great modern ballpark and cheering with synchronized gusto, is an equally dramatic comeback for baseball in Taiwan.

Baseball has a long history in Taiwan. The Japanese taught the game to the Taiwanese in the early 1900s, and the locals then turned around and beat their colonial masters in a landmark tournament in 1930. The game surged in popularity in the 1960s, when Taiwan's Little League team won the first of an eventual 17 world titles. The Chinese Professional Baseball League (CPBL) was launched in 1990, and two years later, Taiwan's national team won a silver medal at the Barcelona Olympics.

Baseball fever in Taiwan peaked in 1996. That year, more than 1.3 million fans poured into the nation's ballparks; television ratings soared. A high-profile gambling scandal in the late 1990s caused the eventual collapse of several teams, and attendance began dropping. By 2002, the game had regained its popularity, and three new baseball parks opened, two on the outskirts of Taipei and a third in Kaohsiung. But new scandals in 2005 and 2008 led to a drop-off in attendance. One team was kicked out, and another folded.

Baseball in Taiwan is not the gentle pastime that American fans are familiar with—it is a loud, raucous affair. Each team is owned by a large Taiwan corporation. The six teams wander the island, playing in ten stadiums. Fans of both teams attend each game. Armed with drums, firecrackers, and noisemakers, they greet every pitch with lots of noise.

In the past decade the sport has gotten a boost from the United States. A number of Taiwanese players have been signed by Major League teams, and hopes are high that Taiwan

The Japanese and Taiwanese remain fierce rivals on the baseball diamond.

will produce a number of stars like Ichiro Suzuki, the Japanese player who has been such a huge success in America. Pitcher Wang Chien-ming emerged as the ace pitcher for the New York Yankees in 2006 and 2007, coming in second in voting for the American League Cy Young Award in 2006, though injuries have severely hampered him since then.

Who's Running the Bases? Lots of East Coast Locals

Attend a professional baseball game in Taiwan and you will no doubt see a large number of local aborigine players, much in excess of the percentage represented by aborigines in the overall population. The majority of these will be from the east coast counties of Hualien and, especially, Taitung.

Baseball is game number one in this area, played by most aborigine youth. Unlike elsewhere (though this is being rectified with a recent government emphasis on physical activity and recreational facilities), there is much open space and access to fields. Most aborigine youth are from lower-income families and often aren't encouraged to fight their way through Taiwan's highly competitive school-examination system. The entire

community looks on pro sports careers as a ticket out of poverty.

In a virtuous circle, baseball also provides many of the heroes and models for the aboriginal community. The Hongye "Red Leafs" Little League world championship team of 1968 (see p. 147) is celebrated on today's NT$500 bill (though what is in fact shown is a later aboriginal championship team). Many of the early championship teams were from the aboriginal areas of eastern Taiwan, and some of these players went on to pro careers in Taiwan, Japan, and even the United States. The country's two most celebrated exports to Japan, Guo Yuan-zhi (Kaku Genji) and Guo Tai-yuan (Kaku Taigen), were both Little League icons of aborigine descent.

National Museum of Prehistory & Beinan Cultural Park

In 1980, workers building the Taitung Railway Station uncovered a major prehistoric culture archaeological site. Excavations revealed the most complete settlement found to date in Taiwan. The site has been preserved and developed into an archaeological park, Beinan Cultural Park, while the nearby National Museum of Prehistory displays the finds, which add up to a fascinating journey through the lives and times of Taiwan's ancient and modern native peoples.

Behind its modern style, the National Museum of Prehistory showcases the pieces of the past.

National Museum of Prehistory

 131 B3

 1 Museum Rd., Taitung

☎ 089/381-166

⊕ Closed Mon.

⑤ $$

www.nmp.gov.tw

National Museum of Prehistory

The museum building seems a hodgepodge design of multi-level roofs of different shapes, randomly placed square and porthole-shaped windows, and multicolored walls in green-tint concrete and redbrick veneer. In fact, it is all rendered to evoke concepts that are found inside

the museum. In the **main plaza** is a circular fountain, centered with a bronze sundial sitting on a columned pedestal.

Follow the stairs from the ground-floor lobby to the second floor and a glass-walled corridor looking down on Shan (Mountain) Square. The **second-floor permanent galleries** present an overview of Taiwan's natural history and Austronesian peoples, showing chronologically the geographic and geological changes of Taiwan, and the different eras of habitation by early peoples, with a timeline to the present aboriginal tribes.

From the galleries a sign leads to a winding ramp—symbolizing the descent into an archaeological dig—that takes you to a myriad of **small themed galleries** that follow Taiwan's natural and ancient histories. First is Taiwan's earliest known culture—the cave-dwelling Changbin people—presented in a life-size diorama. The walls and displays around the diorama include ancient relics dating back some 30,000 years. Subsequent **basement galleries** follow a similar layout.

The museum houses thousands of priceless antiquities, including jade spearheads and carved jade ornaments from the Stone Age; tools and ornaments from the Iron Age; decorated pottery from the Neolithic Age; ritual, ornamental, and funerary objects made from jade, bronze, and iron; plus stone figures and coffins, rock wheels, and richly carved megaliths.

From the basement galleries, an escalator takes you back to the second floor and more modern times to explore galleries that trace the history and cultural development of Taiwan's various groups of indigenous peoples through their hand tools, farming methods, fishing implements, dwellings, musical instruments, icons, clothing, adornments, art, and handicrafts.

Beinan Cultural Park

The expansive, undulating, 328,000-square-yard (300,000 sq m) park at the foot of Mount Beinan (Beinanshan) is the site of a prehistoric Beinan settlement dating back some 2,000 to 3,000 years. The park is designed to give visitors a firsthand view of the ongoing work of archaeologists who are uncovering the settlement. A plaza marks the entrance

INSIDER TIP:

Beinan Cultural Park has guided theme tours (botany, geology, mythology, archaeology) in English—with advance notice.

—RICK CHARETTE
National Geographic contributor

to the park, with a path leading to the **amphitheater,** which is centered with circular marble patterned with jade earring motifs, symbolic of the Beinan people. Another path leads from the amphitheater to the **visitor center,** in the western area of the park. Behind the visitor center is the two-level **Observation Platform,** with a map board and sweeping views of the park and the city of Taitung in the distance.

Another path from the amphitheater winds to the **Excavation Area** on the park's eastern edge. Here you can occasionally observe archaeologists at the canopied dig and learn more from the adjacent exhibit booth. ■

Beinan Cultural Park

- 🅰 131 B3
- ✉ 200 Cultural Park Rd., Nanwang, Taitung
- ☎ 089/233-466
- 🕐 Closed Mon.
- 💲 $
- 🚉 Taitung railway station

Green Island

Green Island (Ludao) is becoming increasingly popular with visitors, most of whom visit for its beaches, weathered rock formations, and dazzling offshore coral. But it also has a darker past. On the island are a number of prisons, including one that incarcerated political prisoners until as late as the 1980s. The prison is now part of a park dedicated to human rights and the suffering of those opposed to the dictatorial rule clamped on Taiwan for nearly 40 years.

Zhaori Hot Springs is one of only a few in the world to be fed by seawater.

Green Island (Ludao)

🏔 131 C2–3

An 11-mile-long (17 km) road encircles the island. Start your trip at the **Green Island Visitor Center** (tel 089/672-510), opposite the airport in Zhongliao Village. Inside the center you will find geological and flora and fauna displays, fish tanks, and photographs of the island's coral reefs and marine life.

From the visitor center, you can walk to the **lighthouse,** rising above a high cape on the island's northwest tip. The 108-foot-high (33 m) structure was built with funds donated by the United States government after one of its ships,

the *President Hoover,* sank in 1937 after striking rocks nearby.

Back at Zhongliao Village, head east along the coastal road for about 1.25 miles (2 km) to the fishing village of **Gongguan,** with its pastel houses lining the edge of a small horseshoe-shaped bay dotted with rock formations.

From here it's another 600 yards (550 m) to the former prison—ironically named Oasis Villa by inmates—where thousands of political prisoners were held during the island's long years of martial law. The prison is now the **Green Island Human Rights Memorial**

Park. Within the park is Asia's only monument to human rights, with the names of all the former incarcerated political prisoners. It stands as an impressive monument to the freedoms that have

INSIDER TIP:

Green Island boasts a rare undersea hot springs accessible by land. But to see the real beauty here you must head underwater.

—YUNGSHIH LEE
National Geographic *magazine's Taiwan edition former editor*

swept Taiwan since the martial law era ended in 1987. The prison's museum highlights the conditions to which detainees were subjected.

Just beyond the memorial park, the road swoops south and heads down the island's west coast. A few hundred yards after the turn you come to **Guanyin Cave.** Inside is a small temple with something quite unexpected: a stalagmite donned in a red cape representing Guanyin, the goddess of mercy.

The island's rugged west coast has some lovely white-sand beaches—although low-lying coral precludes swimming at some. At **Haishenping,** a steep path leads to a small pagoda and panoramic views.

At the island's southeastern tip, right on a rocky beach, awaits one of Green Island's most popular attractions: the unusual **Zhaori Hot Springs** (tel 089/671-133, $$) The springs are one of only three in

the world fed by seawater. Also on the premises is a pavilion, a store, and showers.

About a mile (1.6 km) from the hot springs, in the southwest corner of the island, is **Dabaisha Beach.** A boardwalk takes you to the sand before continuing out into the sea over coral exposed at low tide. At the end of the boardwalk you can jump into the water and snorkel.

A little more than half a mile (1 km) northwest of Dabaisha on the island's west coast are two sea caves, **Longxia** and **Baxian.**

The island's main village of **Nanliao,** about half a mile (1 km) northwest of the caves, is where you can hire motorbikes and bicycles and book glass-bottom boat tours. There are also a couple of dive shops here, where you can arrange diving trips if qualified. ∎

GETTING THERE:
By Air: Flights daily from Taitung Airport on Daily Air (tel 02/2717-1230, reservations center in Taipei; tel 089/362-669, reservations hotline in Taitung). By Ferry: Many departures daily from Fugang Harbor, 10 minutes north of Taitung City on Provincial Highway 11. See p. 238 for more information.

EXPERIENCE:
Heading Under the Water off Green Island

Green Island is where you'll find some of Taiwan's best and most varied coral. The hard and soft coral thrive in the warm Kuroshio (Japan Current), less affected by the pollution attacking sites off the main island. Some 300 species of fish swim these waters. Green Island has emerged as a prime site for snorkelers and divers. For scuba, all outfits require PADI certification and many offer well-priced certification courses. **Taiwan Scuba** (www.taiwanscuba.com) and **Green Island Adventures** (www.greenisland diving.com) are reliable outfitters. You can ask to be grouped with locals for a more authentic experience.

Orchid Island

Orchid Island (Lanyu) lies 40 miles (65 km) off the southeast coast of the Taiwan mainland. This 17-square-mile (44 sq km) isle is dominated by a volcanic landscape of steep mountains soaring high above lush valleys and a precipitous coastline overlooking sweeping bays. It is inhabited by about 2,000 Dahwu aborigines, also called the Yami, one of Taiwan's smallest ethnic groups, which, despite the odds has managed to cling to many of their traditional beliefs.

Elaborately decorated canoes are prized possessions for Orchid Island's native Dahwu families.

Orchid Island (Lanyu)
131 C1

The Dahwu maintain their traditional lifestyle as much as possible, living off the land and sea, building traditional richly decorated canoes for ceremonial occasions, growing yams and taro, foraging for shellfish, and raising pigs and goats.

Some still live in traditional houses built partially underground, dug out of embankments and on hillsides for protection against the severe typhoons that sweep across the island. Low walls of stone or wood surround the structures, and the roofs are thatched. Pavilions are built beside the houses to take advantage of more comfortable weather conditions.

Like the considerably more developed Green Island, Orchid Island has a paved road running along the coast and encircling the island. The island's six villages are dotted along this 31-mile (50 km) road. Ferries arrive near the main village and administrative center of **Yeyou** on the west coast, while the airport is a little farther south at Yuren. At Yeyou you can hire scooters or rent taxis.

Heading north from Yeyou about 2 miles (3 km) brings you to a knob-shaped headland and the island's lighthouse, overlooking rock formations whose names—Crocodile and Tank Rocks—pretty much describe their appearance. The road then tops the northwestern tip of the island and, just before heading east, arrives at the **Wukong Caves,** a series of five huge but shallow adjacent caves burrowed into the side of tall sea cliffs. Cave entrances are marked with crucifixes (missionaries made it to Orchid Island and managed to convert a sizable number of the population), while recesses in the cliff face near the entrances house clay statues depicting scenes from the Bible.

The road then skirts the northern coastline for about 0.6 mile (1 km) before reaching **Langdao,** where you will find the best examples of Dahwu architecture. On a hillside overlooking the Pacific sits a cluster of houses with only the roofs visible. Most of the dwellings have small vegetable gardens and stilted pavilions in their yards.

The island's east coast is studded with a number of unusual rock formations weathered out of the stony coral that makes up the coastline. One of the more interesting is **Twin Lions Rock,** two facing walls sculpted to resemble guardian lions similar to those found in temples, jutting out into the sea at the northeastern tip of the island.

About 1.25 miles (2 km) south on the west coast is **Battleship Rock,** so named because of its hulking ship's-hull shape and outcrops resembling gun turrets. About 110 yards (100 m) farther south, an inviting crystal-clear pool marks the entrance to **Lovers' Cave.**

Just beyond Battleship Rock, **Dongqing Village** is a good place to see fleets of Dahwu fishing canoes resting on the rocky shore. The village sits on a beautiful crescent-shaped bay. ■

GETTING THERE:
By Air: Flights daily from Taitung Airport on Daily Air (089/362-665, reservations center in Taipei; 089/62-669, reservations hotline in Taitung).
By Ferry: Many departures daily from Fugang Harbor, 10 minutes north of Taitung City on Provincial Highway 11. See p. 238 for more information.

Celebrate!

During the spring the Dahwu celebrate **Feiyu Jie** (Flying Fish Festival)— flying fish are a local delicacy and are considered sacred—with the launch of new canoes. The canoes, the pride of a Dahwu family, are a highly regarded possession not least because of the economic well-being they can bring. They are crafted using native timber, with 27 pieces of wood fitted and held together with pegs.

Once completed, the canoes are adorned with splashes of color and designs. During Feiyu Jie, Dahwu men wear loincloths, ceremonial armor made from rattan and silver, and a conical helmet made from silver, which covers the head, with slits for the eyes. The helmets are made by pounding coins. Previously, metal salvaged from shipwrecks and raids was used to craft the prized headgear.

More Places to Visit Along the East Coast

Carp Hill Park (Liyushan)

This Taitung City park sits on a small hill, so named because it is said to resemble a carp. On its eastern slopes is the **Dragon and Phoenix Buddhist Temple** (Longfeng Fotang). Although not a particularly noteworthy piece of temple architecture, you can climb the pagoda for a panorama of Taitung City and the Pacific. The temple has a small collection of ancient artifacts of the Beinan culture found in the area, dating back some 3,000 to 5,000 years, including stone coffins and tools. A looping pathway takes you to the top of the hill for more views, including **Green Island** (Ludao; see pp. 152–153). ⚑ Taitung 131 B3 ✉ Boai Rd., Taitung City

---

Tips for the Road

In Taiwan there are unofficial local "rules" drivers should note. The biggest fish gets the lane—speed and right of way often ignored. Military vehicles go first, their "size" coming from the convoy tucked in behind. Any space "belongs" to the vehicle with nose in first, speed and right of way again oft ignored. Given this rule, lane changes frequently go unannounced; the vehicle beside, a nose ahead, slowly pushes into your space, "advising" you to give way. One car flashing its lights at another is warning the other to give way—not telling the driver to go first.

Ruisui Hot Springs

This top hot-springs spa, built in 1919, has a public bathing area and the rustic Japanese-style **Ruisui Hot Springs Villa** (23 Hongye Village, Ruisui Township, Hualien County, tel 03/887-2170). The water temperature is a scalding 118°F (48°C), and because of its rich iron content, it has an off-putting orange tint. But it is said to be ideal therapy for rheumatism and skin allergies. You can join other bathers in the public pool or rent individual or group tubs. The spa is 47 miles (75 km) south of Hualien on Highway 9. ⚑ 131 C4 ☎ 03/887-5306

Zhiben

The Japanese built Zhiben, one of Taiwan's largest and oldest hot-springs resorts, at the turn of the 20th century. At first glance it's now a rather shabby place of numerous high-rise hotels, but the quality improves as you drive farther up the valley to the newer buildings. Spring water is tapped from the mountain into the hotels for guests and visitors willing to pay. If you feel like having a soak, head to the **Hotel Royal Chihpen** (23 Lane 113, Longquan Rd., Wenquan Village, Beinan Township, Taitung County, tel 089/510-666), which has pleasant outdoor and indoor hot-springs facilities. www .hotel-royal-chihpen.com.tw ⚑ 131 B3

Zhiben Forest Recreation Area

This pleasant park, a few minutes' drive from the Hotel Royal Chihpen, has sculpted gardens, a visitor center, and lots of pictures and information about the park's flora and fauna (only in Chinese). It is also the starting point for a number of trails. The **Scenic Trail** is a nice 45-minute amble through mostly landscaped areas. It ends at the 1.1-mile (1.8 km) **Green Shower Trail,** which takes you through heavily wooded areas of mahogany, ash, and camphor trees. The more challenging 1.3-mile (2.1 km) **Banyan Shaded Trail** climbs through thick forests of ferns, camphor, fig, and giant banyan trees. You have to be in good shape to tackle **Brave Man's Slope,** which takes you straight up to the top of the park via 729 steps. From here—1,600 feet (500 m) above sea level—there are outstanding views of Zhiben resort, Taitung City, and distant mountains. http://trail.forest .gov.tw ⚑ 131 B3 ✉ 3.6 miles (6 km) W of hot-springs resort area at 320 Longquan Rd., Wenquan Village, Beinan Township, Taitung County ☎ 089/510-961 💲 $

Architectural wealth of the colonial city of Tainan (Taiwan's oldest), Kaohsiung's bustling harbor, and the laid-back tropical south coast

The South

The goddess Mazu protects seafarers.

The South

Taiwan's south stretches from the cultural city of Tainan—Taiwan's oldest city and first capital—to the island's glorious tropical tip at Eluanbi in Kenting National Park. The area was once the island's most populated, but since the main economic and political forces moved to the Taipei region, so have many of the people. Kaohsiung, Taiwan's second largest city, still remains the island's most important industrial center.

Surf rumbles onto the shore at Nanwan, one of Kenting's numerous beaches.

Foguangshan, about 40 minutes northeast of Kaohsiung, is well worth the trip. This Buddhist monastery resembles a small town as much as it does a temple complex. What began as a small mountaintop retreat in the late 1960s has grown into the headquarters of the wealthiest of Taiwan's Buddhist sects, featuring grand shrine halls and temples, and museums and art galleries full of priceless artifacts and antiquities.

The most alluring attraction, however, and the one that draws the most people (especially on summer weekends), is Kenting National Park, at the island's southernmost tip. With its white-sand beaches, coral reefs, and turquoise waters, this is the island's tropical playground, popular for its diving, snorkeling, hiking, bicycling, and bird-watching. ■

In the region's northernmost realm, Tainan carries its long history proudly. It is here where the Ming dynasty loyalist Koxinga drove the Dutch occupiers out of Taiwan in 1662; the remnants of a couple Dutch forts are still in evidence. The city is home to nearly a quarter of Taiwan's nationally listed cultural sites, mainly centuries-old temples, and it maintains them with diligence.

At first, the busy city of Kaohsiung may look like a place to avoid. It carries the legacy of an oceangoing port and industrial city, but it has its share of attractions, especially some fine modern museums. Its massive port facilities, where huge container ships squeeze through a narrow channel into Kaohsiung Harbor, are the lifeblood of Taiwan's export-based economy. The city is also known for its raucous nightlife—it is a port city, after all.

NOT TO BE MISSED:

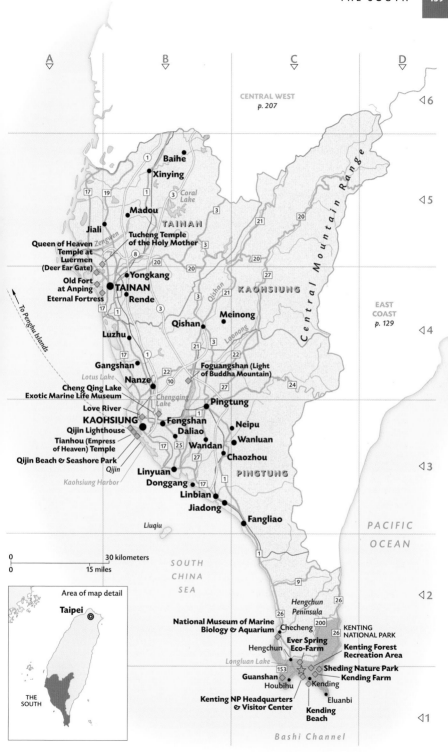

CENTRAL WEST
p. 207

A B C D

Baihe
Xinying

Coral Lake

Madou
TAINAN

Jiali

Queen of Heaven
Temple at
Luermen
(Deer Ear Gate)

Tucheng Temple
of the Holy Mother

Zengwen

Old Fort
at Anping
Eternal Fortress

Yongkang
TAINAN
Rende

Luzhu

Qishan

Meinong

Qishan

KAOHSIUNG

To Penghu Islands

Gangshan

Lotus Lake

Nanze

Foguangshan (Light
of Buddha Mountain)

Laonong

Cheng Qing Lake
Exotic Marine Life Museum

Love River

KAOHSIUNG

Qijin Lighthouse

Tianhou (Empress
of Heaven) Temple

Qijin Beach & Seashore Park

Qijin

Kaohsiung Harbor

Chengqing Lake

Pingtung

Fengshan
Daliao

Neipu

Wanluan

Wandan

Chaozhou

PINGTUNG

Linyuan
Donggang

Linbian

Jiadong

Liuqiu

Fangliao

EAST
COAST
p. 129

Central Mountain Range

PACIFIC

OCEAN

0   30 kilometers
0   15 miles

SOUTH
CHINA
SEA

*Hengchun
Peninsula*

National Museum of Marine
Biology & Aquarium

Checheng

Hengchun

Ever Spring
Eco-Farm

KENTING
NATIONAL PARK

Kenting Forest
Recreation Area

Longluan Lake

Sheding Nature Park

Guanshan

Houbihu

Kending

Kending Farm

Eluanbi

Kenting NP Headquarters
& Visitor Center

Kending
Beach

Bashi Channel

Area of map detail

Taipei

THE
SOUTH

Tainan

Tainan was Taiwan's political and military center between 1624 and 1885 and its capital between 1683 and 1885. It is the island's oldest city and home to nearly a quarter of its nationally listed cultural sites, mainly ancient temples, shrines, and forts. Many of the temples and shrines are found in the city's lanes and alleyways. You may chance upon them, but taking a guided walking tour is recommended.

The Qing dynasty imperial customs building graces the grounds of the Old Fort at Anping.

Tainan

 159 B4

Visitor Information

✉ Tourism Information Service Center, Tainan Branch, 2F, 90 Zhongshan Rd., Tainan

☎ 06/226-5681 or 0800/611-011

One of these structures, the **Eternal Fortress** (3 Guangzhou Rd., Anping District, $), in the western section of the city, was constructed in 1874 in the later years of the Qing dynasty. It was the first Western-style fortification built in Taiwan by the Chinese. A moat surrounds the fort's high walls, which are accessed through a redbrick arched tunnel from a bridge over the moat. The tunnel runs through to a central drill area. To the left of the entrance, you can climb to the fort's ramparts,

where two enormous Armstrong cannon—copies of the originals—face Taiwan Strait.

The **Old Fort at Anping** (82 Guosheng Rd., Anping Distict, $), also in the city's western precinct, was constructed by the Dutch between 1624 and 1634 using bricks imported from Batavia (today's Jakarta) and mortared with a combination of glutinous rice, sugarcane syrup, and crushed sea shells. It was named Fort Zeelandia. All that is left of the original fort these days is part of one wall. During the Japanese occupation (1895–1945), surviving walls were leveled to allow the building of a three-layer platform on top of which the residence of the director of customs was built. The residence's small rooms are crammed with historical relics and illustrations. At the back of the building is a watchtower built with little regard to the fort's architecture. From the top of the tower await city and ocean views.

The Dutch followed the construction of Fort Zeelandia in 1653 with **Fort Provintia** (*212 Minzu Rd., Sec. 2, Central District, $*). All that is left of the original fort is its foundations. After the deified pirate-warrior hero Koxinga forced the Dutch out of Taiwan in 1662, the fort went through a number of incarnations and name changes. In place of the superstructure is what is now called the **Chikan Tower,** consisting of two classical imperial-style buildings. In front of one of the walls of the base are nine inscribed Qing dynasty stelea, each sitting on stone turtles in a moat in which carp swim. A small bridge takes you over the moat, and through a moon gate to the base of the old fort and access to the tower. A limited collection of period artifacts is found in the main building.

Opposite the tower, a long, red exterior wall—notable for its roof moldings and decorative eaves—leads to the entrance of the **Sacrificial Rites Martial Temple** (*229 Yongfu Rd., Sec. 2, Central*

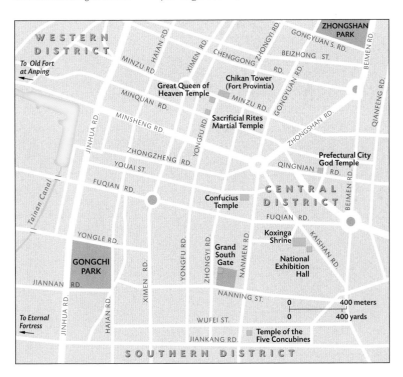

District). Dedicated to Guangong, the god of prosperity and war, the temple is one of the oldest Taoist temples in Taiwan. It was built during the Yongli period of the Ming dynasty (1647–1683), and it is recognized as one of the island's most authentic.

A facade of stone carved in deep relief graces the entrance to the central temple, where the red-faced, bearded Guangong sits inside a shrine. The shrine is decked with sculptured stone panels depicting a menagerie of animals, along with Taoist immortals and old tablets. There is a large pagoda for burning spirit money, and a circular ceiling featuring carved, gilded gods.

INSIDER TIP:

Tainan is famed for its Xiaobei Night Market snacks. Locals love the coffin bread: a fried-bread box filled with meat and vegetables.

—RICK CHARETTE
National Geographic contributor

Nearby, the **Great Queen of Heaven Temple** (*18 Lane 227, Yongfu Rd., Sec. 2, Central District*) is one of 17 temples in Tainan dedicated to Mazu, goddess of the sea. This one is said to be the oldest in Taiwan, built in 1664. The entrance portico leads past stone pillars to a gilded Mazu, sitting on an altar in the main hall and flanked by two stone statues of mythical generals on pedestals. The murals on the walls memorialize Prince Ning Jing, one of the last members of the Ming dynasty royal family, whose palace was made a temple in 1684 to enshrine an icon of the island's most popular deity.

About a half mile (1 km) southeast of the Great Queen of Heaven Temple, you'll find the city's **Confucius Temple** (*2 Nanmen Rd., Central District, $*), the oldest in Taiwan dedicated to the philosopher Zheng Jing, the son of Koxinga, originally built it in 1665, and it has since been renovated nearly 20 times. The temple is a fine example of classical Chinese architecture. Rooftop ornaments and roof-ridge decorations are more subdued than those of the temples of other Chinese religions. The entrance is set in a small park full of banyan trees. From here, the entrance leads to buildings divided by arched gates, corniced walls, and courtyards. Confucius is memorialized in the twin-eave **Central Hall of Great Success** with a spirit tablet, flanked by a gilded wood lattice. The spirit tablets of 12 disciples sit on separate tables. Wooden tablets inscribed with calligraphy written by past emperors and the R.O.C.'s presidents of Taiwan hang from near the ceiling.

The restored **Grand South Gate** (*No. 8 Park, Lane 34, Nanmen Rd., Central District*), about half a mile (1 km) south of the Confucius Temple, is one of just two remaining gates that once protected Tainan from the evils of the outside world. Its outer and inner block-stone and concrete walls surround a classical-style Chinese building. You can now look upon several of the old cannon—though they are not as old as the gate itself—still in place.

East of the Grand South Gate, the **Koxinga Shrine** (152 Kaishan Rd., Central District, $) is another example of classical Chinese architecture—this time in northern Fujian style—without overzealous embellishment. The shrine, set among cool gardens and pavilions, was built in 1875 by Qing dynasty imperial edict but damaged during World War II. This more substantial structure replaced it in 1962.

The shrine is modeled after a traditional courtyard house consisting of a portico entrance, main hall, and rear hall, all framed by colonnaded corridors built off the outside walls. Behind the entrance portico are statues of Koxinga's trusted generals, Gan Hui and Zhang Wandi, while the corridors hold spirit tablets of 114 loyal officers who followed Koxinga to Taiwan from the mainland.

A statue of Koxinga sits in the timber-walled main hall. Koxinga's mother is honored in the rear hall. A contemporary, abstract granite-carved statue of the war hero also sits in the lobby of the **National Exhibition Hall,** to the southeast of the main shrine. The hall exhibits antiquities including pottery, paintings, and documents.

In 1683, Prince Ning Jing, anguished over the imminent fall of the Ming dynasty, decided to commit suicide. On hearing the news, his five concubines preempted their lord and lover by hanging themselves. Ning Jing then took his own life. The **Temple of the Five Concubines**

EXPERIENCE: Yanshui Rocket Hives Festival

Each year on the eve of the Lantern Festival (see p. 44), the 15th day of the first lunar month, one of the world's most unusual festivals occurs in Yanshui town, near Tainan City. Long ago the town successfully used firecrackers to drive off evil spirits causing pestilence; the custom is now an annual celebration. Through the evening and into the night what look like giant beehives are pulled around town, each hole stuffed with small rockets, each hive containing thousands. The rockets are fired down streets, creating Dante-esque scenes. Tens of thousands, including young Westerners, dressed in motorcycle helmets and thick clothing, brave the maelstrom. It is best to take a bus from the nearest town, **Xinying,** caught right outside Xinying Train Station. For details, www.taiwan.net.tw.

(201 Wufei St., Central District) was built to enshrine them. This small temple sitting in an untended park is decorated with a retinue of portrait paintings. Behind the temple you'll find the concubines' tomb.

The **Prefectural City God Temple** (133 Qingnian Rd., Central District) is the largest of a number of Tainan's City God temples. Just beyond the imposing carved stone dragon columns at the entrance portico, the facade is set with gilded timber panels carved into mythological figures and patterns. Inside, timber tablets describe the rules of etiquette and good manners, and two oversize abaci symbolize the number of good and bad deeds done in one's lifetime—which will, it is believed, decide one's fate in the afterworld. ∎

Temple Architecture

Temples in Taiwan tend to be a swirling fusion of different deities, practices, and rituals. Buddhist and Taoist icons reside side by side, often in the same temples, with an iconic representation of the Sage sometimes thrown into the mix outside Confucius temples. Buddhist and Taoist elements are often mixed together, and are sometimes joined by a host of lesser folk gods, many of whom are heroes from Chinese myth.

Taipei's Baoan Temple exhibits decorative eave elements typical of Taiwan's Taoist temples.

You can pick out a Taoist temple by its sweeping roof with long lines of icons marching along the ridges. At or near the apex will often be a pearl, a dragon, or a pagoda, surrounded by a parade of dragons, phoenixes, monkeys, and other animals, and often, Fu, Lu, and Shou, the three wise old men called the star gods that represent prosperity, posterity, and longevity, respectively. Taoist temples are often dedicated to Mazu, goddess of the sea; Guangong, the god of prosperity and war; and Tudigong, the earth

god. You'll also find that Taoist temples are hectic places. Devotees burn incense, throw divining blocks, and set fire to large bundles of faux paper banknotes called spirit or ghost money.

Buddhist temples are quieter than their Taoist counterparts, and are geared more toward reflection than worship. Many are located in monastery complexes, and these have a more hushed and reverent tone. By the standards of many other religions, however, they are not exactly quiet. Guanyin, the goddess of mercy and from the Buddhist pantheon, is featured in many of the island's Buddhist temples.

Some general rules apply to temple layouts in Taiwan. Most temples are designed on a rectangular pattern. The standard layout consists of a front courtyard, and then a wall with three doors—a main door and two side doors that flank it—leading to the shrines. A gate or a fence, which keeps malevolent influences from entering and good luck from exiting, often blocks the main door. The main door is sometimes opened to make way for visiting deities or icons, with great blasts of firecrackers to clear away any lurking evil.

If the main door is blocked, visitors enter through one of the side doors. All doors have curbs that must be stepped over; this keeps ghosts and other baleful influences at bay. Door guards flank the doors leading to the deity: A pair of stone lions might sit at the main portals, and various fierce, brightly painted guardians adorn both main and side doors. Dragons are traditionally carved into the main pillars. To the Chinese, dragons signify all things good:

strength, goodness, wisdom, and fertility.

Larger temples often have three halls, and the main deity is usually in the second hall, with the other halls used for lesser gods or, in Buddhist temples, as classrooms. The main deity is obvious by its size, the magnificence of its surroundings, and its position in the center of the biggest hall, attended by servants and accompanied by a smaller image of the same god. This miniature is sometimes taken from the temple for festivals, to go on local patrol, or to bless the homes and workplaces of devotees. Lesser deities dwell at the sides and in the back of the temple, and on either side is a drum tower and bell tower. The bell summons people to worship, and it is also used to drive out bad spirits.

Temples are key features of every city in Taiwan. The Taiwanese are utilitarian when it comes to religion—they visit temples to seek help, and if it does not come from one god, many will decide to go and appeal to another one. For the most part, temples in Taiwan are relaxed and sociable places, mixing worship and commerce.

Public Superstitions

In Taiwan, everywhere you go you will see age-old superstitions in practice—if you know where to look. In terms of feng shui, which literally translates as "wind and water," the alignment of physical bodies is meant to encourage the flow of good qi and prevent the flow of bad. In banks, hotels, and other public buildings you will rarely if ever see counters facing doors, for this would allow profits to flow out. Aquariums will often be placed facing doors, their reflective panels deflecting ghosts and other baleful influences back out. Any ornamental fish found dead are said to have given their lives by absorbing the evil to protect the premises.

When **Citizen Plaza** was built in front of **Taipei City Hall**, it was feared bad qi could then flow directly down long Renai

Road, across the square, and into the building; the answer was to put up two auspicious lions at the doors, as is done at temples, to deflect any baleful influences.

Among other superstitious practices, note that in some public buildings, especially hospitals, there will be no fourth floor. This is because the Chinese word for "four" rhymes with that for "death." The word for "nine" is a homonym for that for "longevity," and thus is oft used in such places as eatery names and, notably, license plates, for which people will pay good money.

Finally, an old custom familiar to Westerners, too, is to rub the belly of any "laughing Buddha" encountered; the rubbing is thought to please the Buddha, who will grant good fortune.

Kaohsiung

With a population of 1.5 million, Kaohsiung is Taiwan's second biggest city. It is Taiwan's major industrial center and largest port—one of the world's biggest, as well. Kaohsiung can easily keep a visitor busy for a day or two with its wealth of museums and historical buildings, and although its nightlife is not as rambunctious as it once was, it remains lively.

The Love River cuts its way through Kaohsiung, Taiwan's second largest city and one of the world's major ports.

The summit of **Shoushan** (Longevity Mountain), which is mostly given over to parkland, overlooks Kaohsiung's sprawling harbor. On its eastern slopes is **Yuanheng Temple,** which was originally built in 1679 and rebuilt in 1926. Its imposing main hall houses three giant gilded Buddha images, part of a collection of many gleaming images of the Enlightened One inside the multistory temple. Toward the peak of the 1,165-foot (355 m) mountain is the city's **Martyrs' Shrine,** an impressive complex in classical Chinese style featuring sturdy red pillars that support sweeping tiled roofs and huge wooden gates and doors. However, it lacks the pomp of its namesake in Taipei (see p. 79), and the small karaoke cafés outside of the complex tend to denude it of its solemnity. A number of hiking trails in the park take you through wooded areas to sweeping coastal views.

From the shrine, the road winds down toward the exceedingly narrow northern entrance to Kaohsiung Harbor and the restored **Former British Consulate** (20 Lianhai Rd., tel 07/525-0271), $, café display area free), which is on a steep hill overlooking the sea and harbor. Built in 1858, the redbrick consulate is one of the oldest examples of colonial architecture in Taiwan. It displays historical photographs, maps, models, and relics offering insight into the city's past. The consulate's popular café with patio offers fine harbor views.

Liouhe Tourist Night Market—running along Liuhe Second

Road between Zhongshan First Road and Zili Second Road a few blocks south of Kaohsiung Railway Station—offers Taiwanese snacks from hundreds of vendors lining both sides of the street, as well as pubs and beerhouses. Tables and chairs are laid on footpaths and along the road. It opens at 6 p.m., but it's most lively after 9 p.m. The market closes at 2 a.m.

One of the city's most beautiful buildings—the former offices of Kaohsiung's municipal government during the Japanese occupation—is now the **Kaohsiung Museum of History.** The museum, fronted by a paved plaza and trimmed gardens, incorporates both Chinese and Western architectural elements. The building is sided by turretlike walls and topped with swooping tiled roofs, while the facade—with huge windows on its two levels all but forming a glass curtain—is dominated by a grandiose columned entrance, again topped with a classical Chinese-roof structure. Inside, exhibits of artifacts, antiquities, models, and maps trace city history.

To the north of town, the **Kaohsiung Museum of Fine Arts** is located on expansive grounds, including an amphitheater, a sculpture park, and a natural lake. A good deal of the museum's display space is given over to international exhibitions.

Climb the pagoda just inside the entrance to the resort area at **Chengqing Lake,** on the city's northeastern outskirts. There you will find views of the lake—a reservoir supplying the city with water—and surrounding well-tended and peaceful parklands. A path winds through wooded areas around the lake. A nine-cornered bridge cuts across the water in the direction of the **Grand Hotel–Cheng Ching Lake** (see Travelwise p. 255), a big place rendered in classical Chinese-palace architectural style in the image of the more famous Grand Hotel in Taipei (see p. 79).

Qijin

Qijin is an island running parallel with the mainland, its north

Kaohsiung

▲ 159 B3

Visitor Information

✉ Tourist Service Center, Kaohsiung Int'l Airport, Arrivals Lobby, 2 Zhongshan 4th Rd., Kaohsiung

☎ 07/805-7888 or 0800/252-550

✉ Tourism Bureau, Kaohsiung branch, 5F, 235 Zhongzheng 4th Rd., Kaohsiung

☎ 07/281-1513 or 0800/711-765

Kaohsiung Museum of History

✉ 272 Zhongzheng 4th Rd.

☎ 07/531-2560, ext. 309

🕐 Closed Mon.

💲 $

🚌 Bus: 60, 214, 248

http://w5.kcg.gov .tw/khm

EXPERIENCE: Kaohsiung Boat Cruises

A favorite pastime for Kaohsiung residents—couples, families, and friends—is the popular Love Boat cruises (www.kcg.gov.tw) on the Love River and the Kaohsiung Harbor, especially in the evening when city lights twinkle and there is live entertainment aboard. Back on land, folks like to stop for coffee at a Love River boardwalk open-air café. The Love Boats gather at Zhongzheng Bridge for the 20-minute river tour (NT$50) and

Zhenai Pier for the 100-minute harbour tour (NT$100). Tours begin daily at 4 p.m. New in 2010 and tremendously popular are amphibious duck boats that tour Lotus Lake and the surrounding area; another duck boat route plies harbor from Pier 2 Art Center then up Love River to Glory Pier. Each tour is one hour and costs NT$300. For more detail, contact the **Kaohsiung City Bus Service Administration** (2 Jianjun Rd., tel 07/749-8668).

Kaohsiung Museum of Fine Arts

- ✉ 80 Meishuguan Qian Rd.
- ☎ 07/555-0331
- 🕐 Closed Mon.
- 💲 $
- 🚇 KRT Aozidi station then Red 32 bus or Zuoying HRS station then 3 bus

www.kmfa.gov.tw

Chengqing Lake

- ✉ 32 Dabei Rd., Kaohsiung Township
- ☎ 07/370-0821
- 💲 $
- 🚌 Bus: 60 from Kaohsiung railway station, 133 from Zuoying HSR station

tip at the narrow entrance to Kaohsiung Harbor.

The north area–spruced up in recent years–has a collection of sites within easy walking distance of one another. A four-minute ferry ride from a small dock next to the entrance to Binhai fishing wharf lands you on a jetty near the head of **Qijin Seafood Street,** a collection of seafood restaurants and stalls. Rickshaws (*$*) can be rented outside the Qijin ferry terminal.

Seemingly struggling for space among the busy restaurants but clearly holding its own is the lively and colorful **Tianhou (Empress of Heaven) Temple,** dedicated to Mazu, the protector of mariners and fishermen (see sidebar p. 169), and one of Kaohsiung's oldest structures, dating back to 1691. Highly decorative roofs with ship-prow ridges flush with mythical figurines, and rows of cylindrical tiles flowing down the

sweeping roofs, are the temple's most attractive features.

From the temple head north along Tongshan Road to steps leading to the dome-capped **Qihou Lighthouse** (*closed Mon.*) and whitewashed colonial-style watchman's residence, guarding the north entrance to the harbor. As far as lighthouses go, it's small, only 36 feet high (11 m), but there are enthralling views down to huge container vessels squeezing through the harbor entrance. Just to the west of the lighthouse, and also guarding the harbor entrance, are the remnants of the 125-year-old **Qihou Fortress** (*closed Mon.*), a faded redbrick fortification carved into a hillock.

Back over on the western side of Qijin, not far beyond Qijin Seafood Street, is the worth-a-look black-sand **Qijin Beach** and **Qijin Seashore Park,** with an inviting promenade that is interspersed with collections of sea-themed

Qihou Lighthouse guards the north entrance to Kaohsiung's harbor.

artifacts, overlooking parkland and the coast.

National Science and Technology Museum

Located east of Kaohsiung Railway Station in the northeast part of the city, this museum is one of the largest of its type in the world. Wandering its seven floors, through its numerous galleries and exhibits—many interactive—is a fun way to while away an afternoon. If you bring the kids, plan on spending even more time.

Taking pride of place on the museum's entrance floor is the **"Power and Machines"** exhibit, whose official focus is how energy has been harnessed in the industrial age; its unofficial focus: how Chinese invention has contributed to this progress. You are shown how electricity has been utilized over the past couple of centuries at the **"Electronic World"** exhibit, from its discovery to the development of silicon chips and miniature integrated circuits. The **"Food Industry"** section has a "computerized" chef sharing culinary tips. You can experience an earthquake on a simulated earthquake platform at the **"Biological Technology"** exhibit, while an antivibration table shows how architects of modern buildings take earthquakes and typhoons into account during construction. The **"Mitigation of Natural Hazards"** exhibit is all about the brave new world of biotechnology, underscoring how it combines microbiology, biological chemistry, genetics, and electronic engineering for medical diagnosis and treatment, agricultural development, and environmental protection. Jungle drums and smoke signals join telephones and Internet paraphernalia to explain the history of communications in the **"Telecom History of Taiwan"** exhibit. The **"Industrial History of Taiwan"** exhibit demonstrates the almost infinite uses of plastic. A model of a processing tank illustrates how crude oil is refined; the manufacture of a variety of other products is also explored.

The museum's **"Air Navigation and Aerospace"** area has a mock-up of the International Space Station, and an exhibition on the Lockheed F-104 Star Fighter, once considered Taiwan's most sophisticated fighter aircraft.

The museum also has an English-language digital wireless tour and an IMAX theater ($). ■

Beloved Mazu

Technology may rule the day, but the gods still matter. Of the more than one hundred Chinese deities, Mazu is the most popular. The Heavenly Mother and protector of seafarers, she was the real-life daughter of a government official in Fujian Province in the tenth century, said to have the ability to warn fishermen and mariners of impending sea disasters. After she died, a temple overlooking the sea was erected in her honor. Temples sprang up all along China's south coast, and a cult following emerged. Every year on the 23rd day of the third lunar month, Taiwan's grandest of all religious events, the **Dajia Mazu** pilgrimage, kicks off. Over the following week, her image is carried around the entire region amid a riot of costumes, pageantry, and music. A million people watch her image pass by.

National Science and Technology Museum

✉ 720 Jiuru 1st Rd., Sec. 1
☎ 07/380-0089
🕐 Closed Mon.
💲 $
🚇 Kaohsiung main railway station or KRT Houyi station, then Red 28 bus

www.nstm.gov.tw

Lotus Lake

The pagodas and pavilions of Lotus Lake have a wonderful fairy-tale air about them. Perched on the edge of the placid lake, and introduced by colorful and imaginative—and very large—renditions of mythical beasts and gods, these are fun places to explore.

Lotus Lake
- 159 B3
- Huantan Rd., Zuoying District, Kaohsiung
- Zuoying HSR station

The identical and adjacent **Dragon and Tiger Pagodas** reach out into the lake via a nine-cornered bridge. At the end of the bridge you pass through the gaping mouth of a dragon and into its throat to view friezes of China's 24 most obedient sons from its mythology. The walls of the pagodas are embellished with similar paintings, along with scenes of heaven and hell. From the bottom of the Dragon Pagoda, a small bridge connects to the second pagoda, with more friezes on its walls. From here you enter the rear end of a tiger and emerge from its mouth, back onto the nine-cornered bridge.

At the entrance to the **Spring and Autumn Pavilions**—less than 110 yards (100 m) north of the pagodas—is a huge statue of a serene Guanyin, the goddess of mercy, rising above a writhing dragon. Two identical three-story pagodas sit on each side of the statue. A long pier begins between the pagodas and runs to **Wuli Pavilion,** some 200 yards (182 m) out on the lake.

Enclosed by walls enameled in brilliant red and fringed with gold tiles, and done in a somewhat rare—for Taiwan—Song dynasty architectural style, the sprawling **Confucius Temple,** at the northern end of Lotus Lake, is the largest in Taiwan. Its three courtyards and grottoes of potted bonsai plants and trees are divided by corniced walls and moon gates, and like most Confucius temples in Taiwan it eschews the ornate complications of Taoist and Buddhist temples. The original Confucius Temple at this site was built in 1624, but this one was completed in 1976. ■

A nine-cornered bridge zigzags to the fantasy-like Dragon and Tiger Pagodas on Kaohsiung's Lotus Lake.

Foguangshan (Light of Buddha Mountain)

Located northeast of Kaohsiung, this sprawling temple complex began in 1967 as a mountain-top retreat under the guidance of its founder, the Venerable Xing Yun, and has grown into the largest and wealthiest Buddhist monastery in Taiwan and a site of pilgrimage for Xing Yun's followers. It is a remarkable place of funerary niches, shrine and meditation halls, pavilions, gardens, ponds, grottoes, and art galleries, with an extraordinary collection of Buddha statuary.

You enter the monastery from the parking lot, past a hill with a seven-level cemetery containing 50,000 grave niches reserved for followers of Xing Yun. Just above stands a 120-foot-tall (36 m) gilded **statue of the Amitabha Buddha,** flanked by 480 smaller but identical images.

Take the path that leads from beside the Buddha to the **Cultural Exhibition Center,** which exhibits artwork donated by followers. Next, move into a mirrored corridor with marble seated Buddha images lining the wall, to a gallery with knots of twisted timber. The next gallery features the Venerable Xing Yun's published works, along with his robes and a travel case.

The **Main Shrine** fronts the Cultural Exhibition Center, where three huge Buddha images sit under a 65-foot-high (20 m) patterned ceiling. Natural light streams onto 14,000 Buddha images encased in tiny niches. In the corners you'll spot a hanging drum and bell, while on either side of the main altar 33-foot-high (10 m) cones are inscribed with the names of temple benefactors.

The Main Shrine opens to a colonnaded plaza, past the Pilgrims Lodge to another plaza and a grotto backing the monastery's main gate.

Inside the main gate, the galleries of the **Buddhist Cultural Museum** hold a priceless collection of ancient and contemporary Buddha images.

To the right of the main gate is the wonderfully kitschy **Pure Land Cave.** You enter to a wide path lined with images of Buddha's disciples, then pass through a corridor made to resemble a cave, with Buddha's Eight Precepts inscribed on the walls, until you finally reach enlightenment and nirvana. Low-tech animatronic figures abound, and there's a gift shop. ∎

EXPERIENCE:
Buddhist Retreats

When the hectic pace and pressures of life wear on people, one option that folks in Taiwan take is a retreat at a monastery. **Foguangshan** (www.fgs.org.tw) runs a selection of meditation retreats for lay persons—one-day, weekend, and five-day programs. Graduates of these may then sign up for the 49-day retreat. There is straightforward vegetarian fare and 5:40 a.m. wake-up calls; the small guest rooms have TVs. **Dharma Drum Mountain** (www.dharmadrum.org) in northern Taiwan is another option; this is a modern Buddhist center nestled in the tranquil coastal mountains, offering a wide variety of meditation courses and classes.

Foguangshan (Light of Buddha Mountain)

- 🅰 159 B4
- ✉ Dashu Township, Kaohsiung County
- ☎ 07/656-1921, ext. 6203–6205
- 💲 Free English-language tours; contact temple in advance

www.fgs.org.tw

Kenting

Encompassing much of the Hengchun Peninsula, southern Taiwan's crescent-shaped coastline of white sandy beaches, coral gardens, and lush tropical uplands is mostly protected within Kenting National Park, one of Taiwan's natural treasures. This beautiful region, boasting the warmest winters in Taiwan, serves up plenty of opportunities befitting a beach resort.

A sensational sunset paints the shore golden orange at Kenting, Taiwan's tropical playground.

The coastline has been worn ragged by relentless winds and crashing waves. On the park's east coast, windswept sea cliffs overlook broad expanses of the Pacific Ocean, while on its western edges, weird rock formations—including one that resembles a former U.S. President—and huge boulders add drama to the panoramas.

Tablelands of uplifted coral rise quickly inland of this craggy coastline, providing lots of recreational opportunities for hikers, bird-watchers, and nature lovers alike. At Kenting Forest Recreation Area, you can climb through thick rain forest and past pockmarked coral-rock boulders that long ago shoved up from the ocean floor to stunning 360-degree views of the park. Gentle hikes through Eluanbi Park, with its historic lighthouse marking the southernmost tip of the Hengchun Peninsula (and Taiwan), is an enjoyable option. Forested pathways meander past ridges, caves, and curious formations of limestone and coral shaped by wind, waves, and rain. More challenging trails can be found at Sheding and Nanrenshan Parks, although you need permission and a guide from the Kenting National Park Headquarters and Visitor Center, as these are eco-protection areas and as such off-limits to visitors who don't have permits. Cycling, sea canoeing, sea kayaking, pleasure cruises, and fishing are other recreational possibilities in the parks.

Offshore, the south coast has a coral reef teeming with marine life. Diving and snorkeling are understandably two of the most popular pursuits here.

Kending Town, right along the water, and Hengchun, farther inland, are where you'll find most of the hotels, restaurants, shops, and car rental agencies; the national park visitor center is just west of Kending Town.

Kenting National Park

Kenting became Taiwan's first national park in 1982. Each year more than five million people crowd into its 125 square miles (324 sq km), mostly on weekends—making it Taiwan's most popular national park. Visit during the week to avoid the tour buses, traffic jams, and crowds.

The centrally located **Kenting National Park Headquarters and Visitor Center,** just to the west of Kending Town, has displays and photographs of the park's geography, topography, corals, and flora and fauna, making it a good place to get familiar with the park's offerings. Groups with their own transportation can book an English-speaking guide (*free, call ahead or book online*). The visitor center also

has multimedia displays in English and good maps and info.

West from the visitor center along Provincial Highway 26 is **Nanwan** or **South Bay,** a 660-yard (600 m) arc of yellow sand popular with sunbathers, fishermen, and people using personal watercraft. Unfortunately, the number of Jet Skis roaring close to shore makes swimming a risky proposition. If you feel like taking a dip, **Kending Beach** (see pp. 178–179) or **Baisha Beach** (see p. 174) are better bets. The line of guesthouses, souvenir shops, restaurants, and

INSIDER TIP:

Roasted chicken feet and soft vanilla ice cream swirled with green tea flavor are top Kenting beach snacks.

—JAYNE WISE
National Geographic Traveler
magazine senior editor

dive and surf shops opposite the bay add a beach-resort character to the place. Here you can book scuba-diving trips to explore the splendid offshore segment of the park (see pp. 184–187). If the urge hits, you can also take a PADI-certification diving course (see p. 174).

Follow Provincial Highway 26 west to County Road 153, which takes you to the western section of the national park and **Longluan Lake.** This combination of reservoir and wetlands has been touted as one of the best locations in

Kenting National Park

⚠ 159 C1–C2, 179

✉ Kenting National Park Headquarters and Visitor Center, 596 Kenting Rd., Hengchun Township, Pingtung County

☎ 08/886-1321

www.ktnp.gov.tw

EXPERIENCE: Diving Courses at Kenting

About 40 percent of **Kenting National Park** is under the waters of the blue Pacific. On the same latitude as Hawaii, its coral reefs are abundant—scuba diving and snorkeling are popular year-round activities. Coral is especially abundant around **Nanwan** and **Kending Town,** and the seafloor slides away gently, perfect for novices. There are many dive shops at both locations, and a basic three-day open-water **PADI training course,** culminating with international certification, costs about NT$8,000 (U.S. $250), all gear included. Many shops have qualified instructors who speak English, but go through the park's visitor center for the best options.

Taiwan to view migratory waterfowl as they make their way from Japan, mainland China, and Siberia along the Australasian migratory route (see pp. 176–177). From October to May snipes, plovers, ducks, egrets, cormorants, and wild geese fill its placid waters. At the **Longluan Lake Nature Center** (tel 08/889-1456, $), which sits on a bluff overlooking the lake, you can view the birdlife through telescopes.

County Road 153 dips into the stubby peninsula in the west of the national park, passing to **Houbihu,** a small but lively fishing port and marina. Late in the afternoon, bright blue fishing boats with prominent sloping bows return with their catch, some of which is sliced up immediately and dished up sashimi-style at an outdoor harborside market/eating area. Pleasure craft berthed at the marina are available for cruises and fishing trips, and glass-bottom boats leave the marina regularly to explore nearby marine life.

At the tip of the peninsula on which the lake is located, County Road 153 runs to **Maobitou (Cat's Nose Cape) Park** (tel 08/886-7527), which pokes into the Bashi Channel in a jumble of coral-rock formations. The area earns its moniker from some of these formations, which when seen from a distance—and with the use of some imagination—resemble the tip of a crouching feline's nose, with the promontory as the body. Climb the steps to the pavilion at the highest point of Maobitou for superb views of the jagged, coral-rock-fringed coastline.

On the western side of the promontory, a few kilometers from Maobitou Park along County Road 153, **Baisha** (White Sand) Beach, hidden behind a small village also called Baisha, is a 440-yard (400 m) sweep of glittering yellow-white sand locked between rocky knolls and backed by groves of palm and hibiscus trees, and rice paddies. Much of the beach's charm comes from its relative seclusion. It nudges a rustic and peaceful part of the peninsula, complete with hamlets, rice fields, and banana and pineapple plantations. Plans are afoot to develop the area, which will likely eke much of the charm from this delightful spot.

From Baisha, County Road 153 begins a gentle climb north about 3 miles (5 km) to 564-foot-high (172 m) **Guanshan** and more outstanding views. This time expansive vistas sweep north along the coast past fishing villages, and inland to Longluan Lake, South Bay, and the verdant hills to the east. A pathway runs along the edge of Guanshan, with a number of timber observation decks offering more coastal views, before passing though thick groves of banyan, fig, and hibiscus trees to **Fude (Earth God) Temple,** where devotees shove bundles of red paper into a blazing furnace, made ornate by a towering domed chimney, paintings of writhing dragons, and a three-tiered pagoda-style roof. Doing a precarious balancing act next to the furnace is **Feilaishi** (Flown Here Rock), a huge coral-rock boulder named for the shaky premise that it ended up in this spot after being blown here from the Philippines by a hurricane 500 years ago.

From Guanshan, the national park is confined within a narrow strip of western coastline ending near the **National Museum of Marine Biology & Aquarium** (see pp. 182–183), about 6.8 miles (11 km) north. The waters here are flush with Technicolor coral and marine life, and if you take a snorkeling or diving trip, this is surely one of the places you'll end up. Gently sloping reefs teeming with marine life are found at the southern area of the strip. Farther north, the underwater scenery becomes more dramatic, with large slabs of reef broken by deep chasms, forming a wonderland of drop-offs, sea canyons, and tunnels (see pp. 184–187).

Kenting National Forest Recreation Area

This 1,075-acre (435 ha) recreation area was established in 1906 during the Japanese occupation as a botanical garden and herbarium. Although a section of the park is still used for this purpose, the main attractions are its primary tropical forests, weird coral-rock formations, caves, and unsurpassed views of the Hengchun Peninsula. Well-marked paths wind through

(continued on p. 182)

**Kenting
National Forest
Recreation Area**

✉ 201 Gongyuan Rd., Hengchun Township, Pingtung County

☎ 08/886-1211

$ $

http://trail.forest
.gov.tw

Seawater sprays exquisitely weathered rock formations at Kenting National Park.

For the Birds

Taiwan has one of the highest densities of bird species in the world, thanks to its position along the Australasian migratory route and its extensive network of estuaries, coastal marshlands, and sheltered areas along rugged seacoasts and in its mountainous regions.

The vast variety of avifauna on the island includes the graphically elegant jacana bird.

About 500 local and migratory bird species have been identified on the island—which represents about one-twentieth of the world's 8,600 species. This compares with 500 species in Japan, 800 in the United States, and 1,200 in China.

Taiwan's birds and other wildlife often have been disregarded in Taiwan's rush for economic growth, but in the 1980s a conservation movement emerged and gained momentum, beginning to thrive in the late 1990s. Environmentalists have won several significant victories, especially in areas where rare bird species are found. Taiwan has 53 major bird habitats, which cover 18 percent of the island. Eighty-one percent of this area is now protected.

Bird-watching sites are common in Taiwan, as are tours that visit various habitats, most in the mountains, along coastlines, and on outlying islands. The best known areas for waterfowl spotting include Guandu Nature Park on the northwest outskirts of Taipei, the Yilan Delta, Hsinchu's Keya River estuary, central Taiwan's Dadu River estuary, the Zengwen River estuary near Tainan, and the Gaoping River estuary in southern Taiwan.

The most accessible site is **Guandu Nature Park** (*55 Guandu Rd., Guandu, Taipei City,* *tel 02/2858-7417, $, closed Mon.).* This beautiful 148-acre (60 ha) wetland is home to countless birds, both local and migratory. In 2001 the city government bought the site from rice farmers and allowed it to return to its natural state. Within two years it had reverted to a large open wetland filled with tall grasses, small ponds, and native trees, which in turn has lured back some rare bird species. The sanctuary itself is strictly for the birds—entry is carefully controlled—but three shelters provide good sightlines into the sanctuary and of its winged denizens.

People who know their birds are impressed with Guandu. Perched at the confluence of the Danshui and Keelung Rivers, Guandu is a complex ecosystem of marshland and mangrove forest attractive to a wealth of species. Great herons are common here, as are gray herons, egrets, bush warblers, green-winged teals, kestrels, and marsh harriers. Rarer species are also represented; you just might spot ibises and black-tailed godwits. Another famous birding site is **Longluan Lake** in Kenting National Park

A red-combed chicken bird prowls the shallows in search of tasty morsels.

(see pp. 173–174). Chinese sparrow hawks stop at Longluan Lake at the end of September, while the gray-faced buzzard eagle arrives in early October. Many other migrating birds—including snipes, plovers, ducks, and geese—join them. The area also hosts the local bird known as the Taiwan bulbul.

The most famous of Taiwan's 15 species of endemic birds is the mikado pheasant, which is depicted on the New Taiwan one-thousand-dollar bill. Other noted species include the Formosan blue magpie, Taiwan hill partridge, Swinhoe's pheasant, and Taiwan firecrest.

The **Zengwen River estuary** is home to Taiwan's most notorious bird, the blackfaced spoonbill. Of an estimated 2,000-plus black-faced spoonbills in the world, an impressive 800 or so have been known to winter at the mouth of this river.

Taiwan is also a favored stopover for the rare and colorful fairy pitta, with a population estimated at 2,500 to 10,000. The fairy pitta is known in Taiwan as the "eight-colored bird" because of its multihued feathers. It is a summer migratory bird that nests and breeds in the cooler parts of Taiwan during the summer hot months, and heads to tropical areas south of the island for the winter.

EXPERIENCE:
Bird-watching Tours

Kenting National Park, a key rest spot for migratory species, is a prime bird-viewing area. Birders' favorite location is **Longluan Lake,** where there is a viewing center. The Kenting National Park Administration organizes birding trips to the north and south shores, which are off-limits to individual travelers, and to other prime viewing sites. A good time to visit is around October, when migrating gray-faced buzzard eagles and Chinese sparrow hawks pass through in the thousands. The **Taiwan International Birding Association** (*www.birdingintaiwan.com*) organizes regular outings to Kenting and other prime avifauna spots around Taiwan.

A Drive Along the Hengchun Peninsula

Skirting much of Kenting National Park's coastline, this spectacular drive runs along Bashi Channel, dips south to the Hengchun Peninsula's tip at Eluanbi, Taiwan's southernmost point, then heads north along windswept cliffs overlooking the Pacific on the park's east side. Signposts in English lead the way.

Kenting's Sail Rock (on the right) is also called Nixon Rock for its likeness to the late U.S. President.

Start at **Kenting National Park Headquarters and Visitor Center** ❶ (see p. 173), where groups can hire an English-speaking guide (call the day before to arrange) and view displays and photographs of the park's geography, topography, corals, and flora and fauna.

Head southeast from the park headquarters, along Provincial Highway 26 (Kenting Road), through **Kending Town.** On the east edge of town, beyond the prominent, curved-backed **Frog Rock** facing out into the Bashi Channel, you'll spot **Kending Beach (Small Bay)** ❷. This pretty yellow-sand beach sits at the bottom of a small bluff, accessible by wooden steps. The

NOT TO BE MISSED:

Tropical Coastal Forest • Shadao
• Eluanbi Park • Longpan Park

café at the base of the bluff adds some tropical character and is a good place to relax and check out beach life Taiwan style. Unfortunately, roaring Jet Skis have taken over much of the shoreline, allowing only limited roped-off areas for swimming at both ends of the bay. Snorkeling gear can be rented at the dive shop, located on the same boardwalk as the café, to explore the corals just offshore at the southern end of the beach.

Continue southeast along Provincial High-way 26 for half a mile (1 km) to unimpeded views of the Bashi Channel and the curious **Sail Rock ❸** sitting just offshore. This giant 60-foot-high (19 m) boulder is uplifted coral believed to have long ago tumbled down from the tablelands that back the coastline. From a distance it resembles the taut sails of a fishing junk, but as you get closer, its profile begins to resemble that of U.S. President Richard Nixon (1913–1994), earning the boulder its second moniker, Nixon Rock. It even comes with vegetation on top, resembling hair.

Sail Rock marks the beginning of a stretch called the **Tropical Coastal Forest ❹**, which before it was taken to with axes and chainsaws covered 1,250 acres (500 ha) along an 8-mile (12 km) strip of coastline running to the tip of the peninsula at Eluanbi. The forest originally

sprouted from Filipino and Indonesian seedlings carried by the Kuroshiu (Japan Current). All that is left (and protected) these days is a 1-mile (1.6 km) strip, covering just 5 acres (2 ha). But it flourishes with some 180 species of vascular plants, growing from beds of uplifted coral.

Several miles beyond the southern end of the forest are the sparkling sands of **Shadao ❺**, Kenting's most attractive beach. The beach is formed from tiny seashell, coral, and foramin-ifera fragments, which, because of their high calcium carbonate content, make the sand glit-ter. Add to this the crystal-clear waters lapping the shoreline, and you can understand why the

---

See area map p. 159
► Kenting National Park
   Headquarters and Visitor Center
🕒 3 hours
↔ 17.5 miles (28 k)
► Jialeshui

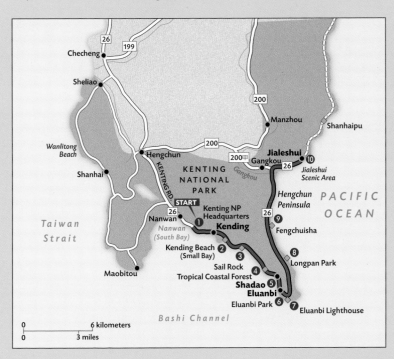

250-yard (220 m) beach at Shadao is such an inviting place. It is also a protected ecological area, so you can't swim there or walk on the sands. Backing the beach is the small **Seashell Sand Exhibition Hall** (tel 08/885-1204), where you can view the sands from its veranda. Inside the center a series of displays explains the phenomenon of the beach.

Continue south half a mile (1 km) past Shadao to **Eluanbi Park** ⑥ (tel 08/885-1101, $), at the tip of the Hengchun Peninsula, where the Bashi Channel meets the Pacific. Much of its 148 acres (59 ha) is given over to cool tropical monsoon forest, with interlaced branches of fig, hibiscus, and banyan trees forming canopies over a maze of winding pathways.

INSIDER TIP:

At Kenting National Park, Taiwan's first, 310 avian species share crowded air space with some 216 kinds of butterflies. The visitor center is excellent.

—JAYNE WISE
National Geographic Traveler *magazine*
senior editor

Here you'll notice an unusual feature of the park: raised walls of pockmarked coral—some as high as 20 feet (6 m)—topped by shrubs and creeping vines. Sections of the park open to panoramic coastline and ocean views, especially from Tough Guy Rock, Ocean Pavilion, and a boardwalk tracing the coral fringed coast.

The park's most impressive man-made feature is **Eluanbi Lighthouse** ⑦, surrounded by whitewashed stone walls. The 70-foot (21.4 m) structure—originally built in 1882 but its most recent incarnation dating from after World War II, when it was heavily bombed—once served a dual purpose: warning passing ships and as a fort to fend off incursions from local aborigines, making it one of the world's few fortified

lighthouses. Next to the gift shop opposite the lighthouse, follow the path down to the ocean and southernmost tip of Taiwan.

From Eluanbi Park, the highway begins to climb north to the grasslands of the peninsula's Pacific coast before opening up to some of the best coastal and ocean views in Taiwan. Make your first stop **Longpan Park** ⑧, about 1.5 miles (2.5 km) north of Eluanbi. From here, a short walk from the parking lot takes you to cliff-top views of the windswept coastline and the Pacific. Although the coral cliffs are not particularly high—about 200 feet (60 m)—nor steep, the views are expansive and spectacular, with the strong prevailing winds keeping the groves of screw pine and pandanus bushes stunted. The area can offer a surprising sense of isolation, a rarity in densely populated Taiwan. Look over your shoulder at the pleasant green rolling pastureland, another rarity for this crowded island. Trails wind along the cliff edge, with some dropping down to sandy beaches.

Farther on, the road dips inland past grass and pastureland before veering back to the coast to **Fengchuisha** ⑨, 1.5 miles (2.5 km) north of Longpan Park. The area is notable for its phenomenal shifting sands, which sweep down from the tablelands to the coast during summer rains, forming at its widest point a 220-yard-wide (200 m) cascade of patterned sand. Winter winds then blow much of the sand back up to the tablelands. Construction of the coastal highway and planting of vegetation by local authorities have ebbed the annual flow in recent years.

The highway continues to offer splendid ocean panoramas as it follows the contours of the coastline for another 3.4 miles (5.5 km)—occasionally dipping down to sea level and sandy beaches—before passing over a bridge at the mouth of the Gangkou River and the fishing village of the same name. Here the road reaches a T-junction. Turn right and go another 1.4 miles (2.2 km) to reach **Jialeshui Scenic Area** ⑩ (tel 08/880-1083), most notable for unusual wind-and-wave-sculpted

Eluanbi Park mixes flower-bedecked parkland and dense tropical forests.

and honeycombed rock formations that run along the coast. From the parking lot, you can follow a walking path for 1.5 miles (2.5 km) for a closer inspection of some of these weird formations, until you reach **Shanhaipu** (Mountain-Sea Falls), where water tumbles down a seaside cliff into the Pacific. Ocean. Alternatively, you can part with a few dollars

and climb aboard one of the fleet of open-decked trucks for a tour.

From Jialeshui, you can backtrack along the coast or head inland at **Gangkou.** This second route, twisting through hills, takes you through a pleasant rural area of rice fields and palm groves, small vegetable farms and hamlets, to **Hengchun,** the main town on the peninsula.

National Museum of Marine Biology & Aquarium

⚠ 159 C2

✉ 2 Houwan Rd., Houwan Village, Checheng Township, Pingtung County

☎ 08/882-5678

💲 $$

🚌 Kenting shuttle bus from Kaohsiung International Airport, Pingtung Bus Co.: every 30–40 min., $$$ one way

www.nmmba.gov.tw

groves of towering palms and eerie forests of banyan trees, then past huge pockmarked outcrops of coral and thick tropical forest to the magical **Fairy Cave.** The narrow, 150-yard-long (137 m) cavern has hundreds of stalactites and stalagmites accentuated by lights. Leaving the cave, you climb a path to the highest point in the park (705 feet/520 m). Here, an elevator in a concrete tower whisks you up to an observation deck and magnificent 360-degree views.

National Museum of Marine Biology & Aquarium

This world-class museum and aquarium, devoted to the education, research, and preservation of Taiwan's marine and freshwater habitats, features visually stunning water tanks, water columns, underwater tunnels, and dioramas filled with live critters to portray Taiwan's various ecosystems. It's educational, and it's also quite a lot of fun.

You are greeted in the front courtyard by an enormous whale, so lifelike it seemingly cavorts in its watery pool.

Upon entering the expansive lobby, you'll spot more life-size models of dolphins, giant squid, whales, and sharks eyeing you from the arched, 69-foot-high (21 m) ceiling.

A tumbling waterfall announces the entrance to one of the museum's three major exhibition areas, the **"Waters of Taiwan."** A procession of tanks traces the voyage that rainwater takes, from high mountain streams, where it first falls, to rivers and reservoirs, into estuaries, and finally ending in the open ocean. The **"High Mountain Stream"** display gives an above-and-below view of a stream's environment, including a number of rare Formosan landlocked salmon swimming about in the tank. From here you move downriver, to mock-ups illustrating the river's ecosystems.

An **oyster rack,** with live oysters hanging underwater from ropes tied to racks, demonstrates traditional oyster farming on Taiwan's west coast, while the rocky intertidal coast display explores the ecosystems that exist where tides ebb and flow.

Opposite the intertidal coast display, a **touch pool** lets you feel sea stars, sea urchins, and other sea life. More of Taiwan's reef ecology is presented in stunning colors at the **"Coral Reef Canyon"** and **"South Bay Reef"** displays.

Life-size whale sculptures greet visitors to the National Museum of Marine Biology & Aquarium.

The second major exhibit is the **"Coral Kingdom Pavilion."** You begin at a floor-to-ceiling, curving water tank teeming with live coral and darting technicolor reef fish. Farther along, in the **"Underwater Tunnel"** exhibition, you enter a clear, 91-yard-long (84 m) underwater tunnel that makes you feel as if you truly are underwater with the rays, reef sharks, snapper, sunfish, dolphin fish, and exceptionally weird-looking bowmouth guitarfish. You finally find yourself in the bowels of a shipwreck, with information on how marine life utilizes sunken ships to create new environments.

After you emerge from the shipwreck, a **"Coral Reef Conservation"** exhibit draws attention to how coral is damaged by industrial waste and other factors. From here you end up at the **sea mammal tank,** beneath the water, where you can get a fish-eye view of the belugas that reside here.

If you arrive at the aquarium before 10 a.m., you can catch the 20-minute feeding show, with the aquarium's four beluga whales doing tricks for enthralled audiences. The performances mainly steer away from the exploitive and are performed more to illustrate how the belugas are taken care of at the aquarium. There is a running commentary (in Chinese) about the mammals: their natural environment; what they eat; their social systems; how they communicate; how they are trained; and so on, with the mammals acting those roles accordingly.

Arrive at the extraordinary **"Open Ocean"** display in time to see the aquarium's residents eat (feeding times: 1 p.m. and 2 p.m.). The display looks on to a huge floor-to-ceiling section of one of the tanks. Watch as hundreds of fish—rays, mud sharks, reef sharks, giant trevally, sunfish, and turtles—all but envelop the diver as he or she submerges with bags of feed.

The third, and newest, major exhibit is the **"Waters of the World"** showcase. In the four theme areas—Polar Seas, Kelp Forest, Deep Sea, Ancient Oceans—visitors step into these environments through "live" or virtual-reality re-creations. The extensive virtual-reality exhibits are a great hit; tell friends you've "been there, done that" when a massive sperm whale battles a giant squid. ∎

EXPERIENCE: New-style Spa Treatments

In Taiwan spa treatment has reached a new level. In the past, the spa experience was exclusive to hot-springs hotels and meant a soak and, possibly, a massage. Many hot-springs locations now have new spa centers (*www.taiwan.net.tw*, click on Hot Springs). Among the new spa options are aromatherapy, massage with heated energy stones, crystal-energy treatment, and callus removal with fragrant salts. **Kenting's resorts** all have top-flight spa centers; among the most popular is the **Caesar Park Hotel** *(tel 08/886-1888, www.caesarpark.com.tw)*, overlooking the main beach.

In **Taipei**, visit **Merry Spa** *(tel 02/731-6431, www.merryspa.com.tw)* or **Being Spa** *(tel 0800/088-228, www.beingspa.com.tw)*.

Underwater Rain Forests

Taiwan is located near the thermal boundary where coral reefs do not thrive. The powerful, warm Kuroshio (Japan Current), however, flows northward from the tropics, splitting in two when it hits Taiwan's southern tip and washing the region with warm water, nutrients, fish, and coral larvae.

A rainbow cloud of parrotfish is just a sampling of Taiwan's dazzling tropical marine life.

The Kuroshio combined with the warming factor of seasonal monsoons creates perfect conditions for corals to thrive. Corals are found in most of Taiwan's waters, but the main area is in the south around Kenting, where a 37-mile-long (60 km) coral reef community, home to some 60 percent of the various species of coral reef to be found in the world, bustles with sea life.

Giant brain corals grow on the rocky bottom closer to shore, joined by staghorn, lettuce, mushroom, and knob coral, while in deeper water undersea meadows of soft coral and grasses wave back and forth in the gentle ocean surge. In all, nearly 300 species of coral live in the offshore waters of Kenting National Park. About 250 types of scleractinian coral have been documented in Kenting, together with 39 species of alcyonarian coral.

Like all coral reefs, the Kenting fringing reef is delicate. To thrive, coral needs a precise combination of factors. It is influenced by the temperature of the sea, intensity of sunlight, nutrient content and ocean currents, number of predators, and amount of sediment in the water. In Kenting, the corals have an ideal natural combination.

The corals of Kenting are blessed by Mother Nature but threatened by the forces of economic development. Destructive fishing is one problem. Dynamite fishing is now rare, but fishing boats ply the waters offshore, and their persistent netting and hooking have removed all but the smallest fish from the waters of Kenting. Scuba divers are often astonished by the tiny size of the tropical fish they see and by the lack of edible fish. Nets are commonly found on the coral reefs, both active and abandoned, and present a hazard to divers and fish alike.

But the biggest danger to Kenting's reefs are silt deposits that are flushed into the sea by tropical storms and seasonal rainfall. Large amounts of silt, coupled with sewage from resort hotels and recreational areas, can suffocate coral and other living organisms. Much of the silt is caused by fast-paced development in Kenting National Park. Construction debris is a persistent problem, and piles of dirt and other refuse lie waiting to be washed into the sea by heavy rainfall. Other detrimental factors have been oil spills and devastating typhoons, not to mention the effects of scuba divers who carelessly trample the reefs—some even carving their names.

There is good news as well. The corals of Kenting are still in reasonably good shape, and authorities in Taiwan are trying to slow the pace and type of development to help preserve them. Kenting National Park was established in 1982; before that, the 81,540-acre (33,000 ha) area was not protected. It was used for agriculture, fishing, whaling, and logging. In addition, it was being subjected to the sort of haphazard sprawl that typified much of Taiwan in the late 20th century. The unplanned growth ended in 1982, although many pre-1982 tenants have been allowed to stay in the park.

Sweeps of fringing coral make snorkeling an attractive alternative to scuba diving.

National parks in Taiwan are not the same as they are in the United States, where building and even access are strictly regulated, and the emphasis is primarily on conservation. In Taiwan, national park authorities try to balance the conflicting interests of business and preservation—with mixed success. There is plenty of construction in Kenting—mostly hotels and other tourist facilities—and the park is a battleground between the forces of development and the forces of preservation. On one side are fishermen, farmers, hotel developers, and Jet Ski operators, and on the other are scuba divers, whale- and bird-watchers, marine biologists, and the national park administration.

The most visible defeat for the national park was the Third Nuclear Power Plant, which looms over South Bay in the heart of Kenting. The Tourism Bureau wanted to build a hotel on the site, but it lost out on this plan, and hot water flowing from the nuclear plant is responsible for some of the coral bleaching that has taken place in Kenting.

There have also been victories for the forces of conservation. Whaling was stopped in 1986, and cyanide and dynamite fishing have been largely stamped out. Despite this turbulence, Kenting's coral reefs still boast some of the greatest biodiversity in the Pacific.

Kenting's Coral Reefs

Caves, grottoes, arches, and ridges covered with dense coral and ornamented with shells, sea lilies, sea stars, and roving fish of every variety await beneath the waves.

1. Reef crest
2. Storm-driven pool
3. Smooth starlet coral
4. Brain coral
5. Coral table
6. Reef slope
7. Pillar coral
8. Vase sponge
9. Anemone
10. Staghorn coral
11. Elkhorn coral
12. Elliptical star coral
13. Sea fans
14. Flower coral
15. Plume worm
16. Cattle egret

17–18. Black-faced spoonbill
19. Chinese crested tern
20. Little ringed plover
21. Whale shark
22. Black marlin
23. Sunfish
24. Silver tip shark
25. Reef shark

26. Manta ray
27. Turtle
28. Angelfish shoal
29. Fire fish
30. Angelfish
31. Lionfish
32. Clown anemonefish
33. Butterflyfish

34. Butterflyfish
35. Moray eel
36. Angelfish
37. *Oxymon acanthus*
38. Clown triggerfish
39. Trigger undulate

More Places to Visit in the South

Cheng Qing Lake Exotic Marine Life Museum

In the Cheng Qing Lake resort area on the outskirts of Kaohsiung, this huge underground bunker complex strengthened by a steel door weighing half a ton (500 kg), was built in 1961 to protect a privileged few against nuclear annihilation by Communist China. As the likelihood of such an event happening diminished, the bunker was transformed into an aquarium, which includes tanks of tropical fish, displays of coral, a whale exhibition gallery, and other marine-themed displays.

🅰 159 B3 ✉ 32 Dabi Rd., Niaosong Village, Niaosong Township, Kaohsiung County ☎ 07/735-6166 💲 $ 🚌 Bus: 60 from Kaohsiung railway station, 133 from Zuoying HSR station

Ever Spring Eco-Farm

This privately run farm, close to Hengchun, is known for its natural, chemical-free farming techniques. Overnight accommodation is available and guests are instructed in organic farming techniques. There is a restaurant, a coffee shop, and a display center with information on organic farming techniques. The farm also sells fruits, vegetables, and flowers grown on the premises.

🅰 159 C2 ✉ 28-5 Shanjiao Rd., Shanjiao District, Hengchun Township, Pingtung County ☎ 08/889-2633 💲 $$

Hengchun

Hengchun, the main town in the Kenting area—lying just outside the national park's boundaries—brags that it is the only town in Taiwan where all four gates are still intact. Built in 1879, the gates were once part of walled fortifications that surrounded the town to protect against attacks from disgruntled aborigines and imperialist forces from the West and Japan. The town has long since spread beyond the walls, and the gates have been all but swallowed up by development. The **West Gate** is in a traffic circle in the center of the town's commercial district. The **North Gate** now breaches the main road, while the **East Gate,** on the outskirts, has a section of the original wall still intact. Follow the road east from here to **Chuhuo** (Fire Coming Out) and a strange geological phenomenon of natural gas seeping from the earth and feeding flames in a rocky pit. Entrepreneurs sell potatoes wrapped in foil to place on the hot rocks and corn-filled foil containers (complete with tin handle) you can hold over the flames to make popcorn. Mud often blocks the fissure in the wet season.

🅰 159 C2

Hengchun History

"Hengchun" means "Eternal Spring," reference to the region's consistently bright weather. The name was bestowed by Qing dynasty officials, who often replaced the names of native settlements after periods of rebellion to denote new beginnings. This region was a neglected frontier because of its remoteness and aggressive native inhabitants. In 1874, Qing inspector-general Shen Bao-zhen fortified the town in anticipation of Japanese invasion (see pp. 34–35). Over the next number of years, massive ramparts of brick and lime were built.

Walls, guard towers, and gates were already in disrepair in 1945 when the Japanese surrendered; sections have been reconstructed in recent times.

There is an informative English-language Taiwan Tour Bus history tour of Hengchun (Ping Tong Travel Service, tel 08/889-1464, www.taiwantourbus.com.tw) that includes some time at the Sanchongxi hot-springs resort in the nearby hills.

An image of the deity Mazu, goddess of the sea, sits amid the gilded grandeur of the Queen of Heaven Temple at Luermen, in Tainan.

Kending Farm

In 1904, Japanese occupiers established this farm as a research facility; it is used for the same purpose today. Locals love Kending Farm for its expanses of pastureland and herds of cattle, both a rarity in Taiwan. Visitors also get to taste freshly pasteurized cow's and goat's milk at the farm's visitor center. There are superb views to the Bashi Channel from the grasslands, where cattle graze freely on the farm's 2,839 acres (1,149 ha). The research station is involved in cattle and sheep breeding and disease prevention among livestock. ▲ 159 C1 ✉ 1 Muchang Rd., Kending Town, Hengchun Township, Pingtung County ☎ 08/732-3180

Love River

The banks of the Love River in Kaohsiung have been turned into a fine park and promenade that comes to life in the evening. Open-air cafés and live entertainment now set the pace on the waterfront. Lovers stroll the promenade hand in hand admiring the lights reflected in the river's waters.
159 B3

Queen of Heaven Temple at Luermen (Deer Ear Gate)

This temple, in Tainan's northwest, groans under the weight of hundreds of figurines prancing along the ridges of its tiered roofs. Under the eaves between each tier are gilded pattern carvings, while the stone facade has been etched with more patterns and mythological scenes. In the main shrine writhing dragons protect Mazu, the queen of heaven. Before her is a row of black camphor-wood images turned out in colorful finery.
Map 159 B5 236 Lane 1, Xiancao St., Sec. 3, Annan District, Tainan City
06/284-1386

Sheding Park

The park shares much of the characteristics of its neighbor, Kenting Forest Recreation Area. It is notable for trees that, against the odds, have grown out of coral outcrops and been worn by northeasterly winter winds to resemble oversize bonsai plants. The park is kept simple, with just a few pavilions—set up for bird-watching—and only a few pathways. 159 C1 Entrance through Kenting Forest Recreation Area; see p. 175

Tucheng Temple of the Holy Mother

What it lacks in antiquity this temple in the northwestern area of Tainan, built in the 1970s, makes up for in size. Its dominant presence and forced isolation—it is surrounded by a wide moat—add to its grandeur. Finely carved stone dragon pillars stand at the entrance, with two large pagodas sitting on either side. The magnificent main shrine is cavernous and luxuriously decorated.
159 B5 160, Lane 245, Chengbei Rd., Annan District, Tainan City 06/257-7547

The parkland banks of Kaohsiung's Love River are popular with strolling couples.

Rugged, windswept, pristine islands—beautiful, yes, but emblematic of more than 60 years of strained relations with mainland China

Strait Islands

A Kinmen eave sports colors galore.

Strait Islands

Separating Taiwan from mainland China, the stormy Taiwan Strait harbors three groups of unspoiled and sparsely populated islands a world away from the bustling major island. Midway between Taiwan and the mainland you'll find the largest island group—Penghu—a scattering of 64 small islands spread over 37 miles (60 km) from north to south, and 13.6 miles (22 km) from east to west.

Water sports rule around the Penghu islands.

Linked by bridges, the group's three main islands—Penghu, Baisha, and Xiyu—are the most visited. The other two archipelagoes, Kinmen and Matsu, each only a mile or so from the Chinese province of Fujian, provide plenty of evidence of Taiwan's tumultuous relationship with its closest neighbor.

Penghu became part of the Chinese empire more than 700 years ago and served for centuries as a way station for immigrants moving to Taiwan. This role has left it rich in cultural and historic sites. Taiwan's first Mazu temple, dating back to the 14th century, can be found here, along with the ancient West Fort Xitai on Xiyu and a wealth of restored houses in the southern Fujian style. Penghu also served as a staging post for the imperial thrusts of the Dutch and French.

There is little industrialization on Penghu and, except for the summer tour buses, little

traffic. The landscape is mostly flat. Combined with basalt-column cliffs rising from the sea, lovely beaches, and fringing coral, these wind-swept isles serve up stark beauty. In winter, however, they are subject to fierce wind and cold.

This harsh climate has made Penghu's 93,000 residents a hardy bunch. They stoically forge their living through peanut, sweet potato, and sorghum farming, and fishing—although tourism is now offering a lucrative alternative for some residents.

On the Kinmen and Matsu Islands, visitors are supplied with more than enough evidence of the friction between mainland China and Taiwan though museums, memorials, and parks memorializing bloody battles. Getting to the outlying islands generally requires taking advantage of local ferry services or joining chartered boat tours. ■

NOT TO BE MISSED:

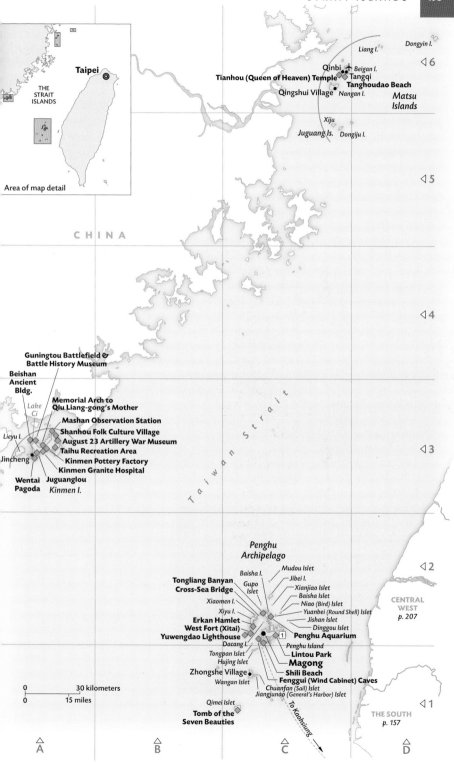

THE STRAIT ISLANDS

Taipei

Area of map detail

CHINA

Dongyin I.

Liang I.

Qinbi
Tianhou (Queen of Heaven) Temple   Tangqi
Qingshui Village   Tanghoudao Beach
Beigan I.
Nangan I.

Matsu Islands

Xiju
Juguang Is.   Dongjiu I.

Guningtou Battlefield &
Battle History Museum

Beishan
Ancient
Bldg.
Lake
Ci
Memorial Arch to
Qiu Liang-gong's Mother
Mashan Observation Station
Shanhou Folk Culture Village
August 23 Artillery War Museum
Lieyu I.
Taihu Recreation Area
Kinmen Pottery Factory
Jincheng
Kinmen Granite Hospital
Wentai   Juguanglou
Pagoda   Kinmen I.

Taiwan Strait

Penghu
Archipelago

Baisha I.   Mudou Islet
Jibei I.
Tongliang Banyan   Gupo
Cross-Sea Bridge   Islet
Xianjiao Islet
Baisha Islet
Niao (Bird) Islet
Xiaomen I.
Yuanbei (Round Shell) Islet
Xiyu I.
Jishan Islet
Erkan Hamlet
Dinggou Islet
West Fort (Xitai)
Yuwengdao Lighthouse
Penghu Aquarium
Dacang I.
Penghu Island
Tongpan Islet
Lintou Park
Hujing Islet   Magong
Zhongshe Village   Shili Beach
Wangan Islet   Fenggui (Wind Cabinet) Caves
Chuanfan (Sail) Islet
Jiangjundao (General's Harbor) Islet

CENTRAL
WEST
p. 207

Qimei Islet
Tomb of the
Seven Beauties

To Kaohsiung

THE SOUTH
p. 157

0   30 kilometers
0   15 miles

A   B   C   D

Penghu

Most visitors to this 64-isle archipelago will probably get to know the main trio first: Penghu, Baisha, and Xiyu—thin, curving islands linked by bridges and encircling Penghu Bay.

Penghu

 193 C2

Visitor Information

✉ Penghu National Scenic Area Administration, 171 Guanghua District, Magong City, Penghu County

☎ 06/921-6521

www.penghu-nsa .gov.tw

Penghu Island

The major island in the group, Penghu is home to the primary city, **Magong,** a sedate and picturesque place where about half of the island group's population resides.

In the city's eastern section, **Tianhou (Empress of Heaven) Temple**—appropriately devoted to the protector of mariners, Mazu—was built in 1593, making it Taiwan's oldest temple. Its interior walls are embellished with finely hewn wooden carvings of patterns and mythical figures, while on the second floor stone tablets recount the expulsion of the "red-haired barbarians," that is the Dutch, from the islands in 1624. These are thought to be the oldest inscribed tablets in Taiwan. A tablet inscribed with gilded characters from Qing dynasty Emperor Qianlong (r. 1736–1796) is also here.

South of the city along County Route 201, on a strip of land near Penghu Bay's south entrance, wind-blown **Shili Beach** stretches more than half a mile (1 km). Its calm, deep blue waters are nicely offset by the fine grains of coral and seashell that make up the inviting beach.

A little farther west along County Route 201 you'll come to the **Fenggui (Wind Cabinet) Caves.** Wind and waves have eroded the sea cliffs into a craggy collection of formations, and plumes of water burst through blowholes and spit onto the rocks.

On County Route 204 east out of Magong, a forest of casuarinas and lintou trees backs a glorious stretch of white sand and clear water at **Lintou Park,** one of the islands' most popular tourist spots. Gardens of tropical flowers add vivid color to the lovely setting. At the park's western end, a military cemetery has a miniaturized version of Taipei's Chiang Kai-shek Memorial Hall.

A stunning ridge of stone columns on Xiyu Island, the most beautiful of Penghu's main island group, stands reflected.

EXPERIENCE: Windsurfing Lessons in Penghu

In the last decade or so, the breezy **Penghu Islands** have emerged as a prime destination for windsurfing in Asia, especially the waters off the main city of **Magong.** Winds sweep up the Taiwan Strait in the summer, and down the strait in winter. International competitions are held here, and many Taiwan locals and expatriates will fly in from the main island on weekends or take longer vacations built around windsurfing.

For travelers, perhaps the best option for windsurfing equipment and lessons is **Liquid Sports** (*www.liquidsport.com.tw*), occupying a spot overlooking the water at Magong. Making things easy, Liquid Sports also offers overnight accommodations. The cost of a two-hour lesson, including use of equipment for a full day, is NT$2,200 (U.S. $70). Lessons are given in the summer, and English instruction is available.

Baisha Island

The fine beaches of Baisha Island are relatively uncrowded. Another lure is the excellent **Penghu Aquarium,** with displays of traditional fishing equipment, aquaculture, life in a fishing village, the evolution of fishing vessels, a futuristic undersea world, mock-ups of a coral reef, and an undersea tunnel for a fish-eye view of local denizens.

The magnificent **Tongliang Banyan,** a tree thought to be more than 200 years old, forms a huge and glorious canopy over the courtyard of **Baoan Temple** in the village of **Tongliang,** on Baisha's western tip. The tree's aerial roots drop down from branches and intertwine to form an eerie fairyland forest that covers 7,100 square feet (660 sq m). The banyan tree is revered by the locals who see its ability to survive and thrive in an inhospitable environment as symbolic of their own lives.

From here, the **Trans-Ocean Bridge** spans the Houmen (Roaring Gate) Channel, linking the islands of Baisha and Xiyu.

At 1.5 miles (2,500 m), it is Taiwan's longest bridge.

Xiyu Island

This island, with its convoluted coastline hiding many coves and small bays, is the most beautiful of the archipelago's three main islands. Midway along County Route 203, off a side road to the island's east coast, you'll come to the **Erkan Hamlet,** a large clan homestead in classical southern Fujian architectural style. Note the finely crafted reliefs embedded above and below the windows and doors and along the eaves.

Close to the island's southern end, in a lofty position at the south entrance to Penghu Bay, is **West Fort (Xitai).** Surrounded by high walls and networked by curved tunnels, the fort was built in 1887 to house up to 5,000 men. You can climb up the ramparts to the gun emplacements for vistas of the Taiwan Strait. From the fort, a road heads west through Waian Village to the island's southwest tip and **Yuwengdao Lighthouse** and expansive ocean views. ■

Penghu Aquarium

🅰 193 C2

✉ 58 Qitou Village, Baisha Township, Penghu County

☎ 06/993-3006 or 06/993-3007

🕐 Closed Mon.

💲 $$

Penghu's Other Islands

Penghu's scattering of islands dishes up a fine mixture of rugged coastal scenery, attractive beaches, crystalline waters, and easily accessible coral reefs. Varying in size from a few square miles to just a couple of hundred square yards, many are uninhabited. There are scheduled ferry services to some of the islands, or you can charter a boat from Magong. Tours depart regularly to the different groups of islands.

Numerous historical buildings add to the natural allure of the Penghu islands.

South Islands

Just outside the mouth of the south entrance to Penghu Bay lies **Tongpan Islet.** Its shoreline is bounded by columnar, stacked, hexagonal-shaped rock formations that offer unusual, sometimes spectacular, scenery. The islands here were formed by volcanic activity, and the columns were formed as lava was quickly cooled by the seawater and shrank. Because of its geology, optimistic local tourism authorities have tagged the island the "Yellowstone Park of the Penghus."

The formations can be explored along a trail that encircles the island. Surrounding outcrops of coral in shallow waters make Tongpan popular with snorkelers. The island's only village houses the small but ornate **Fuhai Temple** at the island's dock.

Just to the southeast of Tongpan, the larger **Hujing Islet** shares a similar, but less spectacular, topography of stacked, hexagonal-shaped rock formations. The waters off the island are among the clearest in the Penghu Archipelago. Legend holds that the Dutch built a fortification here that sank during a particularly fierce battle. In recent years, efforts to find the sunken—and apparently poorly built—fort have been unsuccessful.

To the south, **Wangan Islet** has a population of about 4,000, making it the most populated of the outlying islands. But Wangan is large enough to support that many people and still evoke feelings of isolation, especially along its windswept grasslands. On the western edge of the island's highest point, at 170 feet (52 m), **Tiantaishan** is a small crater that legend holds is the footprint of Lu Dong-bin, one of the Eight Immortals (see sidebar p. 142). It is not particularly impressive, but it does attract travelers because of its mythological significance. On a more earthly note, unhampered ocean vistas can be had from here. **Zhongshe Village,** on the island's western shoreline, has a well-preserved group of Qing dynasty houses, some still used as residences.

About 1 mile (1.6 km) east of Tongpan is the much smaller, but more developed, **Jiangjun-ao (General's Harbor) Islet.**

It earned its prosperity from veined-stone mining, which has now ceased. The island is unusual in the Penghu group because of the number of multistory buildings, leading the local tourism authorities to refer to it as "little Hong Kong." The island celebrated its prosperity by building two richly adorned temples, **Jiangjun** and **Tianhou.** A third, much older temple on the island, **Yongan,** dates back to the Ming dynasty, when a general (source of the island's name) used the piece of land as a base while plotting to expel the Dutch from Taiwan.

INSIDER TIP:

The winds pick up markedly in the Penghus during the cool months, and tourism slows dramatically. This is prime time for windsurfing, with the added bonus of lower hotel rates.

—RICK CHARETTE
National Geographic contributor

Just to the east of the island is **Chuanfan (Sail) Islet,** named for its sail-like shape. You can actually walk there at low tide.

Qimei Island, the southernmost of the Penghu Archipelago, is named for seven legendary local beauties who, it is said, threw themselves down a well rather than have their virtue

Penghu's Other Islands

 193 C1–C2

☎ Penghu County Public Bus & Boat Administration, 06/927-2376

For more Penghu islands, see p. 206.

Penghu Tours

Though the archipelago's individual islands are small, getting around can be time-consuming for those new to the Penghu islands. **Country Travel Service** *(tel 06/921-1431, e-mail: lin .country@msa.hinet.net)* offers two tours of excellent value April through October. The price for each tour is NT$1,500 (U.S. $47) per person (minimum of two). The first is an eight-hour bus tour around Penghu, the main island. Country Travel's second excursion is not a true "bus" tour, for during this 10-hour outing you travel by yacht from the main island of Penghu to the islands of Qimei, Wangan, and Tongpanyu, then return to Penghu to tour it.

despoiled by a gang of marauding pirates. The simple **Tomb of the Seven Beauties** at the island's southern tip honors their sacrifice; the tomb is built over the well.

Columns of basalt rock that have been carved by erosion into myriad shapes rim the island's east coast. At **Longcheng** you'll find a weird landscape of wrinkled and folded rock terraces. **Niumuping** is a slab of stone weathered into a surprisingly accurate shape of the island of Taiwan, which has earned it the moniker "Little Taiwan."

Just off the north coast, an ingenious stone fish trap, built in the shape of two adjoining hearts, draws the crowds; in fact, this type of trap can be found throughout the islands.

North Islands

Tiny **Mudou Islet**—only 2,260 square feet (210 sq m)—on the archipelago's northernmost edge, is dominated by a black-and-white-striped, 131-foot-high (40 m) **lighthouse,** built during the Qing dynasty in 1902. At the island's small, white-sand beach, shallow, crystal-clear waters attract schools of colorful tropical fish of many varieties.

South of Mudou, sparkling beaches of finely ground coral—among the best in the archipelago—scallop the western coastline of **Jibei Islet**. Coral can be found only a few yards off the island's southern tip.

Two sandy bays on the eastern side along with coral reefs flush with marine life lying just off the coast make worm-shaped **Gupo Islet**—situated to the southeast of Jibei—ideal for beach fun and snorkeling. The island has also gained some renown for the seaweed that grows in abundance in its waters and is harvested at the start of winter.

To the south of Jibei and east of Gupo Islet, **Xianjiao Islet** is blessed with wide, white-sand beaches and offshore coral teeming with marine life. Sand makes up much of this little island, giving it a shimmering, mirage-like effect as you approach.

West Islands

The west coast of **Baisha Islet** (not to be confused with Baisha Island), to the southeast of Xianjiao Islet, is strung with a series of white-sand beaches that broaden as you move farther south. Columnar rock formations along the southern coastline are particularly spectacular. Various species of sea terns make their nests within these cliffs, luring bird-watchers, particularly in April.

A few hundreds yards south is **Niao (Bird) Islet,** although it has no birds. What it does have are stacked rows of basalt columns

INSIDER TIP:

While basalt rock formations in such shapes as lions and a miniature map of Taiwan are top draws on the Penghu islands, the double-heart-shape stone fishing traps are breathtaking.

—CHERYL ROBBINS
Tribe-Asia Indigenous Arts founder

forming high sea cliffs along its eastern shore. Below the cliffs, blowholes spit spray onto the cliff faces. Cliffs along the island's northern coast have been weathered into onion shapes.

Between Niao Islet and the main Penghu island group, impressive columnar rock formations rim **Yuanbei (Round Shell) Islet'**s northern coast. On the east coast, the fan-shaped rows of basalt columns resemble pleated skirts. Waters between Yuanbei and Baisha and Niao Islets are rich with coral beds.

South of Niao Islet, **Jishan** comprises two islets, which are "connected" at low tide. Sea cliffs almost totally enclose the smaller island, making it fairly inaccessible for people and thus a terrific haven for birds.

To the southeast, **Dinggou Islet'**s rock columns have been weathered into an array of angles and differing heights, giving the impression of a gigantic petrified forest. Seabirds flock here in the thousands from March to September, setting up colonies among the craggy landscape. Their overhead wheeling and screeching makes for a memorable experience. ∎

Workers repair fishing nets in an "endangered" scene. More and more locals are being employed by the tourism industry.

Kinmen

Off the south coast of mainland China's Fujian Province, the Kinmen archipelago was the site of fierce fighting between Communist and Nationalist forces soon after the latter withdrew from the mainland in 1949. The island group, along with Matsu (see p. 203), was also bombarded by mainland Chinese artillery in 1958. The Kinmen islands remained under martial law until 1992, and civilian visits to the islands were prohibited up until that time.

Dug into solid rock on Mount Taiwu, Qingtian Hall was long used for military purposes; it now is sometimes open for public tours and concerts.

Not surprisingly, Kinmen now relies on its military past to attract visitors. But the archipelago also has its share of natural beauty (though the highlight of **Kinmen National Park** might well be the cave theater **Qingtian Hall),** along with a wonderful collection of restored Qing and Ming architecture.

Kinmen is the main island, and **Jincheng** is Kinmen's main town, offering most of the accommodations, restaurants, and other services. Here you'll also find **Juguang Tower,** one of a number of monuments, buildings, and museums glorifying and memorializing the feats of Taiwan's military against mainland China.

This particular one is the earliest, built in 1952. The imposing structure comprises a two-story granite-wall "base" topped by a Chinese palace-style roof. Be sure to see the room on the first floor that's given over to a multimedia and cultural artifacts presentation of Kinmen's history.

In Kinmen's Jincheng District, at the island's southwestern end, the five-story, hexagonal **Wentai Pagoda** was originally constructed in 1387. The granite tower served as a navigational marker for ships negotiating the treacherous waters near Kinmen.

On Kinmen's northwest tip, in Jinning District, the **Guningtou Battlefield** was the scene of a 56-hour bloodbath that began when Communist troops landed on the shore in the early hours of October 24, 1949. The Communists initially made inroads but were eventually pushed back out to sea by the Nationalist forces. According to the victors, the end result was a total of 3,000 Nationalist troops and 12,000 Communist troops killed. You enter the battlefield through a Chinese-style city gate. A memorial tablet on the waterfront commemorates the battle.

The facade of the nearby **Guningtou Battle Museum** resembles a medieval fortress. Three charging soldiers made of bronze and set on a plinth guard the museum's main entrance, while large bronze reliefs of heroic battle scenes line the outside walls. Inside the museum, you'll find 12 large oil paintings that depict various moments during the battle,

along with materials, documents, and photographs relating to the fighting and ensuing victory.

Bullet holes from the battle pockmark the **Beishan Ancient Building** on the shores of nearby Lake Ci, which the Communists used as a command post before being overrun by the Nationalists. A tablet in front of the derelict building records in Chinese the events that took place here. **Lake Ci** is now used mainly for fish farming.

Erected in 1812, the **Memorial Arch to Qiu Liang-gong's Mother,** on Juguang Road in Jinhu District, to the east of

Wind Lions

During the Ming dynasty, Kinmen was denuded of forest by the voracious shipbuilding appetite of **Koxinga,** the famed warrior who, among other things, forced the Dutch from Formosa. The island became desolate. For salvation, the villagers turned to the wind lion—who they believed could control the savage winter winds and protect from evil spirits. Reforestation efforts begun under the Nationalists have resulted in significant forest cover, but the wind lion still features prominently. You will find its statue at the edge of every village and guarding important buildings and places, standing upright and often bedecked with a red bib.

Kinmen

 193 A3

Visitor Information

✉ Kinmen National Park Administration Center, 460 Boyu Rd., Sec. 2, Jinning District

☎ 082/313-100

www.kmnp.gov.tw

Jinning, celebrates the virtuous mother of Qiu Liang-gong, a governor-general of Zhejiang Province in mainland China who was a resident of Kinmen. His mother was deemed virtuous because she lived 28 years in widowhood without remarrying. Carved stone beams, figurines, and inscriptions adorning the stone monument mark that fact.

INSIDER TIP:
Kinmen's cleavers make good souvenirs. They are crafted out of the steel from shell casings lobbed here in the hundreds of thousands by China's Communists. History meets function.

—RICK CHARETTE
National Geographic contributor

The **Kinmen Pottery Factory** turns out embellished containers for the local firewater, Kaoliang (sorghum) spirits, which are snapped up by souvenir hunters and collectors. To the west, **Kinmen Granite Hospital** burrows deep into the granite of Kinmen's highest mountain, 830-foot (253 m) **Taiwushan.**
Mashan Broadcasting and Observation Station sits on a tongue of land on the island's northeastern tip in Jinsha District. From here, mainland China is only 1.3 miles (2.1 km) away. A trench takes you to a bunker equipped with powerful binoculars, so you can check out fishing villages on the mainland shore opposite.

A showcase of Qing architectural style is found at the **Shanhou Folk Culture Village,** featuring neatly packed rows of 28 southern Fujian-style houses dating from the turn of the 20th century, some of which are still lived in. The houses feature orange-tiled roofs shaped like ships' prows. One residence built by a senior imperial official stands out, with intricately carved beams and elaborate wall murals.

Taihu Recreation Area ($) centers around Lake Taihu. Three small islands in the lake are topped with elegant pavilions, and a handsome Ming dynasty–era residence in the park has been fully restored.

Also in the recreation area, the **August 23 Artillery War Museum** commemorates the 587 soldiers lost during a 44-day bombardment by mainland Chinese of Kinmen in 1958, in which 470,000 shells—including 57,500 in the first 24 hours—rained down on the island. The names of those who died are carved on either side of the entrance gates. The museum has a collection of tanks, aircraft, and artillery on its grounds. Inside, 12 display areas take you through the battle with photos, documents, models, relics, and, of course, numerous spent artillery shells.

Guningtou Battlefield, Guningtou Battle Museum, August 23 Artillery War Museum, and Taihu Recreation Area are all part of Kinmen National Park. ■

Matsu

Like Kinmen, Matsu nestles along the coast of mainland China's Fujian Province. It is an isolated place with a large military presence. Few visitors journey to the island group, which in itself is a good reason to visit, as the islands are not without attractions. The group consists of 18 islands, though some are off-limits to visitors.

The isolated Matsu island group has some golden beaches but very few visitors.

Beigan

If you fly to Matsu, this is where you'll arrive. This island is the group's second largest and has a population of 1,360 civilians. A paved road leads east from the main settlement of **Tangqi Village** to **Tanghoudao Beach,** a spit of sand connecting Beigan's two mountainous sections. On the north coast, the village of **Qinbi** is largely made up stone houses. The **Tianhou (Queen of Heaven) Temple,** dedicated to Mazu, fronts **Banli Beach** on the south coast.

Nangan

This is Matsu's largest and most populous island, with 3,800 civilians sharing just 4 square miles (10.4 sq km). You'll find a few attractions in and around **Qingshui Village.** The **Wenchien History and Folk Culture Museum** ($) covers the area's marine life, history, and culture. Next door, you can't miss the **Fushan Illuminated Wall,** a huge sign declaring: "Sleep with one's sword ready." Its purpose was to brace the islands' Kuomintang troops and warn off the Communist troops just across the waters.

In nearby **Qingshui Park,** a pretty reservoir sits amid gardens. The park is home to the display-rich **Matsu Military History Museum.** ■

Matsu
🅰 193 C5–C6, D6
Visitor Information
✉ Matsu National Scenic Area Administration, No. 95-1, Renai Village, Nangan Island
☎ 083/625-630
www.matsu-nsa .gov.tw

Trouble Across the Strait

Economically speaking, Taiwan and China couldn't be much closer. Taiwanese investment in China has surged over the past few decades, and the mainland absorbs the lion's share of Taiwan's exports. Politically, the two countries are enemies. China considers Taiwan a breakaway province and repeatedly threatens to take it back by force, while Taiwan prefers to remain independent.

Threats leveled by mainland China to someday retake the island fuel the Taiwan military.

Most Taiwanese prefer the status quo. Polls consistently show that the vast majority of citizens want to remain separate from China. That stance has strengthened in the past two decades, as the China-born "mainlander" generation has lost much political influence, and a pro-Taiwan identity has emerged.

The Taiwanese see no reason to rejoin China, which they view as a badly governed country where business is dominated by corrupt officials, personal freedom is limited, and quality of life is low. However, China insists that Taiwan return to the motherland, and threatens to use military might to achieve unification. By

constantly threatening to use force, including launching missiles near Taiwan in 1995 and 1996, China has left itself little room for diplomatic maneuvering.

Despite having opposite goals, the two sides have talked. In 1992 and 1993, discussions were held under a One China platform, which held that Taiwan and China were one country, but with two governments. That was the high point of the relationship.

The third major player in the ongoing tug-of-war—the United States—does not promote Taiwanese independence. But the Taiwan Relations Act, a 1979 declaration by the U.S. Congress, implies that the United States will provide Taiwan with sufficient defensive weaponry, and will help defend it against attack.

As the political stalemate drags on, Taiwan continues to behave like an independent country, electing its own leaders and conducting its own foreign policy. It is not a member of the UN, but it has nearly 25 diplomatic allies.

Nor has Taiwan neglected its military. Its Air Force has bought 150 Lockheed F-16 fighter jets and 60 French-built Mirage 2000 fighters, and built 130 locally designed Indigenous Defense Fighter jets. Military service is mandatory, and nearly 300,000 soldiers serve full time. In early 2010 the United States enraged China by agreeing to a $6 billion arms-sale package for Taiwan.

Looking back, in March 2000, the two countries looked like they were headed for a crisis, as Taiwan first elected an independence-minded president, Chen Shui-bian (1951–). Just as they did in 1996—when they elected Lee Teng-hui (1923–)—Taiwan's voters ignored threats from China and elected the candidate most

Taiwan has a large, modern, and efficient military, with all manner of weapons and equipment, including missiles and aircraft. A readiness to defend its borders is a natural outgrowth of its past.

disliked by Beijing. China reacted cautiously, but repeated its main theme: There is but one China, Taiwan is part of China, it can never be independent. Tensions have eased since the reelection of a pro-China Kuomintang government in 2008, with much economic opening occurring, but China still declares its "right" to impose a military solution.

Meanwhile, on Taipei's streets, China is not discussed much, and daily life remains the same regardless of the political tension. The presence of a vague threat does little to dampen spirits.

More Places to Visit in the Strait Islands

Dacang Island

This island, located in Penghu Bay and encircled by the three main Penghu islands, is known for its huge tidal movements. You can walk the 2 miles (3 km) to the island from Baisha Island during the lowest tides. It takes about an hour. ⚠ 193 C2 **Visitor Information** ✉ See Penghu National Scenic Area Administration, p. 194

Juguang Island

This is the southernmost inhabited island in the Matsu archipelago, actually consisting of two islands, Dongju and Xiju. About 600 civilians live on the islands, most in the village of **Dapu,** in the center of **Dongju.** At the island's northern tip is the **Dongju Lighthouse,** built by the British after the Opium Wars of the mid-19th century and still in use. A stone tablet—the Tapu Inscription—recounting the adventures of a local Ming dynasty general who drove away marauding pirates some 400 years ago, sits on a cliff about half a mile (1 km) southwest of Dapu Village. **Xijyu** is a little more lively, but you'll likely be the main attraction, given the island's lack of actual tourist sights. ⚠ 193 C5 **Visitor Information** ✉ See Matsu National Scenic Area Administration, p. 203

Lieyu Island

This island, about 2 miles (3 km) west of Kinmen Island, is also referred to as Little Kinmen. You can catch a ferry from Jincheng on the main island. Natural beauty is practically upstaged by military history. From the pier at **Xizhai Village** on Lieyu, you pass through **Victory Gate**—celebrating Nationalist troop heroics against the mainland Communists—and through to the **Bada Memorial,** which honors the local soldiers who died in 1933 in the Sino-Japanese War. ⚠ Map 193 A3 **Visitor Information** ✉ See Kinmen National Park Administration Center, p. 200

Xiaomen Island

A bridge links small, scenic Xiaomen, sitting at the edge of the Houmen Channel, to Xiyu, one of the major islands in the Penghu group. On the island's northwestern coast is **Whale Hole,** a large gap in the cliffs said to resemble a whale, but only when viewed from a distance.

Golden sand covers a small plateau to the southeast of Whale Hole, making it one of Taiwan's few arid landscapes. ⚠ 193 C2 **Visitor Information** ✉ See Penghu National Scenic Area Administration, p. 194

Penghu Celebrates Its Abundant Seafood

The annual **Penghu Seafood Carnival** (tel 06/926-2620, www.penghu.gov.tw) runs from the end of August to the end of September—coinciding with an important fishing season. Carnival visitors are presented not only with many special offers for seafood dining at local restaurants, but also with activity opportunities such as feeding the fish at saltwater fish farms, learning about oyster farming, fishing for squid from a boat, guided tours to fishing villages and—a highlight—a visit to the village of Erkan (see p. 195) and its exquisitely crafted early 20th-century residences.

Perhaps the most popular tours bring visitors right into the ancient-style fish traps that dot the coastline, made by piling up stone walls and trapping fish at low tide; tour visits are, for logical reason, also at low tide.

But eating reigns. Many culinary events are held; the islands are especially known for oysters, cobia, and grouper.

Taiwan's exquisite landscapes of the Central Mountain Range in contrast to urbanized and industrialized areas along the coast

Central West

Pineapples thrive in abundance in the fertile central west.

Central West

Almost every square inch of land here is utilized in landscapes of urban, industrial, and rural life. The outskirts of one city merge into the beginnings of the next. In between, paddies of rice and patchworks of pineapple and banana plantations nudge the perimeters of factories and the fences of suburban homes. On the east side, in contrast, coastal plains abruptly yield to the towering peaks of the Central Mountain Range.

Jingming 1st Street is the place to stop for an afternoon snack in Taichung.

the highway branches; one route continues northeast to Yilan County and the other east to Dayuling. At Dayuling is another split, where one branch heads east through to Taroko Gorge (see pp. 134–139), while another swings southwest, reaching its highest point near the snow-dusted slopes (in winter at least) of Hehuanshan before a steep, winding descent to picturesque Wushe, nestled in a lush valley and surrounded by mist-shrouded mountains. About 16 miles (25 km) southwest is the city of Puli, near the geographic center of Taiwan. (Note that because of instability the Central Cross Island Highway has been closed indefinitely from just east of Guguan to just west of the Deji Reservoir. All traffic now goes through the Puli-Wushe branch.)

The central west region radiates from the urban hub of Taichung, Taiwan's third largest city, easily accessible from Taipei along the arterial Sun Yat-sen Freeway and Formosa Freeway. Many visitors use the city as a base for trips to the region, drawn not only by its geographical convenience, but also by a night-life that many say surpasses that of Taipei.

While the coastal area does have a few attractions, including the historic former river port of Lugang and the riotously ornate Chaotian Temple in Beigang, it is the region's mountains that attract most interest.

A little northeast of Taichung, at Dongshi, begins the north branch of the Central Cross Island Highway, an engineering marvel that climbs to over 10,000 feet (3,300 m) on its 172-mile (277 km) serpentine journey to the east coast. High up into the mountains at Lishan,

NOT TO BE MISSED:

Area of map detail

Taipei

CENTRAL
WEST

AROUND TAIPEI
& THE NORTH
p. 91

Xueshan
3,885 m

Wuling
Recreational
Farm

◁ 4

Dajia
To
Taipei

Houli

Qingshui

Dongshi

TAICHUNG

Deji
Res.
(closed)

Lishan Guest
House
Lishan

Shalu

Fengyuan

Guguan

Dragon
Valley Falls

Dayuling

Beitun

Tunghai University

Fushoushan
Rec. Farm

To Taroko
Gorge

CENTRAL CROSS ISLAND HWY.

Nantun

TAICHUNG

Changhua

Taiping

Qingjing Rec. Farm

Hehuanshan
3,420 m

Lugang

Baguashan Scenic Area

Wushe

Lushan
Wanda Res.

◁ 3

Taiwan Folk Village

Huatan

Puli

Xihu

CHANGHUA

Yuanlin

Caotun

Taiwan Geographic
Center Monument

Erlin

Nantou

Jiji
Railway
Line

Shuishe
Village

Wenwu Temple

Formosan Aboriginal
Culture Village

Zhuoshui

Erhshui

Jiji

Lalu
Island

Sun Moon Lake

Xuanzang Temple

Huwei

Douliu

Xitou Forest
Rec. Area

SUN MOON LAKE
NAT. SCENIC AREA

EAST
COAST
p. 129

◁ 2

YUNLIN

Alishan
Forest
Railway

Xitou

NANTOU

Shanlin Stream Forest Rec. Area

Chaotian
Temple

Fengshan

Monkey
Rock

Dongpu Hot Springs

Beigang

Ruili

Taihe

Zhushan

Dongpu

Minxiong

Zhuqi

Alishan

Batongguan
Historic Trail

CHIAYI

Fenqihu

Yushan Main Peak
3,952 m

Puzi

Tataka
Visitor Center

YUSHAN
NAT. PARK

Shuishang

CHIAYI

Budai

ALISHAN
NATIONAL
SCENIC
AREA

Baiyun
Cottage

0   30 kilometers
0   15 miles

◁ 1

THE SOUTH
p. 157

Taiwan Strait

A   B   C   D

South of Puli, the evocative beauty and serenity of Sun Moon Lake has made it one of Taiwan's most popular resorts, especially among honeymooners.

The narrow-gauge Alishan Forest Railway begins its amazing 44.7-mile (72 km) climb into the mountains of Alishan National Scenic Area from the city of Chiayi. The railway climbs from 100 feet (30 m) above sea level to 7,460 feet (2,274 m) in three and a half hours.

You'll find the head of Taiwan's most popular trail, leading to the peaks of the country's tallest mountain, Yushan (Jade Mountain), about 12 miles (20 km) east of Alishan. Tackling the summit of Yushan Main Peak (the highest peak at 12,966 feet/3,952 m above sea level) and other nearby peaks is for experienced climbers only. Views from the peaks reveal the drama of Taiwan's Central Mountain Range at its best. ■

Taichung

With a population of about one million, Taichung is Taiwan's third largest city. Its economic success comes from its wealth of small and medium-size enterprises. It also has a reputation as an educational and cultural center, and its nightlife is renowned around the island. The city is a good base for travel in the region.

Taiwan's third largest city, Taichung has one of the island's liveliest nighttime entertainment scenes.

Taichung

 209 C3

Visitor Information

✉ Greater Taichung Visitor Information Center, 2 Dacheng Rd.

☎ 04/2225-8988

🕑 Closed Sat.–Sun.

National Museum of Natural Science & Botanical Gardens

✉ 1 Guanqian Rd.

☎ 04/2322-6940

🕑 Closed Mon. & Chinese New Year holidays; open Mon. if national holiday

💲 $ (free Wed. before 10 a.m.)

Boutiques, tea shops, cafés, restaurants, and art galleries flank busy **Jingming 1st Street,** a pedestrians-only road in the city's hotel and shopping district—a popular place for locals and travelers alike to gather.

Fronting the city's Botanical Gardens, about half a mile (1 km) east of Jingming 1st Street, the **National Museum of Natural Science** has interactive exhibits to keep you—and the kids—amused. At the entrance, the **Path of Evolution** runs 240 yards (220 m), with plants and trees arranged to represent Taiwan's different seasons and climactic conditions. There are also IMAX shows in the Space Theater. The adjoining

Botanical Gardens, with its enormous area that simulates a tropical rain forest, is worth a look.

From the Botanical Gardens, a belt of parkland runs south for a mile (1.6 km) to the gardens of the **National Taiwan Museum of Fine Arts.** In the gardens, along with numerous sculptures, are 50 stone tablets embellished with calligraphy representing different calligraphic schools and styles from imperial China. The museum, which was badly damaged during the September 1999 earthquake but since rebuilt, concentrates on Chinese art and antiquities; it also has temporary Western art exhibitions.

Heading east from the National Museum of Natural Science

along Jianxing Road, you can't miss the blue glazed-tile roof of **Baojue Temple** *(140 Jianxing Rd., tel 04/2233-5179).* The temple's showpiece is a gilded statue of a portly, laughing seated Buddha. The 88-foot-high (26.8 m) image sits on a hollow pedestal inscribed with Chinese characters meaning "happiness to all." Smaller potbellied Buddha images are scattered around the temple complex.

At the end of Jianxing Road, a right turn onto Shuangshi Road, Section 2, brings you to the **Martyrs' Shrine**—a fine example of classical Chinese palace architecture. Among other heroes of China's military past, it commemorates 72 Chinese who were beheaded in 1911 by the Manchu court at the beginning of the republican revolution. Next door, the **Confucius Temple** *(30 Shuangshi Rd., Sec. 2, tel 04/2233-2264, closed Mon.*

& Sept. 15–28 for Teachers' Day prep) differs from other temples dedicated to China's famous philosopher because of its Song dynasty palace-style architecture, where the section of temple roof extending over the eaves curves downward rather than flaring heavenward.

The **Folklore Hall** in **Taichung Folklore Park,** north of Baojue Temple on the city's outskirts, is built in splendid Hokkien architectural style, with its characteristic U-shaped layout and needlepoint roofs. The park's plaza is used for cultural and folk performances.

For something different, head to the 74-acre (30 ha) **Encore Garden,** 6 miles (10 km) northeast of the city center. The neatly kept patchwork of European- and Japanese-style landscaped gardens is dotted with models of famous European statuary. ∎

National Taiwan Museum of Fine Arts
- ✉ 2 Wuquan West Rd., Sec. 1
- ☎ 04/2372-3552
- 🕐 Closed Mon.
- 🚌 Bus: 59, 71, or 89 from Taichung train station

www.ntmofa.org.tw

Taichung Folklore Park
- ✉ 73 Luxun Rd., Sec. 2
- ☎ 04/2245-1310
- 🕐 Closed Mon.
- 💲 $
- 🚌 Bus: 31, 33, 105

Encore Garden
- ✉ 41 Boyuan Ln., Minzheng Ward
- ☎ 04/2239-1549
- 💲 $$$
- 🚌 Bus: 2, 60

EXPERIENCE: Join in the KTV Song-Fest Fun

The people of Taiwan love to sing, and a night out at a KTV (an abbreviation of "karaoke TV") is a favorite way to spend an evening. In a gesture of Taiwan-style hospitality, foreign visitors are often invited to a KTV night out by new local acquaintances; conversely, a good way to make local friends is to treat them to a KTV song-fest.

KTV lobby and waiting areas are typically sumptuous, decorated with ostentatious themes such as Versailles and the Taj Mahal. Each group gets its own den-like soundproof room; shyness in front of strangers isn't part of the program. Rooms have large TVs and sound systems, with song books containing thousands of tunes, including familiar English ones.

There are extensive food and beverage menus; customers can also bring their own booze. As the libations flow—as at any Taiwan party, there is always much toasting—vocal chords loosen and inhibitions disappear. Most KTVs are open 24 hours or close near dawn. **Holiday KTV** *(www.holiday.com.tw)* and **Cashbox Partyworld** *(www.cashboxparty.com)* are the two dominant chains, both with guaranteed quality and good English-song selections. The most popular Cashbox location in Taichung *(111 Ciyou Rd., Sec. 2, tel 04/2223-6666)* is near the train station. The lobby is a mix of dark wood and marble with a grand piano in one corner. Safety equipment and staff emergency training are top-notch.

Changhua

Changhua is a nondescript city just to the southwest of Taichung, generally visited briefly as a transit point for international travelers on their way to the nearby historic town of Lugang (see pp. 213–214). But locals flock here to see its famous hilltop Buddha image. A few other sights in the town and surrounding countryside nicely round out a visit.

Changhua

🗺 209 B3

Visitor Information

✉ Cultural
Affairs Bureau,
Changhua City
Govt., 416
Zhongshan Rd.,
Sec. 2

☎ 04/728-7844

www.chcg.gov.tw

On the eastern outskirts of Changhua City, the main attraction at **Baguashan Scenic Area** (13-7 Guashan Rd., Changhua City, tel 04/728-9608, www.trimt-nsa .gov.tw), is the 100-foot-tall (30 m) black concrete statue of the Buddha at **Great Buddha Temple.** The Buddha—which weighs 300 tons (272 metric tonnes)—is hollow, which means you can climb inside and check

out the surrounding views through the image's ears and eyes. Dioramas inside the statue trace the Buddha's life, teachings, and philosophy. Behind, a pavilion and a pagoda flank a three-story temple.

The city's **Confucius Temple** (6 Gongmen Rd.) was built in 1726, making it one of Taiwan's oldest Confucius Temples. Although it has been rebuilt eight times, the temple maintains some original Qing dynasty architectural elements. The temple is notable for its carvings in the main shrine and inscribed tablets praising Confucius.

About 3 miles (5 km) south of Changhua, along County Route 137 in Huatan, the **Taiwan Folk Village** (360 Sanfen Rd., Wanya Village, Huatan Township, tel 04/787-3988, closed Mon., $$$) showcases traditional Taiwanese culture—and more. In the "Historic Taiwan" section, about a hundred buildings—houses, workshops, small factories—are modeled after typical Taiwanese and ethnic-minority structures. The village also includes areas devoted to "Taiwan Today," with arcade games and waterslides; "Taiwan of Tomorrow," with an aquarium and biology museum; and "Space-Time Performance," featuring a boat ride in which visitors experience natural disasters. ∎

You can walk inside Changhua's giant hilltop Buddha to view dioramas of Buddhist teachings.

Lugang

During the Qing dynasty, Lugang bustled with the arrival of immigrants and trading junks from the mainland Chinese province of Fujian. But the Japanese closed this river port soon after they occupied Taiwan in 1895 to stop the flow. The port's waters silted over, and the town became a place of little consequence. These days, the restored Qing dynasty architecture—much of it hidden in narrow, winding lanes—along with temples and craftsmen's shops lure visitors.

Lugang's Putou Street exhibits comfortable, inviting charm.

Most of Lugang's attractions lie on the main avenue of **Zhongshan Road,** which cuts through town, or in the lanes that run off it. Off the southern end of Zhongshan Road, on Qingyun Street, more than 300,000 sacred texts are housed at the **Civil Shrine/Martial Temple/ Wenkai Academy,** a combination of shrine, school, and temple built in 1824. Classical buildings with sweeping tiled roofs and minimal ridge ornamentation, along with detailed wall inscriptions, lend a peaceful air to the compound, befitting its history as a center for Taiwan's 19th-century Taiwan's scholars and literati.

North from the academy along Zhongshan Road—just past the junction with Changlu Road—a left on Sanmin Road leads to the **Longshan Temple,** devoted to Guanyin, goddess of mercy. Longshan, or Dragon Mountain, was built early in the 17th century and moved to its present location in 1786. It is regarded as one of

Lugang

🅜 209 B3

Visitor Information

✉ Lugang Town Office, 168 Minquan Rd.

☎ 04/777-2006

www.lukang.gov.tw

Taiwan's most architecturally significant and best preserved Qing dynasty temples, famed for classical murals by famed artist Guo Xin-lin and the circular carved ceiling in its main hall that towers above the enshrined image of the goddess. Its courtyards and halls exude a more tranquil ambience than other Taoist temples, enough to earn it the moniker "Taiwan's Forbidden City."

INSIDER TIP:

Walking along Lugang's old streets is like a trip back in time. Watch as artisans make delicate paper lanterns and wood carvings.

—CHERYL ROBBINS
Tribe-Asia Indigenous Arts founder

Looking distinctly out of place in a town that sells itself as a Chinese cultural center is a European-style villa housing the **Lugang Folk Arts Museum** (*152 Zhongshan Rd., tel 04/777-2019, $*). The building, designed for a wealthy local landholder by a Japanese architect in 1919, is imposing with its bold, cream-colored facade, arched windows, and flanking cupola-topped cylindrical towers. Inside, displays include furniture, jewelry, photos, handicrafts, clothing, and plenty of interesting Chinese curios.

Farther north along Zhongshan Road, a left turn on Minzu Road takes you to the brick-paved Nine Turns Lane (Jinsheng Lane). The narrow lane, often called

Breast-Rubbing Lane because people have to turn sideways to pass, was built to prevent the entry of bandits and protect against strong northeasterly winds that hit the town in September.

Traditional handicraft shops—some dating back more than a hundred years—line Zhongshan Road. A number of them craft religious images, decorations, and paraphernalia (given the number of temples in the town, that's not surprising), while others turn out wooden furniture, tinware, fans, lanterns, embroidery, and pottery. Worth a visit is the **Wu Dun-hou Lantern Shop** (*312 Zhongshan Rd., tel 04/777-6680*), where Taiwan's greatest master of this delicate craft creates exquisitely painted lanterns. A few doors up (No. 439), the smell of sandalwood pervades the 200-year-old **Shi Jin-yu Incense Shop** (*tel 04/777-9099*), which uses a secret blend of ingredients to produce handmade incense famous throughout Taiwan.

Running parallel to Zhongshan Road, **Old Market Street** comprises three narrow lanes—Putou, Yaolin, and Dayu—edged with renovated Qing dynasty-style shop-houses selling crafts, toys, clothing, and other nostalgic paraphernalia.

The image of Mazu, enshrined in the town's **Tianhou (Empress of Heaven) Temple** farther north at 430 Zhongshan Road, is thought to have been brought to Lugang in 1684 after Qing dynasty forces took the island from Ming dynasty loyalists. This legend has made this ornate temple extremely popular with pilgrims. ■

Nantou County

Lying at the geographical heart of Taiwan, Nantou County is mainly mountainous. A number of forest recreation areas that can be explored by car or on foot exemplify its natural beauty.

Vast groves of bamboo in Xitou Forest Recreation Area explain its wide use as a building material.

Xitou Forest Recreation Area is where National Taiwan University cultivates more than one million tree and bamboo shoots every year on its terraced nurseries; they are distributed throughout Taiwan for reforestation. The recreation area also comprises vast groves of bamboo (40 percent of Taiwan's bamboo comes from here), cypress, cedar, and pine. Numerous trails lead through the forest. The most popular hike follows a creek south from the main gate for about a mile (1.6 km) to a 150-foot (46 m) cypress tree, reckoned to be 2,800 years old. Shops at Xitou's tourist village, just outside the main gate, sell souvenirs made mainly from bamboo.

About 12.5 miles (20 km) south, higher into the mountains, **Shanlin Stream Forest Recreation Area** (contact Nantou Cty. Govt. Tourism Bureau) presents a more rugged face. From just inside the tollgate, a trail leads off along a boulder-strewn creek and through forests of cedar and pine for about half a mile (800 m) to tumbling **Green Dragon Waterfall.**

East of Shanlin Stream, **Dongpu Hot Springs** (Dongpu Rd., Dongpu, tel 049/270-1616) is a high-mountain resort that combines hot-springs soaking with some scenic--and rigorous--hikes. After hiking all day, soothe your muscles at any of a number of the hotels that have spring water tapped into their premises. ∎

Nantou County
🅰 209 C3
Visitor Information
✉ Nantou County Government Tourism Bureau, 660 Zhongxing Rd., Nantou City
☎ 049/222-2106, ext. 226 & 308
www.nantou.gov.tw

Xitou Forest Recreation Area
✉ Visitor center, 9 Forest Ln., Neihu, Lugu Village, Nantou County
☎ 049/261-2111

Central Cross Island Highway

The Central Cross Island Highway stretches for 172 miles (277 km) from Dongshi, northeast of Taichung, to Taroko Gorge on the island's east coast, with branches going north to Yilan and southwest to Puli. The route offers continuous beauty unsurpassed in all of Taiwan. You get it all: subtropical forests, waterfalls tumbling from cliffs, roaring rivers, placid lakes, hot springs, cloud-filled valleys, forests, and mountain peaks that—if you're lucky—are dusted with snow.

Glorious Deji Reservoir is just one of the many splendors along the Central Cross Island Highway.

Some ten thousand workers—many decommissioned Nationalist soldiers originally from the mainland and with little or no means of financial support—toiled on the construction of this spectacular engineering project for four years.

The impressive highway, completed in 1960, covers a wealth of various terrain, following early aboriginal trails, widened by the Japanese, through tortuous ravines, under cliff faces, and along steep mountainsides.

From **Dongshi,** a town severely damaged in the September 21, 1999 earthquake (see sidebar p. 218), the highway passes emerald rice paddies and orchards for 12 miles (20 km) before reaching **Guguan (Valley Pass),** a hot-springs resort that received its share of earthquake damage.

Beyond the resort, a mile-long (1.6 km) hiking trail leads through a lush valley to the 250-foot (76 m) **Dragon Valley Falls.**

From Guguan, the highway climbs steeply, winding to the mountain resort of **Lishan,** a spectacular two-hour drive from Guguan. However, the Central Cross Island Highway has been closed indefinitely from just east of Guguan to just west of the Deji Reservoir. All vehicular traffic now must go through the Puli-Wushe branch.

Lodges and restaurants cling to precipitous mountainsides flush with apple, pear, and peach orchards. Trails take you to views of towering peaks, broad valleys, and the vast emerald green **Deji Reservoir** below, just to the north of the village.

Less than half a mile south of Lishan village, an arched gate marks the entrance to **Fushoushan Recreational Farm** (29 Fushou Rd., Lishan Village, Heping Township, Taichung County, tel 04/2598-9205, $). The farm grows a variety of temperate-climate fruits on its terraced hills, which you can gaze upon from a lookout. Ponds and pavilions dot the farmland, while walking trails head farther up into the mountains. The farm is especially beautiful between March and May, when peach and apple trees blossom and flowering azaleas and mountain dandelions carpet the hillsides.

From Lishan, you have a choice. You can go northeast on the Yilan branch to Xueshan and Wuling Recreational Farm, or you can head southwest toward the junction at Dayuling.

Yilan Branch

If you choose the northern route, in **Wuling** you can arrange mountaineering expeditions to **Xueshan,** or Snow Mountain, Taiwan's second highest peak at 12,749 feet (3,886 m). The difficult ascent begins at Wuling and takes 10 to 12 hours. Views on the way up are magnificent. The climbing seasons are between October and December and March and April. At other times, snow, rain, wind, or the chance of landslides make the ascent too risky.

INSIDER TIP:

Wuling Farm is a great place to escape Taipei's summer heat. You'll see a panorama of terraced tea fields and endless wildflowers.

—EMILY HAILE
Travel Telegraph *blogger and former* National Geographic Traveler *magazine researcher*

The popular mountain resort of **Wuling Recreational Farm** (3 Wuling Rd., Pingdeng Village, Heping Township, Taichung County, tel 04/2590-1259, www.wuling-farm .com.tw, $$ per vehicle) was established in 1963 to provide work for decommissioned military servicemen. Orchards and tea plantations, spreading over 1,730 acres (700 ha) of terraced hillsides, flourish in the crisp alpine air. Trails lead to magnificent views of surrounding mountains.

Central Cross Island Highway
209 C3–D4

Late 20th-century Earthquake

Taiwan gets its share of earthquakes. The one that occurred on September 21, 1999, measured a devastating 7.3 on the Richter scale. With its epicenter near Sun Moon Lake, the quake was so violent that it toppled buildings in Taipei, 93 miles (150 km) away. A total of 2,405 people were killed, 10,718 injured, and 100,000 left homeless. Around 30,000 buildings were destroyed and 25,000 damaged. Visit the **921 Earthquake Museum of Taiwan** (*46 Zhongzheng Rd., Gengkou Village, Wufeng Township, Taichung County, tel 04/2339-0906, www.921emt.edu.tw, $*), built around the ruined buildings of a school campus right on the fault line.

Hehuanshan

 209

Visitor Information

 Hehuanshan National Forest Recreation Area Visitor Center, 33 Guanyuan Fushi Village, Xiulin Township, Hualien County

☎ 049/280-2732

http://trail.forest
.gov.tw

South to Dayuling & Beyond

If you go south from Lishan, you'll come to Dayuling in 19 miles (30 km), and another choice: You can go east to the unforgettable **Taroko Gorge** (see pp. 134–139). Or, you can take the highway southwest, rising steeply along wide expanses of grassland and arrow bamboo, with stands of pine, with views to distant rocky summits, to **Hehuanshan**—the Mountain of Harmonious Happiness—rising 11,207 feet (3,416 m) above sea level. Gentle slopes and a relatively regular winter snowfall once made Hehuanshan the only place in Taiwan suitable for skiing, but warmer climactic conditions over the past few decades have affected ski conditions, and the ski lift has been dismantled. Even so, as soon as the media report that one of the infrequent snows is expected, droves of people show up for the unusual Taiwan experience.

Even without snow, Hehuanshan serves up plenty of nature-appreciation opportunities. From highway stopping points near the summit, you can take a

INSIDER TIP:

In Nantou, Taiwan's only inland county, the café and restaurant scene at Qingjing Recreational Farm is worth exploring.

—IVY CHENG
Taipei's Community Services Center cooking teacher

number of short hikes that offer riveting views. The **Hehuanshan East Peak Trail** leads up past the site of the old ski lift to the summit of the mountain's eastern peak, offering fantastic views of the Central Mountain Range. The round-trip takes about two hours.

Heading southwest beyond Hehuanshan, the highway begins a steep, winding descent, past the grassy plains of Kunyang and the maple forests of Yuanfeng, before reaching **Qingjing Recreational Farm** (*170 Renhe Rd., Datong Village, Renai Township, Nantou County, tel 049/280-2748, www.cinqjing .gov.tw, $ for each of two separate areas*), one of the numerous farms that offer urban Taiwanese the chance to watch cattle and sheep graze in lush green fields.

Misty mountains all but enclose the aboriginal settlement of **Wushe** *(visitor center, 2 Renhe Rd., Renai Township, Nantou County, tel 049/280-2205),* 2 miles (3 km) south of Qingjing. In 1930 a bloody uprising by local aborigines was put down by Japanese troops, leaving 1,000 aborigines and 200 Japanese officials dead. A plaque in the village's temple recalls the event. The village has a few stores selling artifacts and handicrafts. Nearby, a trail winds down to the emerald **Wanda Reservoir.**

The hot-springs resort of **Lushan,** 5 miles (9 km) east of Wushe, sits on both sides of a rock-strewn river gorge. A long, slightly swaying suspension footbridge high above the river joins the two sections, giving you a choice of soaking at hot-springs inns on either side of the river.

Following the highway's southern section for another 16 miles (26 km) southwest brings you to sprawling **Puli.** The city suffered greatly from the 1999 earthquake, as the many vacant blocks (now cleared of rubble from ruined buildings) attest. The town is famous for its beautiful women, pleasant weather, and its rice wine, which is said to get much of its taste from the high quality of the area's water.

The **Puli Winery** *(219 Zhongshan Rd., Sec. 3, Puli, tel 049/290-1649)* was founded in 1917, when it began producing its famous Shaohsing rice wine. It has a small museum and display center, and offers samples. The **Taiwan Geographic Center Monument,** half a mile (1 km) northeast of town, by the Central Cross Island Highway, marks the dead center of Taiwan. ■

The scenery at Qingjing Recreational Farm appears more alpine than Asian.

Sun Moon Lake

Sun Moon Lake is one of Taiwan's most popular resorts, especially favored by honeymooners. It is at its best at dawn and dusk, when the low-set sun washes its waters in gentle hues of orange and red and mist swathes the surrounding hills in a scene redolent of a classical Chinese painting. On bright, cloudless days, the lake waters sparkle with stunning intensity. The temples and pagodas that dot Sun Moon Lake's shoreline only add to the area's natural beauty.

Sun Moon Lake's mood changes moment to moment, according to the whims of light and mist.

The lake gets its name from two lakes, Sun and Moon, which existed side by side before a hydroelectric dam project undertaken by the Japanese flooded them into one. The construction of the dam had an upside. Sun Moon became Taiwan's largest lake, spreading over 3.5 square miles (9 sq km) and creating an evocative place.

The dam project, however, also had it downside. The Thao, a local aboriginal tribe that lived and still lives by the lakeshore, were forced off the slopes of the high hill sitting between the two lakes to allow flooding of the basin. The top of the hill—today's **Lalu Island**—is still exposed, but the tribe's burial grounds on the lower reaches were flooded, as was their main village. The Thao consider the isle a spiritual place—the maples you see on it are sacred—and local authorities are no longer allowed to cruise boats or to land tourists on the island. The government is working toward reconciliation with the Thao. The isle is now in the tribe's control, and they use the surrounding waters for aquaculture—their results can be savored in lakeside restaurants. The tribe also has been given a say in the development of **Sun Moon Lake National Scenic Area,** established in response to the 1999 earthquake to help bring back tourism and help locals recover more quickly from the devastation (see sidebar p. 218). The scenic area comprises the lake and surrounding hills.

On its north shore, **Shuishe Village** is the lake's main settlement, with a number of hotels, restaurants, and souvenir shops. It is also one of a number of places you can rent rowboats, canoes, and paddleboats, or take an organized lake cruise out of Shuishe Pier (*tel 049/285-5054*) and a water shuttle to select points. A lovely boardwalk reaches around the lake; the various shore-hugging sections will eventually be connected to circle the lake.

Driving Around the Lake

A winding road rings the lake, serving up some lovely lake and mountain views along its route and allowing you to reach most attractions without too many navigational problems.

East from Sun Moon Village, past the scenic area's north tollgate, is **Wenwu Temple,** built grandly into the hillside in three ascending levels. At the lower levels, shrines honor warrior deities

Guangong and Song dynasty hero Yue Fei. A hall dedicated to Confucius sits on the upper level, the lofty positioning symbolizing the power of knowledge over the path to war. At the foot of the stone steps leading to the temple, balancing on concrete globes, are the two largest stone lion temple guardians in Asia. Both, painted bright red, look suitably fearsome. The absence of statuary along the ridges enhances the graceful lines of the temple's classical many tiered roofs, which sweep over the colorful patterned eaves and are supported by carved dragon columns. Meticulously trimmed bonsai and animal topiary decorate the temple's courtyards, while ornate colonnades and stairways connect its side halls and pavilions. From the hill behind the Confucius shrine you can gaze down over serene Sun Moon Lake.

Above the northeastern shore of the lake, nearby **Peacock**

Sun Moon Lake

 209 C3

Visitor Information

✉ Sun Moon Lake National Scenic Area Administration, 163 Zhongshan Rd., Sun Moon Lake, Yuchi Township, Nantou County

☎ 049/285-5668

www.sunmoonlake .gov.tw

EXPERIENCE: Boating on Sun Moon Lake

Time spent on the tranquil waters is a must with locals—and for visitors. The vistas change with time of day and season. Rowboats can be rented inexpensively from beside the car park at the village of **Shuishe** by the hour. The most popular type of outing, however, is on small yachts that launch from four piers—the main one at Shuishe—for 1.5-hour tours. A lower cost option is the regular "bus boat" service, with a day ticket allowing multiple journeys to various points of interest. For details, visit *www.sunmoonlake.gov.tw* and click on **Traffic Information.**

Garden ($) was built in 1968 at the behest of President Chiang Kai-shek, who reasoned it would help bring tourists to the lake. It's unlikely you'll ever see more peacocks gathered in one spot.

The road meanders south to **Dehuashe,** on the lake's southeastern edge. What had been a halfhearted attempt to portray

---

Sun Moon Lake Ropeway

A cable-car system *(www .ropeway.com.tw)* that went into operation in 2009 gives a picturesque aerial ride between **Sun Moon Lake** and **Formosan Aboriginal Culture Village** (FACV), traveling over the hills and valleys between the two. Cars take seven to ten minutes to travel the 1.1-mile (1.78-km) route, and operate from 10:30 a.m. to 4 p.m. weekdays, 5 p.m. holidays. The round-trip fare is NT$300 ($9.50 U.S.); combined cable-car and FACV entry gets you a discount.

---

an authentic aboriginal village is now in the control of the Thao, who have reclaimed the area as ancestral land and developed it into a community whose housing and lifestyles reflect traditional styles. The settlement, which because of its concentration of aboriginal denizens is also appropriately called Sun Moon Village, has a handicraft center and holds cultural performances for tourists.

Xuanzang Temple perches high on a bluff off the lake's ring road along the lake's southern shore. It was built in 1965 to house and display some of Taiwan's holiest Buddha relics. Illuminated in a gold, jewel-encrusted, miniature pagoda on the altar in the main shrine are seven *shelizi* nuggets—found among the cremated ashes of highly revered monks that Tang dynasty monk Xuanzang brought back from his pilgrimage to India.

Like many temples in Taiwan, Xuanzang Temple combines Buddhism and Taoism, evidenced by the shrine to Guanyin, the goddess of mercy, on the second floor. A small pagoda on the third floor holds what is believed to be a piece of the skull of Xuanzang.

Near Xuanzang Temple, a 550-yard (500 m) steep climb leads to **Ci En Pagoda** (Pagoda of Filial Virtue). Climb to the top level of the 157-foot (48 m) structure for superb lake views. This is one of the more peaceful places you'll find in the area, on weekdays at least. Decorative elements lace the ridges of its nine roof tiers, while its white balustrades contrast neatly with the tower's ocher walls. Chiang Kai-shek, who had the pagoda erected in honor of his mother, inscribed the tablet over the front archway entrance.

At the tip of the same promontory on which Xuanzang Temple sits is the similarly named minor **Xuanguang Temple.** From a pier in front, you can hire rowboats or motorboats for the short trip around Lalu Island. ■

Formosan Aboriginal Culture Village

Sprawling over 153 acres (62 ha) about a mile and a half (2.5 km) northeast of Sun Moon Lake, the Formosan Aboriginal Culture Village presents a cultural and historical microcosm of Taiwan's ten government-recognized aboriginal groups. Tacked on are an unsettlingly incongruous European-style chateau and garden, plus an enormous amusement park, which can't overshadow the serious showcasing of Taiwan's indigenous minorities.

The **Aboriginal Village Park** organizes the Dahwu/Yami, Ami, Atayal, Saisiat, Tsou and Thao (together in one area), Bunun, Puyuma, Rukai, and Paiwan ethnic minority groups each within its own "traditional village." You can catch a cable car (see sidebar p. 222) from the entrance to the park's highest point, then wander along pathways leading down the hillside to explore the "villages."

Despite the park's exploitative tinge, much effort has gone into the reproduction of the dwellings and attendant arts and crafts of the minority groups, with authentic materials used in their construction. The aboriginal village employs aborigines from each of the tribes to work in the "villages," acting as guides, creating local handicrafts, selling inexpensive traditional snacks, and putting on song and dance performances. Signs throughout the park let you know of the times of performances.

The seemingly out of place **European Gardens** is an expanse of lawn, beds of flowers, statuary, and fountains fronting a faux-baroque chateau. A restaurant inside the chateau attempts to bridge the incongruity, serving Chinese and Western dishes.

Future World, another nod to generic entertainment, offers several movie theaters, including the Showscan Theater, with its enormous screen.

Between the European-style gardens and the Aboriginal Village Park, **Amusement Isle** serves up some adrenaline-surging rides. At its entrance, **Cultural Square,** festooned with aboriginal totems and sculptures, features aboriginal music and dance performances as well as demonstrations of traditional craftmaking. ∎

Structures and lifestyles of Taiwanese aboriginal groups are displayed at the Formosan Aboriginal Culture Village.

Formosan Aboriginal Culture Village
🗺 209 C3
✉ 45 Jintian Ln., Dalin Village, Yuchi Township, Nantou County
☎ 049/289-5361
💲 $$$
www.nine.com.tw

Taiwan's Aborigines Today

The fortunes of Taiwan's 500,000 indigenous peoples (or aborigines, as they are called on the island) have followed a similar path to those of the native peoples of the United States, Canada, and Australia, where recognition and appreciation of their culture exists, but when it comes to mainstream society they are still marginalized.

Aboriginal groups joyously celebrate the Harvest Festival every summer/autumn.

Beginning in 1945, during Nationalist rule, little thought was given to the welfare and cultures of the aboriginal groups. Many had been assimilated, adopting Chinese names, while a dwindling number still held to their traditional lifestyles high in the mountains and in more remote areas in the east and offshore. The physical resemblance of some of the aborigines to the Chinese led to a "don't ask, don't tell" policy, in which people of native heritage kept their origins to themselves.

In the 1990s, the fortunes of Taiwan's aborigines began to improve. In keeping with a global trend, the groups became more assertive in their demands, and the government responded. In 1992 it launched a six-year plan to promote aboriginal culture and provide subsidized medical care, legal advice, and business loans. At the same time, it began to improve roads that link isolated aboriginal villages with nearby cities, and native land in mountainous regions was zoned as reservation land and cannot be sold to non-natives.

The government programs fueled a renewed interest in all things aboriginal. The first native theme bars opened in Taipei in the early 1990s, and the trend picked up as aboriginal restaurants became popular and native food items appeared on Chinese restaurant menus. Aboriginal music and dance became trendy, and annual tribal festivals are now well attended. Wood carving demonstrations are common in public parks in Taipei, native-motif clothing is fashionable, and authentic souvenirs—some of them very expensive—decorate homes and outdoor public spaces around the island.

Even the standard Chinese appellation has changed, from *shandiren,* or mountain people, to *yuanzhumin,* or original people. Some aborigines are beginning to forsake their Han Chinese names and return to traditional tribal names.

The overall educational and income levels of Taiwan's native peoples, however, lag behind those of the Chinese-descent majority, and many suffer from chronic social problems like alcoholism, unemployment, and prostitution. Another concern is the fading away of native languages and traditions.

Facial tattooing is long gone, and shamanism has largely given way to more conventional religion, especially Christianity. Aboriginal languages are still spoken, but native speakers are declining in number, and young people are speaking Mandarin and Taiwanese. Tribal chiefs and other traditional leaders are still respected, but elected officials hold the real power and

The aboriginal elders maintain traditions, most visibly in their clothing and adornments.

have undermined their traditional authority.

A faltering movement in Taiwan seeks to return portions of tribal lands to the aborigines and to give them autonomy in those lands. Such a process—combined with the assertiveness of the aboriginal tribes and the surge of interest in aboriginal culture—would go a long way to help ensure that fragile tribal traditions are maintained.

EXPERIENCE: Living Aboriginal Culture

Over the past decade the homestay experience has taken hold in Taiwan, and many members of the country's various indigenous tribes have opened their homes to outsiders, proud to explain their cultures to those who show an interest. Former Chashan village chief Li Yu-yan runs the **Old Village Chief's Guesthouse** *(60, Lin 3, Chashan Village, Alishan Township, Chiayi County, tel 05/251-3122 or 0937/356-402)* in **Alishan National Scenic Area** (see pp. 227–229), a Bunun and Tsou tribe region. Rooms are spartan and spanking clean; monkeys, rabbits, chickens, and ducks live on the compound; fresh eggs and vegetables grace the table each morning. In the same village is the two-room **Jhih Zai Cih Shan Jhong Guesthouse** *(82, Lin 4, Chashan Village, Alishan Township, Chiayi County, tel 05/251- 3352 or 0921/684-258),* run by a Hakka woman and her Tsou husband, with a coffee shop, and a shop with the couple's handicrafts. The husband's brother takes guests on kayak trips. For more: *http://info. taiwan.net.tw/homestay.english/index. html.*

Beigang's Chaotian Temple

Beigang is famed for its outstanding Chaotian Temple, dedicated to popular deity Mazu, the goddess of the sea. Of the 500 or so Mazu temples in Taiwan, Chaotian—originally constructed in 1694—is one of the most important. It stands out as an extravagant example of temple architecture, exceeding the riotous flamboyance found in most of Taiwan's temples.

Chaotian Temple
- 209 B2
- 178 Zhongshan Rd., Beigang, Yunlin County
- 05/783-2055

More than a million pilgrims visit Chaotian Temple (Palace Facing Heaven) every year, so it is usually crowded. During the week-long festival running up to Mazu's birthday, which falls on the 23rd day of the third moon of the lunar year (April or May), it erupts into a cacophony of noise and color.

Chaotian's most striking element is its multitiered roofs, with their ridges, eaves, and curving beams piled high with glazed ceramic figurines and images that depict a vast array of mythological characters and scenes.

A curving beam rising heavenward tops the main shrine hall. In the center sits a pagoda flanked by two balancing dragons. A colorful muddle of ceramic deities, beasts, and mythological scenes supports the beam. Below, rising from both sides of the ridge of the top tier, dragons and other figures balance on more curving beams. The central tier is completed with large ceramic figures of the star gods of longevity, prosperity, and posterity.

INSIDER TIP:

Mazu celebrations at the Chaotian Temple involve direct godly dialogue instigated by men wielding self-flagellation devices.

—RICK CHARETTE
National Geographic contributor

The intricate and masterly stone dragon pillars inside the main building were carved in 1775. A lot of the other decorative work inside also dates from the Qing dynasty. In the temple's courtyard, devotees burn paper offerings at a three-level pagoda, while the temple's benefactors—of which there are many—are honored in tall Buddha image cones flanking the temple's altars, with each cone featuring hundreds of small images of the Buddha lit up by a small light. ∎

Pilgrims flock to Chaotian Temple, one of the island's most important temples honoring Mazu, protector of seafarers.

Alishan

Alishan is one of Taiwan's most famous tourist attractions. People come here mainly to see the sunrise at Zhushan, when thick clouds throw a fleecy white carpet of clouds into the valleys, leaving only jagged mountain peaks pointing heavenward. Alishan can be reached by road, but a far better journey is on the scenic Alishan Forest Railway, which departs from Chiayi.

Alishan Forest Railway

The delightful Alishan Forest Railway is one of the world's great short train rides, not least because of the superlative scenery and the magnitude of the feat of engineering involved in its construction. From the town of **Chiayi** (see pp. 232–233), locomotives haul postcard-pretty red-and-cream carriages from 100 feet (30 m) above sea level on a narrow-gauge railway for 45 miles (72 km), reaching 7,461 feet (2,274 m) above sea level at Alishan National Forest Recreation Area, home of one of the world's highest altitude railway stations. Along the way, the railroad crosses 77 bridges and passes through 50 tunnels. In 1899 the Japanese, intent on exploiting these inaccessible and heavily forested mountains for logging, began building the railway. It was not until 1912 that the line reached Alishan.

The railway begins its three-and-a-half-hour climb in a mundane fashion, rumbling past fields of banana and pineapple plantations on the outskirts of Chiayi for 8.5 miles (14.2 km), before beginning its dramatic climb into the mountains. It corkscrews around lofty **Dulishan** before pushing farther up the mountain along precariously steep inclines.

Ushering in a new day, the sun peeks over the mountains at Zhushan in Alishan. Many come here to watch the day begin.

The train negotiates the final, and steepest, section of the climb through a series of switchbacks before pulling into Alishan.

Along the way, passengers are treated to scenes of precipitous pointed peaks shrouded in mist. Bamboo forests dominate the lower reaches of the track before giving way to dense cedar and pine forests on steep mountainsides.

The main destination for most people is the **Alishan National Forest Recreation Area,** Alishan's main hub, the jewel in the much larger Alishan National Scenic area. From the recreation area, toylike steam locos pull carriages

Alishan
🔺 209 C2

Alishan Forest Railway
✉ Taipei Main Station 02/ 2311-1024, Chiayi Beimen Station 05/ 276-8094, Alishan Station
☎ 049/289-5361
🕐 Leave Chiayi at noon & 1:25 p.m. daily; Alishan at 11 a.m. & noon daily.
💲 $$$

www.ht-alishan .com.tw

**Alishan National
Scenic Area**

🏔 209 C2

✉ 3-16 Chukou
Village, Fanlu
Township, Chiayi
County

☎ 05/259-3900

💲 $ (certain
sections,
including
Alishan
National Forest
Recreation Area)

www.ali-nsa.net

Unsinkable!

At **Laiji**, south of Fengshan on County Route
149, you can peer over a
sheer mountain precipice
shaped like the sharpened
bow of a huge ship that
drops more than 200 feet
(60 m). Scary? Yup. But
there's a trustworthy
safety rail between you
and the abyss. The name
of this great hunk of
mountain: **Titanic Rock.**

---

even farther into the mountains
to nearby **Zhushan** and Alishan's
famous sea of clouds; the Mianyue
Line branches off along the way,
going 5.7 miles (9.2 km) from
Alishan Station north to the end
of the line at **Monkey Rock,** 8,041
feet (2,451 m) above sea level.

Alishan National Forest Recreation Area

This forest recreation area has
plenty of hotels, restaurants, and
other amenities. Peaceful and
serene during the week, Alishan
metamorphoses into a noisy, jam-
packed mess of traffic, tour buses,
and people on weekends.

Roads and a number of trails
wind around the recreation area,
taking you to all the requisite
sights, although trying to find a
decent map of the trails can be
the most challenging part of the
experience.

The easy-to-negotiate, 2.5-mile
(4 km) **Alishan Loop Trail** begins
from behind Alishan House—spectacular in springtime with its many

blossoms. Among its many sights
are the thousand-year-old **Three
Generations Tree,** a massive
cypress crowned by a 10-foot-high
(3 m) second tree, and **Tree Spirit
Pagoda,** which commemorates
a stand of noble and ancient
trees ignobly cleared in 1936. It
also passes by two temples, the
simple Buddhist **Ciyun Temple;**
and the ornate Taoist **Shouzhen
Temple,** reconstructed in 1969.
The peaceful **Sister Ponds** are
said to be the manifestation of
two aboriginal girls who drowned
themselves rather than submit
to the demands of a brutish local
chief. This part of the trail, called
the Wood Forest Corridor, slices
through one of Taiwan's densest
stands of ancient red cypress.

Zhushan

An early morning, 30-minute train
journey from Alishan's quaint
railway station takes you farther
up the mountain to Zhushan,
famed for its beautiful sunrise
views of sawtoothed peaks poking
out of a sea of fluffy clouds. The
clouds move in huge billowing
waves, which sometimes swallow
the island-like mountain peaks.
Because of fickle weather, this
unforgettable sight cannot always
be guaranteed. Dress warmly; it's
always fairly cold before dawn on
the mountaintop.

It's best to start the trip up
the mountain about 45 minutes
before sunrise. Your hotel will tell
you when the sun will rise and
wake you in time to catch the
train or minibus.

Zhushan can also be reached
on a one-hour walk along a paved

path and stone steps. The route is easy to pick out in the dark, especially if you visit on a weekend when hundreds of others lead the way. At the top, a board points out the positions of Yushan (see pp. 230–231) and other mountains. You can buy local breakfast

INSIDER TIP:

Spend the night in Alishan, rise well before dawn, and go up the mountain to Zhushan to see the sunrise turn foggy cloud-filled valleys cotton candy pink.

—JODI COBB
National Geographic photographer

foods while you wait for the sun to appear. When it does, peeking above a ridgeline, the crowd gasps, cameras click, and the rush for a space on the train for the ride back down begins.

Other Areas in Alishan

The scenery around the small village of **Fengshan,** northwest of the forest recreation area, is a magnificent collection of primeval forests, steep rocky precipices, and tumbling waterfalls set in one of the most pristine environments in all of Taiwan. Hiking is the main attraction here, with a number of forest trails leading off to superlative vistas of the mountains, including 7,008-foot-high (2,136 m) **Xiaotashan,** which spends most

of the year shrouded in mist.

The **Ruitai Old Mountain Trail** wends its way east–west through a magnificent bamboo forest for about 2 miles (3 km) between the towns of Ruili and Taihe, west of Laiji. Alishan's bamboo forests are exceptionally tall, rising as high as 30 feet (10 m) in some areas, producing a still, eerie effect. You can get to Ruili from the Alishan Forest Railway's Jiaoliping Station by shuttle bus.

About halfway between Chiayi and Alishan along the Alishan Forest Railway is a lesser known gem of a place. **Fenqihu,** a heavily forested and scenic area, is sidestepped by most travelers, who head straight to the Alishan National Forest Recreation Area, so it is decidedly less crowded. A number of trails lead from the small settlement into the surrounding forests. One trail winds its way toward the peak of **Dadongshan,** where sunrise-watching crowds also gather. ∎

Take the train: The Alishan Forest Railway winds its way up into the mountains from Chiayi to Alishan.

Yushan National Park

Rising 12,966 feet (3,952 m) above sea level, Yushan—Jade Mountain—is Taiwan's highest. Trails leading to its peaks are well maintained, but exposed ridges and steep inclines make them challenging. If you're experienced, fit, and equipped, this is the place to discover the intimidating beauty of Taiwan's mountains.

Yushan, Taiwan's tallest mountain, has numerous peaks rising over 10,000 feet (3,000 m). Climbing any of these peaks requires a high fitness level and experience—plus a permit.

Yushan National Park's 407 square miles (1,055 sq km) are found within the Central Mountain Range, including 11 connecting peaks that form a cruciform shape, with Yushan Main Peak at the apex. Broadleaf forests dominate the park's lower altitudes, giving way to coniferous and bamboo forests at mid-altitudes and, finally, at the highest elevations, to arrow bamboo, conifers, and rocky outcrops. On the mountainsides, endangered species, including the Asiatic black bear and sambar deer, are staging a come-back, though sightings of these animals are rare. You are more likely to see Taiwan macaques and goatlike serows.

Among the park's six hiking routes, the most popular is the **Yushan Peaks System,** which allows you to reach six of Yushan's 11 peaks, including Yushan Main Peak. The starting point of the main trail is reached from **Tataka Visitor Center,** 8,563 feet (2,610 m) above sea level. From the visitor center, it's a 1.7-mile (2.7 km) walk along the Tatajia Saddle to the trailhead for the Yushan main trail. Another 4.1-mile (6.6 km) climb brings you to **Baiyun (White Cloud) Cottage,** used as a base for tackling the peaks of the Yushan Peaks System. It is the usual first day goal and the only place on the mountain that has accommodations; it sits 11,550 feet (3,520 m) above sea level.

If you want to catch the sunrise at **Yushan Main Peak,** you'll need to awake at about 3 a.m. for the up-to-two-hour walk to the summit. Along the last bit, you climb on bare rock face, where fences and chains have been erected to help negotiate the tricky footing, as well as protect climbers against blasts of wind along the exposed rocky area known as **Wind Tunnel.** At the top await the magnificent panoramas of the Central Mountain Range to the east, Alishan's peaks to the west, and drop-offs to lowlands thousands of feet below.

The trail to the 12,175-foot (3,711 m) **Yushan South Peak—** a series of rocky peaks cut with deep valleys either side—branches off from the Main Peak path a short distance above Baiyun Cottage. The views are just as spectacular as those at the Main Peak, but fewer climbers give the South Peak a more isolated feel. It takes longer (about three and a half hours) to reach the South Peak, but the climb is less arduous.

The 11,575-foot (3,528 m) **Yushan West Peak,** a 2.5-mile (4 km) hike from Baiyun Cottage, is the easiest of Yushan's peaks to climb. The trailhead is found directly behind the cottage.

To get to the summit of 12,575-foot (3,833 m) **Yushan North Peak** from Baiyun Cottage, take the trail toward the Main Peak until it reaches the last ridge before the peak. Instead of turning right to the Main Peak, turn left and head down the steep ridge. The round-trip takes about three hours. An alternate descent route is the **Batongguan Historic Trail** (see p. 232), which links Yushan North Peak to the hot-springs resort of Dongpu. ∎

Yushan National Park

🗺 209 C2

Shuili Visitor Center

✉ 515 Zhongshan Rd., Sec. 1, Shuili Township, Nantou County

☎ 049/277-3121, ext. 605

Tataka Visitor Center

✉ 118 Taiping Rd., Tongfu Village, Xinyi Township, Nantou County

☎ 049/270-2200

🕐 Closed 2nd & 4th Tues. every month unless a national holiday

www.ysnp.gov.tw

Before You Lace Up Your Hiking Boots

A special mountaineering permit ($) is necessary for some mountain areas, notably those above 9,852 feet (3,000 m)—this includes Yushan—and for special eco-protection areas. These are obtained at the Foreign Affairs section of any local police department or at the police detachment in a national park. An application must be filled out, and a passport, visa, or Alien Resident Certificate shown. The application is evaluated immediately. The Tourism Bureau website (www.taiwan.net .tw) has a downloadable application, or you can call the National Police Administration (tel 02/2357-7377).

There are two levels of restricted area; for the more highly restricted zones, a guide is necessary. The **ROC Alpine Association** (www.mountaineering.org.tw) can arrange for an experienced English-speaking guide for a group of four or more. Note: If the area is within a national park, a park entry permit is also required.

More Places to Visit in the Central West

Batongguan Historic Trail

The 95-mile (152 km) trail was completed in 1875 to link the east and west coasts. Much of it is now overgrown, but one section, linking Yushan North Peak in **Yushan National Park** (see pp. 230–231) to the hot-springs resort of **Dongpu,** is maintained for hikers. The route offers an alternative descent route back down from Yushan Main Peak. Instead of returning to the base camp at Baiyun Cottage, you can continue down the trail to Yushan North Peak. Follow this trail until it leads steeply off to the right down a gravel slope; the routes to the North Peak and to the Batongguan trail are marked at the fork. A chain fence helps keep you from slipping.

The actual trailhead is found 3.7 miles (6 km) beyond. This leads down to spectacular views of Yushan. The trail continues to fall gradually, with meadows giving way to forested areas. Just before Dongpu, at Father and Son Cliff, the trail has been carved out of a perpendicular rock face. From here, a steep section of the trail leads to Dongpu. The trip from Baiyun Cottage to Dongpu takes about ten hours, so you need to start early.

🏔 209 C2   **Visitor Information** ✉ See Yushan National Park, pp. 230–231

Chiayi

This small city between Tainan in the south and Taichung is the departure point for the wonderful **Alishan Forest Railway** (see pp. 227–228). If you plan on traveling up the mountain by train, you'll likely find yourself staying here for at least one night. The city is pleasant enough, but it does not have a lot to offer visitors. The city has a number of temples. On Minquan Road, in the center of town, **Beiyu Temple** (North Hell Temple) is worth a look for the image of its god, the king of hell, housed on the seventh floor of the temple's main tower. The temple was originally built in 1697 to house the image,

---

EXPERIENCE: Making Ceramics

Even in the electronics-ruled 21st century, the handcrafting of ceramics remains a thriving industry in Taiwan. That said, there are few places where the average person can try his or her hand at creating something from clay. Here is a sampling of places, in various parts of the country.

Shuili Snake Kiln (tel 049/277-0967) in Nantou County (about a 90-minute drive from Taichung and southwest of Sun Moon Lake) is the site of the island's oldest and most representative traditional wood-fired kiln. Here, craftsmen assist visitors to make their own utilitarian items, such as simple housewares, then help to fire them. Those who cannot wait for pieces to dry can have them mailed to them, for a fee. The kiln was founded in 1927 by master potter Ling Chiang-sun, who chose the location for its quality clay and timber for heating the kilns. He built a workshop and named it Snake Kiln in recognition of the its long traditional kiln of brick set out on a slope. It is best to visit with a tour group, for staff speak no English.

The **Yingge Ceramics Museum** (see p. 121; www.ceramics.tpc.gov.tw) has regularly scheduled Hands-On Activity sessions, for both adults and kids, in English. Advance booking is required. Various ceramics shops in Yingge, just south of Taipei, offer do-it-yourself ceramics activities, most easily accessed via Taiwan Tour Bus tours (www.taiwantourbus.com .tw, request kiln access in advance) because English is sporadic and your guide can help with arrangements on the scene.

Stone lions guard most temples in Taiwan. This one, at a Taichung temple, also serves as a hat stand.

which was brought by immigrants from mainland China. It was completely renovated in the 1970s.

As you would expect in a temple enshrining such a fearful god, there is a lot of appeasement going on by way of food offerings and paper burning. Near the railway station in the

city's center, the **Wenhua Road Night Market** is a good place to nibble on a variety of Taiwanese snack foods, especially the Chiayi specialties. ▲ 209 2B **Visitor Information** ✉ Chiayi City Govt. Tourism Bureau, 199 Zhongshan Rd., Chiayi City ☎ 05/229-4593, *http://travel.chiayi.gov.tw.*

Jiji Railway Line

Early in its 70-plus-year history, this narrow-gauge railway between Changhua and Nantou Counties primarily hauled logs from the forest to a lumber mill in the picturesque village of Jiji. Later on, it transported passengers, bananas, rice, fruit, and timber to the towns along the line.

Today, the Jiji Line is Taiwan's most popular scenic railway. The trip, which takes just under an hour, starts from the restored colonial-style railway station at Jiji and winds through forests and past spectacular mountain backdrops for 19 miles (30 km). Conveniently, the visitor center was recently moved into the fully renovated station in Jiji. The railway station was severely damaged in the 1999 earthquake. A Taiwanese entrepreneur helped provide the funds necessary to get it back up and running. Photographs taken of the station right after the earthquake are among the items displayed at the Jiji Railway Culture Museum.

🅼 209 B3 ✉ Jiji Train Station, 75 Minsheng Rd., Jiji, Nantou County ☎ 049/276-2546

Taichung Metropolitan Park

Expansive Taichung Metro Park sits on a plateau at Dadushan, on the northwest edge of the city of Taichung. The park's centerpiece is a large semicircular man-made pond set amid willow trees, while its grounds are scattered with assorted artifice. It is a favorite spot for stargazers and lovers taking in romantic views of Taichung's twinkling lights and the city's harbor on the coast.

A walkway leads from the pond to a plaza and a convex chart set into the ground that maps the heavens. After dark, the map is lit up and can be used to plot the current positions of the stars and constellations, with reference by dates printed on its outer rim.

A path winds through a protected area of thick acacia groves on the park's periphery, which in the evening comes alive with chirping cicadas and blinking fireflies. The best way to experience the park is via bicycle. You can rent one right at the main gate.

http://taichungmp.cpami.gov.tw 🅼 209 C3 ✉ 30-3 Xiping South Ln., Xitun District, Taichung ☎ 04/2461-2483 💲 $

Tunghai University

The university—a 20-minute drive northeast of downtown Taichung—has one of Taiwan's most attractive campuses. Spread over 343 acres (139 ha) of largely wooded area, many of the campus's buildings have been created in the Tang dynasty style, which incorporates a more graceful and subtle form from the more ornate Ming period architecture. The unadorned tiled roofs of the buildings sweep over wide colonnaded eaves, evoking a suitably cloistered air. Clashing with this calm is the university's postmodernist **Christian Chapel,** made to look like two hands in prayer pointed skyward; it was designed by notable Chinese-American architect I. M. Pei.

The university, open since 1955, has always embraced a holistic learning philosophy, stressing a strong, well-rounded general education over the more popular leaning toward specialization.

www.thu.edu.tw/english/enindex.htm 🅼 209 B3 ✉ 181 Taichunggang Rd., Sec. 3, Taichung ☎ 04/2359-0121

What You Need to Know About Public Toilets

Always bring your own toilet paper when moving around. Even if provided, numbers mean paper is quickly used up in public washrooms. Toilets come in sit-down and traditional squat varieties. To avoid touching the sit-down seat, locals will often stand on it and squat, leaving shoe marks, or will lay down a ring of tissue, not always removed. Locals do not ask if a stall is occupied, rapping sharply on the door. The person inside sometimes raps in response, often not. A surprising number of people do not lock stall doors, so after rapping, open slowly.

Travelwise

Straw figures add quirky whimsy outside a Zhudong shop.

TRAVELWISE

PLANNING YOUR TRIP

When To Go

Taiwan is enjoyable any time of the year, although the weather is at its most delightful across the island from mid-September until November. During these months, the skies are sunny, humidity low, and there is little rainfall.

Travel is difficult over the Chinese New Year holidays (January or February). Public transportation is packed (taxis hike rates); hotels are heavily booked and their rates may double; and shops, offices, and government departments close.

During Ghost Month—late August or early September—many superstitious locals are reluctant to travel, so sites are less crowded.

Locals tend to visit major tourist sites on weekends. Try to organize your itinerary so that you explore cities on the weekend and favored countryside spots during the week.

Climate

Taiwan straddles the Tropic of Cancer, with two distinct seasons—chilly and damp, and hot and humid. Between December and March, when the winds come from the northeast, the north and east coastal regions are cool with heavy cloud cover and frequent drizzle. Temperatures start to rise in April as the winds shift to the south-southwest. By May across the island, temperatures consistently rise above 86°F (30°C), and days begin to feel sticky. The average daily temperature is a comfortable 72°F (22°C), with lows ranging from 54° to 63°F (12° to 17°C).

Rains start in May, with the heaviest downpours in June, July, and August. These are typically short, afternoon thunderstorms,

but the skies are clear and sunny between showers. Rainfall drops off and temperatures become milder by mid-September. This is the harbinger of the island's "winter." In the mountains, summer rainfall is heaviest, but temperatures are mild and afternoon fog common. Winters are drier and colder at higher elevations, but snowfall is not common.

The southwestern section of the island is more subtropical, with two distinct seasons. Characterized by mild to warm sunny days, the cool season runs from November to March. Average temperatures during the hot months hover around 86°F (30°C)—marginally cooler than Taipei. During the hot season, afternoon thunderstorms usually last a couple of hours.

Taiwan is subject to frequent buffeting by typhoons, usually between July and October. Due to the island's closeness to the Asian landmass, temperature swings vary during the winter. Chilling monsoon winds sweep down from Central Asia and can send the mercury plummeting 20°F (11°C) in just a few hours.

What to Bring

For general guidelines, see sidebar p. 11. If you plan to hike, bike, or motorcycle, high-quality wet-weather gear is a must. But there is no need to buy it before you come—this type of gear and camping equipment is inexpensive in Taiwan.

Footwear should include dress shoes for the best restaurants, sneakers, and sandals. A sturdy pair of hiking boots is also recommended if you plan on taking to the mountain trails.

How you dress can determine how you are treated. Clothes

should always be clean and neat. Women should dress modestly. Although long shorts are acceptable street wear, you might feel more comfortable in a skirt or light slacks. For men, clean shorts, T-shirts, and sandals are acceptable city wear. Flip-flops are not proper street wear, nor are vests without a shirt.

Carry toilet paper with you, as most public rest rooms do not supply it. Although sanitary napkins are widely available, tampons are not.

Insurance

Arrange for travel insurance to cover penalties for missed flights, medical costs for illness and injury, and lost or stolen property. If you plan on active pursuits such as cycling, surfing, or paragliding, you may require additional coverage.

If renting a car, check the coverage included in the rental price. You should be able to purchase additional insurance from the car rental company.

Theft or loss of property covered by insurance should be reported to the Foreign Affairs Police (see Emergency Numbers, p. 243). You will need a police report to file a claim.

Entry Formalities

Visas

Citizens of the United States, Canada, Australia, New Zealand, Britain, Japan, and a number of European and other countries (31 in total) can stay in Taiwan for 30 days without a visa. On arrival, foreign visitors from these countries can obtain a 30-day single-entry visa by filling out a form, supplying two passport photos, and handing over NT$1,600 ($51 U.S.). Visitors must have outbound tickets and valid visas (if required) for their next destination. Their passports need to be valid for at least six months. If a longer stay is required, an application must be made at representative offices overseas. These types of visas allow you to stay 60 days, and they can be extended twice for a maximum stay of 180 days.

If you overstay your visit, you could be subject to a grilling by police and immigration, and a fine. If you have overstayed, it is best to report to the immigration department first. Trying to explain yourself at the airport could result in a missed flight.

For visa extensions or overstays, contact the Bureau of Consular Affairs, Ministry of Foreign Affairs, 3rd Floor, 2-2 Qinan Rd., Sec. 1, Taipei, tel 02/2343-2891, www.boca.gov.tw.

You can get visas for Taiwan from these representative offices:

United States
Taipei Economic & Cultural Representative Office–Washington, D.C.
4201 Wisconsin Ave., N.W.
Washington, DC 20016-2137
Tel 202/895-1800
Fax 202/363-0999
E-mail tecroinfodc@tecro.us

Taipei Economic & Cultural Office–Los Angeles
3731 Wilshire Blvd., Ste. 780
Los Angeles, CA 90010
Tel 213/389-1158
Fax 213/389-1094
E-mail info@tecola.org

Taipei Economic & Cultural Office–New York
1 East 42nd St., Ste. 9F
New York, NY 10017
Tel 212/867-1632
Fax 212/867-1635
E-mail nyo@tbroc.gov.tw

Australia
Taipei Economic & Cultural Office
Ste. 1902, MLC Center, King Street,
Sydney, NSW 2000
Tel 2/9223-3233
Fax 2/9223-0086
E-mail syteco@bigpond.com

Canada
Taipei Economic & Cultural Office
151 Yonge St., Ste. 501
Toronto, ON M5C 2W7
Tel 416/369-9030
Fax 416/369-1473
E-mail yyz@mofa.gov.tw

United Kingdom
Taipei Representative Office
50 Grosvenor Gardens
London SW1W OEB
Tel 20/7881-2650
Fax 20/7730-3139
E-mail tro@taiwan-tro.uk.net

Customs
Those 20 or over may import one liter of alcoholic beverages, 25 cigars, 200 cigarettes, or one pound of tobacco products duty free. Things prohibited and in some cases punishable by heavy fines and imprisonment include counterfeit currency or forging equipment, gambling apparatus or foreign lottery tickets, pornographic materials, publications propagating communism, weapons (including real or toy gun-shaped devices and assault knives), illicit and narcotic drugs, pirated or copyright-infringed goods, and endangered animals or animal parts.

When leaving Taiwan, an outbound declaration form is required if taking out: gold, antiques over $10,000 in U.S. currency (or foreign equivalent), or over NT$60,000 currency notes, and commercial samples or dutiable items such as personal computers or professional photo equipment that will be brought back into the country for sale. For information, contact the Directorate General of Customs, Ministry of Finance, 13 Dacheng St., Taipei, tel 02/2550-5500 ext. 2116, http://eweb.customs.gov.tw.

Drugs & Narcotics
Taiwan bans all restricted substances and drugs that are nonprescription or nonmedicinal. Like most places in Asia, Taiwan does not take kindly to illicit drugs. Trafficable amounts of cocaine, opium, heroin, methamphetamines, and other narcotic drugs can bring the death penalty. Even small amounts of marijuana for personal use can result in a prison term. Clearly label medicines for personal use and have a doctor's prescription. If you are required to carry a large amount of pharmaceuticals, have a letter from your doctor to that effect.

HOW TO GET TO TAIWAN
Airlines
Taiwan is served by Taiwan Taoyuan International Airport in Taipei, and Kaohsiung International Airport in the south, which serves mainly Asian destinations. Some 40 international airlines fly to Taiwan's Taiwan Taoyuan International Airport, including American, Northwest, and United from the United States. Taiwan's flag carrier, China Airlines, and more respected EVA Air also have daily flights from North America, Europe, Oceania, and most of Asia. Other major carriers include British Airways, KLM, and Cathay Pacific.

The flight time from New York is 18 hours. London, 13 hours. Sydney, 9 hours.

International airline offices in Taipei
Air Canada, tel 02/2511-7799
American, tel 02/2563-1200
British Airways, tel 02/2512-6888
Cathay Pacific, tel 02/2715-2333
China Airlines, tel 02/2715-1212
Continental, tel 02/2719-5947
Delta Airlines, tel 02/2551-3656
Eva Air, tel 02/2501-9599
KLM, tel 02/2711-4055

Northwest, 02/tel 2772-2188
Qantas, tel 02/2559-0508
United Airlines, 02/tel 2703-7600

Taipei's Airport

Taiwan Taoyuan International Airport is connected to downtown Taipei by expressway—about 28 miles (45 km) away. There are two terminals, the aging though renovated Terminal I and the newer Terminal II.

The Taiwan Tourism Bureau has a desk in the arrivals hall of both terminals—in Terminal I at the baggage-claim area (tel 03/398-3341) and in Terminal II at the arrivals hall exit (tel 03/398-3341). The helpful staff will provide maps, book you into a hotel at a discount rate (just about every hotel in Taipei is on their list), and arrange a limo for a fixed rate of NT$1,300 anywhere in the city. In the arrivals halls are a number of hotel representative desks, where you can book a room and arrange limo transport. The cost is NT$1,300–NT$1,500, just slightly higher than taxi fare. Limo charges can be added to your hotel bill, and no driver tip is necessary.

Alternatively, you can follow the signs in the terminals to the taxi stands, where waiting taxis will transport you downtown or its environs. A 50 percent surcharge is added to the fare—at least NT$1,000. There is no surcharge for taxis to the airport, but drivers will be reluctant to take you there for less than NT$1,000. Four bus companies provide frequent service from the airport terminals, stopping at designated spots in Taipei, including major hotels. One-way fares range from NT$85 to NT$140. Car rentals are also available at both terminals.

There are currency exchange booths at the airport, as well as ATMs where you can withdraw cash from credit card accounts or from banking networks such as Cirrus and Maestro.

GETTING AROUND
Traveling in Taiwan
By Automobile

You need a valid international driver's license and steely nerves to drive in Taiwan. It certainly takes getting used to. Traffic laws are both enforced and flaunted. Most roads are heavily traveled, and impatient drivers seemingly have no qualms making death-defying passing maneuvers. Trucks, buses, and military vehicles demand, and usually get, right of way.

If you are not familiar with road conditions, it may be best to hire a driver along with the car. Most hotels can arrange this. A good idea is to use public transport between cities, and hire a car and driver for in and around the cities.

Many road signs are not in English, and English-language road maps are hard to find. Cars in Taiwan are driven on the right, and all occupants must wear seat belts.

By Domestic Airline

Taiwan's domestic airline network is extensive, though shrinking. Flights go to other major cities and to the offshore islands of Kinmen, Matsu, and Penghu. However, the operations of the convenient high-speed rail system (HSR) have deeply affected the airlines, and only three remain. Their operations have been severely curtailed, flights to west coast cities also served by the HSR have been ceased except among Taipei, Taichung, and Kaohsiung, and both Green Island and Orchid Island are served out of Taitung City. Fares are inexpensive—a flight from Taipei to Kaohsiung costs about NT$2,200. You can usually buy tickets at the airport before the flight, but it is better to book ahead. You will be required to show your passport before boarding any flight.

Domestic Airlines

Mandarin Airlines,
tel 02/2717-1230
UNI Airways,
tel 02/2715-6969

By Ferry

A regular network of ferries links Taiwan proper to its outlying islands. Travel agents can book trips. Because of frequent inclement weather, service is unpredictable. Always confirm ahead by phone.

Strait Islands

Keelung to Matsu takes 8 hours.
Nangan, tel 083/626-655 (Dongyin) or 083/677-555 (Matsu)
Xinhua Navigation, tel 02/2424-6868 (Keelung) Kaohsiung to Kinmen takes 10 hours.
Hefu Marine, tel 07/551-3112
Jinhan Marine, tel 07/332-9588
Kaohsiung to Magong (Penghu Islands) takes 4.5 hours.
Tai Hua Shipping, tel 07/551-5823

East Coast Islands

The ferry from Taitung to Green Island takes 35 to 50 minutes; from Taitung to Orchid Island takes 2 to 3 hours; and from Green Island to Orchid Island takes 1.5 to 2.5 hours.
Victory, tel 08/928-1047
Jiou-Xin Ferry, tel 08/932-0413
Green Island Star,
tel 08/928-0226

By Intercity Bus

Frequent and inexpensive luxury coaches travel almost everywhere in Taiwan. You can purchase your tickets through a travel agent, your hotel, or at the bus station. During the holidays, expect to be caught up in crowded conditions. Allow for extra time.
Intercity Bus Companies
Aloha Bus, tel 02/2550-8488
Guoguang Bus Corp., tel 0800/010-138

Free Go Express,
tel 02/2586-3065
Toward You Air Bus Co.,
tel 0800/088-626
United Highway Bus,
tel 02/2995-7799

By Train

Taiwan's rail network is comprehensive, inexpensive, and efficient, albeit a little complicated. It can be crowded on long weekends and holidays, so it is best to avoid trains at these times.

Four main lines—western, eastern, northern, and southern—form the core of the network. Making a reservation through a travel agent assures you of a guaranteed seat. The air-conditioned services are Ziqiang, the rapid express; Juguang, the first-class express; and Fuxing, a limited express. The Putong service is slow and non-air-conditioned and has no reserved seating.

The information counter at Taipei Main Railway Station (tel 0080/765-888 or 02/2371-3558) is very helpful in arranging round-trip tickets. Information desks at larger stations generally have someone who speaks English and will be helpful in arranging tickets, but you may need to insist if you want to reserve a seat.

Reservations for express trains can be made up to 14 days in advance; pick up your ticket within three days. You will need to show your passport for identification. You can also book online at www .railway.gov.tw.

Some classes provide complimentary snacks, while meals are available in a casual dining car.

A 215-mile (345 km) high-speed rail (HSR) from Taipei to Kaohsiung came online in January 2007 with stations at Taoyuan, Hsinchu, Miaoli, Taichung, Changhua, Yunlin, Chiayi, and Tainan. It slices travel time from 4.5 hours to just 90 minutes (www.thsrc.com.tw).

Traveling in Taipei

By City Bus

Buses run from 6 a.m. to 11:30 p.m. and cost NT$15 for each leg of the route. Drop the money in a coin box next to the driver when getting on the bus if you see a SHANG sign (with Chinese character). Pay again if the same character shows in red when you get off. Each of the many city routes has both a number and starting–ending points written in Chinese, now often in English, which means it can get a little confusing. For further info and route maps: www.e-bus .taipei.gov.tw. You can get to most places in the city by combining the MRT and inexpensive taxis, diminishing the need for a bus.

By MRT

Taipei's mass rapid transit (MRT) system is one of the best in Asia. Its five interconnecting lines can take you to, or close to, most of the city's attractions. The system's signs, maps, and information are in English. Tickets vary from NT$20 to NT$65 depending on distance, or you can purchase a one-day pass for NT$200. You can also purchase a stored-value card called the EasyCard, which brings a discount of 20 percent for each trip. This card is now also almost universally used on public buses, and can also be used at public parking lots, roadside parking spaces, Xinyi District bike-rental kiosks, and elsewhere. Charts at the ticket machines show how much money you need to get to your destination, and exits are clearly marked. Maps in English are also posted in stations. The MRT runs from 6 a.m. to midnight.

Metro Taipei Service Hot Line, tel 0800/033-068 or 02/2181-2345 (24 hours).

By Taxi

Taipei and other major cities have an abundance of taxis that can be hailed virtually anywhere. Fares around the cities are cheap, with most intracity trips costing around NT$100 to NT$130. Longer trips in the city or to suburbs may cost NT$300. Charges in Taipei are NT$70 for the first 0.7 mile (1.25 km) and NT$5 for each additional 0.2 mile (250 m). An additional NT$5 is charged for every 1 minute and 40 seconds that the taxi is waiting or moving less than 5 kph, and a 20 percent surcharge is added to fares that start between 11 p.m. and 6 a.m. For out-of-town or long-distance trips, meters are not used, so negotiate a fare beforehand.

Most drivers do not speak English, so have the hotel staff write your destination in Chinese. Hotels have name cards available with their name and address written in English and Chinese. Always carry one. Taipei has a young English-language learning program for drivers, and graduates can carry a special identifying marker in their window, but don't expect much. For complaints you can call the Traffic Division, Taipei City Police Dept., tel 02/2394-0997 (day) or 02/2321-9166 (night).

PRACTICAL ADVICE
Communications
Post Office

Taiwan has fast and efficient postal service. Mail takes five to seven days to reach the United States. The post office's express mail service speeds the delivery time by about two days, and is less expensive than international courier services. Most articles are delivered within Taiwan in 24 to 48 hours. Post offices are open from 8 a.m. to 6 p.m. Monday through Friday. Some of the bigger post offices are also open from 8 a.m. to 4 p.m. on Saturday.

Taipei's Central Post Office *(tel 0800/099-246)* is at the North Gate intersection close to Taipei Main Railway Station. Staff in the international section speak English.

Most hotels will mail items. Otherwise, drop stamped articles into red mailboxes. The left-hand slot is for airmail, right for prompt delivery. With green mailboxes, the right-hand slot is for mail within the city, the left-hand for elsewhere.

Telephones

The international dialing code for Taiwan is 886. To call Taipei from overseas, add the prefix 2 to the local number. To call Taipei from within Taiwan, the prefix is 02. From Taiwan dial 002 for international direct dialing access.

For directory assistance in English, dial 106. An international operator can be reached at 100 from private phones only. Dialing 108 will get the reverse-charges operator.

Both local and international calls can be made from pay phones. Local calls are NT$1 per minute. To keep talking, keep adding coins. The digital display keeps count of how much time you have left. There are also phones that require stored-value cards. These magnetic-strip stored-value cards sell for NT$100, and there are NT$200 and NT$300 IC cards. They can be purchased at convenience stores, railway stations, bus stations, and major scenic sites. For international calls, buy phone cards, International Direct Dial cards (IDDs) from any of the 7-Eleven convenience stores on the island, and find a pay phone that is marked as IDD capable. Some hotels have phones that take major credit cards.

If you bring a mobile phone, buy a replacement SIM card that will give you a local number and a certain number of minutes. Cards can be purchased from mobile phone retailers. Before the number

can be used, you must register and provide a few details and passport number. This is done by dialing the number provided on the SIM card packaging. A card with a hundred minutes of calling time will cost about NT$700. This can be added to by buying a phone card from convenience stores with a number code. You dial the number code on your mobile phone and the extra time is allocated.

Alternately, buy a mobile phone when you arrive. Fierce competition has made them available at knock-down prices. The penetration rate of mobile phones in Taiwan is over 90 percent, so you shouldn't have a problem phoning someone.

Internet

There are many Internet cafés in the cities—usually inhabited by teenagers playing video games—where you can send e-mails or surf the Web. They are cheap, averaging about NT$30 per half hour. Hotels have Internet access from computers in their business centers, and charge about NT$200 per hour or more.

Conversions

Taiwan uses the metric system for weights and measures. An ancient Chinese system is also used in some circumstances. It's not necessary to know, but be aware it exists.

1 kilometer = 0.6 mile
60 kph = 37 mph
1 kilo = 2.2 pounds
1 liter = 1.75 pints
Temperatures are in centigrade
0°C = 32°F
Chinese system weights
1 liang (tael) = 1.2056 ounces
1 jin (catty) = 16 liang = 1.32 pounds

Electricity

Taiwan uses the same standards for electricity as the United States: 110V, 60 Hz AC. Flat

two-pin plugs are used for connection. If your devices do not match these, you will need to bring a power adapter and plugs. Hotels also have adapter plugs.

Holidays

The Taiwanese keep in touch with their traditions and culture with numerous festivals throughout the year. Most have their origins in Taoism, Buddhism, or Chinese folk religion, so the dates vary based on the lunar calendar. In many cases they are raucous and riotously colorful affairs rich in costume, action, and religious symbolism. With the exception of the sedate Chinese New Year festival, it is worth planning your visit to coincide with one of the island's major festivals.

January 1 Founding Day of the Republic of China
January/February Chinese New Year (Lunar New Year's Eve and first, second, and third day of first lunar month)
February 28 Peace Memorial Day
April 5 Tomb Sweeping Day
May/June Dragon Boat Festival (fifth day of fifth lunar month)
September/October Mid-Autumn Festival (fifteenth day of eighth lunar month)
October 10 Double Tenth National Day

Liquor Laws

You must be 20 to buy and consume alcohol in Taiwan. Bars and pubs open between 5 p.m. and 7 p.m. and stay open until around 3 a.m.—some stay open until 5 a.m. Eating and drinking are commonly combined into a single pursuit at restaurants. Beers and spirits are sold in convenience stores.

Media

Magazines

Regional and international magazines such as the *Far Eastern*

Economic Review, Time, Newsweek, and *The Economist* are sold at large bookstores and in hotels. Other national English or bilingual magazines in Taiwan include the news and current events magazine *Taiwan Review. Taiwan Panorama* covers social and political issues. *This Month in Taiwan* is a travel and listings magazine, as is *Travel in Taiwan.*

Newspapers

Taiwan enjoys a high degree of press freedom and a vibrant and competitive newspaper industry. There are many Chinese-language papers, along with the English-language dailies: *China Post, Taiwan News,* and *Taipei Times.* English publications are available at most newsstands and hotels.

The regional *Asian Wall Street Journal* and the *International Herald Tribune,* printed in Taipei, are available on newsstands and in hotels. *USA Today* is also widely available.

Radio

ICRT (International Community Radio Taipei) is Taiwan's only English-language station. Its FM channel broadcasts Western pop music, talk shows, and community service segments. It's at FM100.7MHz (100.1 in Hsinchu and farther south) and AM576MHz.

Television

About 80 percent of Taiwan homes have cable TV with more than 100 channels available. Most hotels have cable TV with English-language international satellite and cable channels, including National Geographic, Australia Asia Pacific Television, BBC World, Cinemax, CNBC, and CNN.

Money Matters

The New Taiwan dollar (NT$) is the unit of currency. While it varies slightly from day to day, the exchange rate generally hovers around NT$33 to the U.S. dollar and NT$42 to the euro. You will find 1, 5, 10, 20, and 50 dollar coins, and 100, 200, 500, and 1,000 dollar bills. A 2,000-dollar note is in circulation but is rarely encountered in everyday use.

Major foreign currencies can be exchanged for NT$ at larger banks (smaller banks do not deal in foreign exchange), international hotels, and the island's international airports in Taipei and Kaohsiung. Most banks charge a fee for cashing traveler's checks.

Traveler's checks generally can only be cashed at banks and hotels. To exchange money at a hotel, you may need to be a guest—almost always the case for cashing traveler's checks—and hotels tend to exchange at lower rates.

Receipts are given when exchanging currency. Keep them! They must be presented in order to redeem unused NT$ before departure. Wait until you are at the airport to change back your money. The foreign exchanges there are more familiar with the process and have more currencies. (It can be difficult to exchange NT$ outside of Taiwan.) Note, there are no foreign exchange booths once you pass through immigration and customs at the airport.

Many ATMs accept international credit cards, allowing you to withdraw local currency. A growing number of worldwide ATM networks are found at banks and convenience stores.

Banks are open Monday to Friday from 9 a.m. to 3:30 p.m.

Major credit cards are widely accepted.

Opening Times

Business hours are generally 9 a.m. to 5 p.m.; government hours are 8:30 a.m. to 5:30 p.m., Monday through Friday. Some government offices close for lunch from 12:30 p.m. to 1:30 p.m.

Department stores are open seven days a week, usually opening between 10 a.m. and 11 a.m., and closing at 9 p.m. or 9:30 p.m. Most other retail outlets open 9 a.m.–10 a.m. and close around 10 p.m. The 7-Elevens and other convenience stores stay open seven days a week around the clock.

Reading Maps & Signs

The various transliterations of Chinese place-names into English is guaranteed to be a major frustration for visitors. Too often, maps, street directories, and road signs fail to follow the official national Hanyu Pinyin system, circumventing it for regional nomenclature. For example, a major road may be variously labeled Pate, Pateh, and Bade. And that's an easy one.

Religion

The main religions in Taiwan are Taoism and Buddhism, with many temples incorporating elements of both faiths. There is a significant Christian minority on the island. Churches can be found in most cities and major towns. Protestants make up about 80 percent of the Christian population, mainly Presbyterian, with the remainder Catholic. The island's Muslims number around 60,000.

Taiwan Tourism

For information on visiting Taiwan, contact the Tourism Bureau R.O.C and the Ministry of Transportation and Communications (see p. 9). You may also contact the tourist offices abroad (see p. 242), at the Taiwan Taoyuan International Airport (see p. 238), and Kaohsiung

International Airport *(tel 07/ 805-7888)*. The Tourism Bureau also has travel information service centers in Taiwan's major cities.

Taipei
240 Dunhua N. Rd., tel 02/2717-3737 or 0800/011-765, e-mail tisc@tbroc.gov.tw

Kaohsiung
5F-1, 235 Zhongzheng, 4th Rd., tel 07/281-1513 or 0800/ 711-765

Taichung
4F, 216 Minquan Rd., tel 04/2227-0421 or 0800/422-022

Tainan
10F, 243 Minquan Rd., Sec. 1, tel 06/2226-5681 or 0800/611-011

National park and forest recreation area visitor centers provide maps and brochures of varying quality and quantity—not always in English. The Tourism Bureau manages all national scenic areas and provides English materials.

Time Differences
The time difference from Greenwich mean time (GMT) is +8 hours. From New York it is +13 (one hour less during daylight savings time). From Sydney, the difference is -2 hours in winter and -3 hours in summer.

Tipping
Taiwan does not have a tipping culture, so there is no need to encourage it. Most hotels add a 10 percent service charge to their restaurants and room service. Bellhops are tipped NT$20 per piece of luggage. Some upscale restaurants also have a service charge. Leaving a few coins in a check tray has become a more common practice in bars and cafés that don't have a service

charge. Taxi drivers don't expect to be tipped.

Tours
The Taiwan Tourism Bureau (officially known as the Republic of China Tourism Bureau) has a wealth of suggestions for tours and related contacts (see p. 241).

Travelers With Disabilities
Modern buildings have wheelchair access ramps, but the law does not require them in older buildings. Most top hotels have facilities for people with disabilities, but it is a good idea to ask in advance.

Taipei's MRT system has elevator access for those in wheelchairs. But the crowds during rush hours can make for an uncomfortable travel experience. Other public transport, save the high-speed rail system, does not provide for disabled passengers. On the streets, high curbs and uneven surfaces make things difficult, although ramps onto sidewalks in the big cities are becoming common. Taipei is also working hard to widen and level sidewalks.

Street overpasses and underpasses present insurmountable problems for people with walking disabilities. Although most intersections in cities and towns are now equipped with time-countdown "walk" signals, drivers unfortunately often ignore them.

Most government museums and art galleries have facilities for the disabled.

Tourist Offices Abroad
United States
Taipei Economic & Cultural Office–Los Angeles
3731 Wilshire Blvd., Ste. 780, Los Angeles, CA 90010, tel 213/389-1158, fax 213/389-1094, e-mail latva@pacbell.net

Taipei Economic & Cultural Office–New York
Travel Section, 1 East 42nd St., Ste. 9F, New York, NY 10017, tel 212/867-1632 or 212/867-1634, fax 212/867-1635, e-mail nyo@ tbroc.gov.tw

Australia
Taipei Economic & Cultural Office Travel Section, Ste. 1902, King St., MLC Centre, Sydney NSW 2000, tel 02/9223-3233, fax 02/9223- 0086, e-mail info@ cultural.teco.org.au

Canada
Taipei Economic & Cultural Office Tourism Representative, Travel Section, Ste. 1960, 45 O'Connor St., Ottawa, ON K1P 1A4, tel 613/231-5025, fax 613/231-7414

United Kingdom
Taipei Representative Office, Tourism Representative, Travel Section, 50 Grosvenor Gardens, London SW1W OEB, tel 20/ 7881-2650, fax 20/7730-3139

EMERGENCIES IN TAIWAN
Representative Offices
Taiwan has formal diplomatic relations with fewer than 25 countries. Other countries are represented by trade and commerce offices in Taipei and a few other cities. These places are not embassies, but they do provide similar functions, such as issuing visas and replacing lost or stolen passports.

United States
American Institute in Taiwan, 7 Lane 134, Xinyi Rd., Sec. 3, tel 02/2162-2000, www.ait .org.tw

Australia
Australian Commerce Office, 27F, President International Tower,

9-11 Songgao Rd., tel 02/8725-4100, www.australia.org.tw

Canada
Canadian Trade Office, 13F, 365 Fuxing North Rd., tel 02/2544-3000, www.canada.org

United Kingdom
British Trade & Cultural Office, 26F, President International Tower, 9-11 Songgao Rd., tel 02/8758-2088, www.ukintaiwan.fco.gov.uk

Emergency Phone Numbers
Fire, ambulance, tel 119
Police, tel 110
Taipei Foreign Affairs Police, tel 02/2556-6007
Taichung Foreign Affairs Police, tel 04/2327-3875
Kaohsiung Foreign Affairs Police, tel 07/221-5796
English-language directory assistance, tel 106

Lost or Stolen Credit Cards or Traveler's Checks
Visa, tel 00801/444-123
American Express, tel 2719-0606

Medical Services
Hospital treatment in Taiwan is of a high standard and compared to Western countries inexpensive. Hotels can call a doctor on short notice, and hospitals have outpatient facilities. Emergency services are available 24 hours at most hospitals, including:

Taipei
Taiwan Adventist Hospital
424 Bade Rd., Sec. 2, tel 02/2771-8151
Mackay Memorial Hospital
92 Zhongshan North Rd., Sec. 2, tel 02/2543-3535
Veterans General Hospital
201 Shipai Rd., Sec. 2,

tel 02/2875-7628
Chang Gung Memorial Hospital
199 Dunhua North Rd., tel 02/2713-5211

Kaohsiung
Kaohsiung Chang Gung Memorial Hospital, 123 Dabei Rd., Niaosong Township, Kaohsiung County, tel 07/731-7123
Chung Ho Memorial Hospital
100 Ziyou, 1st Rd., tel 07/312-1101

Taichung
China Medical University Hospital
2 Yude Rd., tel 04/2205-2121

Health
No special precautions or inoculations are necessary to visit Taiwan, and there are very few risks to your health. There have been some occurrences of the mosquito-borne virus Japanese B encephalitis, and dengue fever, passed by mosquitoes.

Hepatitis A is prevalent in rural areas where sanitation is poor. Make sure eating and drinking utensils are clean in these areas. Unused, paper-wrapped chopsticks are the best idea. You can buy a number of sets, for personal use, as a precaution.

Tap water in major cities and towns is drinkable, but health authorities advise it should be boiled first. It may be best to stick to bottled water.

Hepatitis B and C, present in Taiwan, can be contracted from blood transfusion or sexual contact. Although HIV prevalence is relatively low in Taiwan, it is still a threat, along with other sexually transmitted diseases.

Over the past decade the country has been affected by the international scares regarding SARS, bird flu, and swine flu, but the strength of its advanced public-health system has meant there has been little impact, and tourism has

each time returned in strength after these scares have waned.

Taiwan's subtropical climate can cause problems for the unprepared. If hiking or cycling during hot, humid weather, drink plenty of bottled water to prevent dehydration. Wear a wide-brimmed hat and apply liberal amounts of sunscreen (SPF 15 and above), even under cloudy conditions.

Weather conditions change rapidly in mountain areas. You may start your hike with clear skies and warm temperatures, but these conditions can quickly deteriorate. Carry wet-weather gear and warm clothes with you.

A prescription is not always required for drugs in Taiwan. However, if you are taking any medications, bring a prescription from your doctor in case you need a refill or the drugs are lost. If you are carrying large quantities of prescription drugs for your own use, have a letter from your doctor saying so in case you are questioned by customs on arrival.

Many Taiwanese place faith in both traditional Chinese medicine practitioners and Western medical practices. Traditional medicine is geared to prevention rather than cure. Taiwan is an ideal place to get checked over by such a practitioner.

Hotels & Restaurants

There are many hotels in Taiwan—especially Taipei—that are of international standard and reasonably priced compared to Western countries. Service is generally efficient and friendly, although you may encounter language problems, even in the best hotels. The variety and quality of food in Taiwan makes it one of the best places in the world to sample the many styles of Chinese cuisine. From cheap noodle shops to classy establishments, the food is consistently good.

Hotels

The best establishments are generally found in the center of the cities as this is where business people stay. Here, amenities are slanted toward corporate travelers, with business centers, secretarial services, executive floors, and in-room fax and Internet connections. The better hotels tend to offer health clubs, swimming pools (some both indoor and outdoor), spacious guest rooms, and quality restaurants.

Outside Taipei and the cities of Kaohsiung and Taichung, choices are more limited. Many of the island's midsize cities have what are called "regular tourist hotels." Don't expect special services.

The more popular tourist areas, such as Kenting, Sun Moon Lake, and the north coast, have resort hotels with the emphasis on recreation. But again, the choice of luxury hotels in these areas is limited.

Rooms in the best hotels in Taipei start at around U.S.$185 and generally belong to chains such as Hyatt, Sheraton, Inter-Continental, and Shangri-La. There are also a number of fine hotel chains under local management, including the Landis, Howard, and Sherwood, with guest-room prices starting at around U.S.$120. Equivalent hotels in other major cities tend to be a little less expensive. A buffet breakfast—often excellent—is normally included in the room rate at most hotels, but ask before booking if you are not sure.

The prices of the hotels noted here are the published rack rates—a 10 percent service charge is often added. Most establishments offer discounts of 30 percent or more if you book ahead, and possibly more if you book online. The plethora of Internet hotel booking services often offer larger discounts.

It is best to book hotel airport transfers before you arrive (or check the Taiwan Tourism Bureau desks at the airport). Taipei's Taiwan Taoyuan International Airport is a fair distance from downtown (see p. 238). The cost of a hotel limo, which can be added to your hotel bill, is about the same as the taxi fare (NT$1,200–1,500).

Smoking in hotels is illegal.

Restaurants

Taiwan offers innumerable choices for Chinese cuisine (see pp. 24–29). People from all over mainland China have settled in Taiwan, bringing their culinary traditions with them. You never have to walk far to find a good restaurant. Increasingly, culinary talents from elsewhere around the world are also finding Taipei a good place to set up.

If you are new to Chinese food, dining rooms at the better hotels are a good place to begin. Here, staff are more familiar with Western tastes. Menus in Chinese restaurants can be extensive and present a challenge to ordering. Frequently creative use of English can also present a challenge.

Taipei has plenty of quality international restaurants, with many found in the top hotels, where buffet meals are a good value and often have choices of Western and other Asian dishes.

PRICES	
HOTELS	
An indication of the cost of a double room in the high season is given by **$** signs.	
$$$$$	Over $235
$$$$	$185–$235
$$$	$120–$185
$$	$70–$120
$	Under $70
RESTAURANTS	
An indication of the cost of a three-course meal without drinks is given by **$** signs.	
$$$$$	Over $50
$$$$	$25–$50
$$$	$12–$25
$$	$5–$12
$	Under $5

Restaurant prices are reasonable, and meals at small local Chinese eateries often cost only a few dollars.

Smoking in restaurants is illegal.

Hygiene standards in Taiwan, generally, are very high. There should be no problem eating food from market stalls.

Organizations & Abbreviations

The hotels and restaurants have been arranged alphabetically by price range and within each region. Credit cards are abbreviated AE American Express, DC Diner's Club, MC MasterCard, and V Visa.

■ TAIPEI

HOTELS

⊞ EVERGREEN LAUREL HOTEL TAIPEI

$$$$$

63 SONGJIANG RD.

TEL 02/2501-9988

FAX 2501-9966

www.evergreen-hotels.com

A boutique hotel known for outstanding service. In a busy area, soundproofing handles external noise. Italian furniture brings a continental ambience. Each room has wireless LAN, free broadband Internet, walk-in closets, facilities for physically handicapped. Superior food and beverage offerings.

ⓘ 95 P ⊖ ⊠ 👕

⟨S⟩ All major cards

SOMETHING SPECIAL

⊞ FAR EASTERN PLAZA HOTEL

$$$$$

201 DUNHUA SOUTH RD., SEC. 2

TEL 02/2378-8888

FAX 2377-7777

www.feph.com.tw

Western and Chinese tastes blend in this Shangri-La–managed hotel. Spacious rooms feature rosewood furnishings against light-colored walls. If you feel like indulging, stay in a spa suite with sauna, steam, and Jacuzzi. Spectacular views from the rooftop pool. The **Marco Polo** (see p. 247) wine list is among the best in Taipei.

ⓘ 420 P ⊖ ⊠ 👕 ⟨S⟩ All major cards ⊠ Technology Building

⊞ GRAND FORMOSA REGENT

$$$$$

41 ZHONGSHAN RD., SEC. 2

TEL 02/2523-8000

FAX 2523-2828

www.regenthotels.com

This hotel boasts some of the largest guest rooms in Taipei.

Floor-to-ceiling windows and marble bathrooms with soaking tubs are a delight. Some suites open to a Japanese garden. Views of the city from the rooftop pool. Seven food and beverage outlets.

ⓘ 538 P ⊖ ⊠ 👕 ⟨S⟩ All major cards ⊠ Zhongshan

⊞ GRAND HYATT TAIPEI

$$$$$

2 SONGSHOU RD.

TEL 02/2720-1234

FAX 2720-1111

www.taipei.hyatt.com

The rooms are finished in warm pastels with marble bathrooms. The heated outdoor pool has a bar and an underwater sound system. Haute cuisine and an extensive wine list enhance its **Pearl Liang** restaurant (see p. 247). authentic Italian food at **Ziga Zaga** (see p. 250).

ⓘ 856 P ⊖ ⊠ 👕 ⟨S⟩ All major cards ⊠ Taipei City Hall

⊞ HOTEL ROYAL TAIPEI

$$$$$

37-1 ZHONGSHAN NORTH RD., SEC. 2

TEL 02/2542-3266

FAX 2543-4897

www.royal-taipei.com.tw

The Royal Taipei rooms employ beige colors with floral bedspreads and seat cushions. A lovely greenhouse full of blazing tropical flowers sits next to the rooftop swimming pool.

ⓘ 202 P ⊖ ⊠ 👕 ⟨⟩ ⟨S⟩ All major cards ⊠ Zhongshan

⊞ IMPERIAL HOTEL

$$$$$

600 LINSEN NORTH RD.

TEL 02/2596-5111

FAX 2592-7506

www.imperialhotel.com.tw

Designed to attract the corporate traveler with a well-equipped 24-hour business center. Spacious rooms are decorated in warm tones, rich wood, and art. The Front Page bar is a favorite haunt for

Taipei's longtime expatriates during happy hour and as a jumping-off point for the Zone bar area immediately behind the hotel.

ⓘ 288 P ⊖ ⊠ 👕 ⟨S⟩ All major cards

SOMETHING SPECIAL

⊞ LANDIS TAIPEI HOTEL

$$$$$

41 MINQUAN EAST RD., SEC. 2

TEL 02/2597-1234

FAX 2596-9223

www.landistpe.com.tw

This small, classy hotel with lobby and guest room done in art deco style. The hotel has 87 suites, with starting rates not much higher than the standard rooms. The **Paris 1930** French restaurant (see p. 247) ranks as one of the city's best.

ⓘ 209 P ⊖ ⊠ 👕 ⟨S⟩ All major cards

⊞ SHERATON TAIPEI HOTEL

$$$$$

12 ZHONGXIAO EAST RD., SEC. 1

TEL 02/2321-5511

FAX 2321-5511

www.sheraton-taipei.com

This Taipei landmark has a grand feel. There's a fitness center and rooftop outdoor pool. The nine cafés and restaurants serve quality cuisine, among them the fine French dining in the **Antoine Room** (see p. 246). The lobby café is a classic meeting spot.

ⓘ 688 P ⊖ ⊠ 👕 ⟨S⟩ All major cards ⊠ Shandao Temple

⊞ THE SHERWOOD

$$$$$

111 MINSHENG EAST RD., SEC. 3

TEL 02/2718-1188

FAX 2713-0707

www.sherwood.com.tw

The rooms here don't scrimp on quality furnishings. The decor contains a mix of classical and modern European styles, embellished with original artwork. The indoor, glass-roofed atrium swimming pool is a special treat. The business center operates 24 hours.

ⓘ 350 🅿 🚻 🏊 🟥 🚇 All major cards 🚇 Zhongshan Junior High School

🏨 TAIPEI FULLERTON HOTEL EAST
$$$$$

32 NANJING EAST RD., SEC. 5
TEL 02/2763-5656
FAX 2767-9347
www.taipeifullerton.com.tw
The nearby World Trade Center and financial district make this hotel popular with business travelers. Sleek furniture adds a stylish appeal. Standards and service for the Fullerton chain are very high.

ⓘ 225 🅿 🚻 🚇
🟥 All major cards

🏨 THE WESTIN TAIPEI
$$$$$

133 NANJING EAST RD., SEC. 3
TEL 02/8770-6565
FAX 8770-6555
www.starwoodhotels.com
One of Taipei's newer hotels built for the business traveler. Decor is a muted blend of Western and Asian. The ten food and beverage outlets provide for all tastes. **Danieli's** (see p. 247) is one of the city's elite Italian restaurants.

ⓘ 288 🅿 🚻 🏊 🚇 🟥 All major cards 🚇 Nanjing East Road

🏨 CAESAR PARK
$$$$

38 ZHONGXIAO
WEST RD., SEC. 1
TEL 02/2311-5151
FAX 2331-9944
www.caesarpark.com.tw
Formerly the Taipei Hilton, now managed by a homegrown hotel group with a fine reputation, the Caesar Park maintains first-class standards. Rooftop garden with open-air massage pool (closed Nov.–March).

ⓘ 395 🅿 🚻 🏊 🚇
🟥 All major cards
🚇 Taipei Main Station

🏨 THE GRAND HOTEL
$$$$

1 ZHONGSHAN
NORTH RD., SEC. 4
TEL 02/2886-8888
FAX 2885-2885
www.grand-hotel.org
The red-columned facade, classical Chinese tile roof, and hilltop location give this hotel a special presence. The decor changes with each floor, representing a specific dynastic period. Balconies have views of Taipei city or the mountains.

ⓘ 490 🅿 🚻 🏊 🚇 🟥 All major cards 🚇 Jiantan

🏨 HOWARD PLAZA HOTEL
$$$$

160 RENAI RD., SEC. 3
TEL 02/2700-2323
FAX 2700-0729
www.howard-hotels.com
Chinese rosewood furniture and original artwork lift the large rooms a notch. Brunch and afternoon tea in the leafy atrium restaurant are favored by locals. Upscale boutiques ring the atrium on four levels. Charges for in-room Internet.

ⓘ 606 🅿 🚻 🏊 🚇
🟥 All major cards
🚇 Zhongxiao-Fuxing

🏨 SAN WANT HOTEL
$$$$

172 ZHONGXIAO RD., SEC. 4
TEL 02/2772-2121
FAX 2721-0302
www.sanwant.com
It's a bit confusing when you first enter the hotel and don't see a check-in counter—it's on the fourth floor. Rooms are comfortable but small. Excellent location, however, with a MRT station at the doorstep.

ⓘ 268 🅿 🚻 🚇 🟥 All major cards 🚇 Zhongxiao-Dunhua

🏨 HOTEL RIVERVIEW
$$$

77 HUANHE SOUTH RD., SEC. 1
TEL 02/2311-3131
FAX 2361-3737
www.riverview.com.tw

Its location in the colorful old Wanhua section of the city near the Danshui River makes the Riverview a little out of the way. But the lower room rates make up for this. Rooms are large and river views are a bonus, especially from the glass-roofed restaurant.

ⓘ 201 🅿 🚻 🚇
🟥 All major cards

RESTAURANTS

🍴 ANTOINE ROOM
$$$$$

SHERATON TAIPEI HOTEL
12 ZHONGXIAO EAST RD., SEC. 1
TEL 02/2321-5511
This French restaurant has been around for two decades. Top-notch ingredients and thoughtful presentation give it much appeal. Try the luxurious seafood salad. This place possesses one of the best wine cellars in the city. Jackets required. No children under 12.

🪑 90 🟥 All major cards

🍴 BEL AIR
$$$$$

GRAND HYATT TAIPEI
2 SONGSHOU RD.
TEL 02/2720-1200, EXT. 3198
The high-quality continental cuisine infused with Asian elements emphasize the Bel Air's attention to healthy dining. Classical decor combines muted colors, soft lighting, and natural skylight.

🪑 80 🟥 All major cards

🍴 BEN TEPPANYAKI
$$$$$

2 LANE 102, ANHE RD., SEC. 1
TEL 02/2703-2296
Experienced teppanyaki chefs prepare choice cuts of Masusaka, Kobe, and Omi beef to perfection. While most diners come to try the Japanese beef, a set meal of quality U.S. beef is also prepared with skill.

🪑 160 🟥 All major cards

🏨 Hotel   🍴 Restaurant   ⓘ No. of Guest Rooms   🪑 No. of Seats   🅿 Parking   🚇 Metro   🕐 Closed

CHEZ JIMMY
$$$$$
27 LANE 50, TIANMU EAST RD.,
TIANMU
TEL 02/2874-7185
Attentive waiters in natty
French-style uniforms. Diners
rave about the steamed egg
in the shell topped with Hol-
landaise sauce and caviar. The
unfussy roast spring chicken
flavored with garlic is a popular
main course.
🛗 90 🔶 All major cards

DANIELI'S
$$$$$
THE WESTIN TAIPEI
2F, 133 NANJING EAST RD., SEC. 3
TEL 02/8770-6565
If the descriptive term "casual
elegance" means anything
in the reviewer's lexicon, it
would apply here. Notable
are the antipasto selections.
The seafood *guazzetto*, a spicy
concoction of broth brimming
with clams, shrimp, and
scallops, with garlic and chili
pepper, zings with flavor.
🛗 80 🔶 All major cards

IBUKI
$$$$$
FAR EASTERN PLAZA HOTEL
7F, 201 DUNHUA SOUTH RD., SEC. 2
TEL 2376-3241
Indoor dining in "outdoor"
Japanese gardens, with
aquariums recessed into the
walls. Chefs are brought in
from Japan, specializing in
sushi, sashimi, teppanyaki, and
kaiseki. The most popular dish
is deep-fried oysters coated in
a soymilk skin.
🛗 106 🔶 All major cards

MARCO POLO
$$$$$
FAR EASTERN PLAZA HOTEL
201 DUNHUA SOUTH RD., SEC. 2
TEL 2376-3156
The panoramic views from
this 38th floor are engaging at
night. The multicultural and
mouthwatering Sicilian Maine
lobster Catalana style and the
tagliatelle with shrimp and

asparagus are standouts.
🛗 144 🔶 All major cards

MOMOYAMA RESTAURANT
$$$$$
SHERATON TAIPEI HOTEL
2F, 12 ZHONGXIAO EAST RD.,
SEC. 1
TEL 02/2321-1818
The nearest you'll get to true
Japanese dining in Taiwan.
Kaiseki cuisine recipes and
preparation techniques are followed precisely. The selection
of sashimi arriving at your
table exemplifies the emphasis
on freshness. The yamagata
beef sirloin steak—sirloin strips
grilled on a volcanic rock
brought from Japan—all but
melts in your mouth. The sushi
bar offers both Western-style
and tatami-room dining.
🛗 140 🔶 All major cards

SOMETHING SPECIAL

PARIS 1930
$$$$$
LANDIS TAIPEI HOTEL
41 MINQUAN EAST RD., SEC. 2
TEL 02/2597-1234
Start with the signature stuffed
piquillo pepper with olive oil
mash and/or the roast goose
liver with corn-seed beer pancake at this renowned French
restaurant. Its whole pressed
duck must be ordered ahead.
The service is flawless, and the
French wine list is extensive.
🛗 80 🔶 All major cards

PEARL LIANG
$$$$$
GRAND HYATT TAIPEI
2 SONGSHOU RD.
TEL 02/2720-1200, EXT. 3198
Novel interpretations of
Chinese seafood and dim
sum are served in elegant and
sophisticated surroundings.
The wine cellar is one of the
most extensive in a Taipei
Chinese restaurant.
🛗 176 🔶 All major cards

RUTH'S CHRIS STEAK HOUSE
$$$$$
2F, 135 MINSHENG EAST RD.,
SEC. 3
TEL 02/2545-8888
www.ruthchris.com
Among the best steak houses
in Taiwan. Lots of polished
wood, brass, glass, and mirrors.
All cuts of U.S. prime beef
are available—New York strip,
rib-eye, T-bone, porterhouse.
Service is friendly and efficient.
🛗 218 🔶 All major cards

TUTTO BELLO
$$$$$
15 LANE 25, SHUANG-
CHENG ST.
TEL 02/2592-3355
www.tuttobello.com.tw
The menu is mainly northern
Italian. Rolled spinach pasta
with fresh and smoked
salmon, mushrooms, and
herbed cream sauce is pasta
perfection. The tasting menus
offer excellent value.
🛗 55 🔶 All major cards

CAFÉ
$$$$
GRAND HYATT TAIPEI
2 SONGSHOU RD
TEL 02/2720-1200, EXT. 3198
There are more than 160
dishes on the buffet tables.
Fresh salads are in abundance
and the sashimi is deliciously
fresh. Part of the joy is watching the 50 chefs in the open
kitchen.
🛗 314 🔶 All major cards

CAPONE'S ITALIAN AMERICAN DINNER-HOUSE
$$$$
312 ZHONGXIAO EAST RD., SEC. 4
TEL 02/2773-3782
www.capones.com.tw
Checkered tablecloths, a long
bar, and photographs on
the walls evoke the gangster
theme. The "Italian American"
in the restaurant's name

indicates the fare served. It's a good place for a late-night supper, staying open to 2 a.m. on weekdays and 3 a.m. on weekends. Live bands.

🪑 148 💳 All major cards

🍴 CHEZ MOI
$$$$

28 LANE 240, GUANGFU SOUTH RD.

TEL 02/2772-7265

The garden entrance adds charm to this stylish French restaurant. Baked escargot and Burgundy-style appetizers are prepared with butter, cheese, garlic, and herbs. Delectable lamb chops and duck's leg. The set menus offer good value.

🪑 50 💳 All major cards

🍴 CHIKURINTEI
$$$$

2F, SPRING CITY RESORT HOTEL 18 YOUYA RD., BEITOU DISTRICT

TEL 02/2897-5555, EXT. 25

Grand views of hills and valley from one of Beitou's most popular hot-springs hotels. Fare—seasonal—is Japanese. Be sure to try the Taraba crab hot pot.

🪑 90 💳 All major cards

🍴 CHING YEH RESTAURANT
$$$$

1 LANE 105, ZHONGSHAN NORTH RD., SEC. 1

TEL 2551-7957

This place has a rightful claim to being Taipei's best Taiwanese restaurant. Among the numerous house specialties are fried oysters with fermented soybeans and braised pig's foot with peanuts. For dessert, try the sweet soup with rock sugar, lotus seeds, and snow fungus.

🪑 122 💳 All major cards

🍴 DAN RYAN'S CHICAGO GRILL
$$$$

8 DUNHUA NORTH RD.

TEL 02/2778-8800

This pub/restaurant emulating a Chicago speakeasy of the 1930s and '40s serves healthy portions (for Asia) of familiar American dishes. New England clam chowder, Caesar salad, and buffalo wings appear for starters. Steak is the favored main course.

🪑 150 💳 All major cards

🍴 FENG ZHUAN TAIPEI
$$$$

B1, 225 DUNHUA SOUTH RD., SEC. 1

TEL 02/2751-2277

Asian decor evokes a tranquil ambience. French and Chinese dishes—primarily seafood—are cooked to bring out natural flavors. Treats include abalone in oyster sauce and shrimp dumplings. Set lunch and dinner menus go easy on the wallet.

🪑 80 💳 All major cards

🍴 IRODORI
$$$$

GRAND HYATT TAIPEI 2 SONGSHOU RD.

TEL 02/2720-1200, EXT. 3198

High-quality Japanese food spread out on buffet tables is an irresistible draw, so go before the lunch crowds arrive at noon. Sample the extensive array of sushi, sashimi, tempura, teppanyaki, and other styles of Japanese cuisine.

🪑 160 💳 All major cards

🍴 L'AMICO RISTORANTE ITALIANO
$$$$

10 LANE 55, MINSHENG EAST RD., SEC. 4

TEL 02/2719-3688

Classic European decor, intimate size, and hideaway location on a narrow lane evoke a romantic ambience. Layers of eggplant and courgette with mozzarella is a tasty antipasto choice. Tender veal dishes smothered in an assortment of sauces are tempting.

🪑 56 💳 All major cards

PRICES

HOTELS

An indication of the cost of a double room in the high season is given by **$** signs.

$$$$$	Over $235
$$$$	$185–$235
$$$	$120–$185
$$	$70–$120
$	Under $70

RESTAURANTS

An indication of the cost of a three-course meal without drinks is given by **$** signs.

$$$$$	Over $50
$$$$	$25–$50
$$$	$12–$25
$$	$5–$12
$	Under $5

🍴 LE JARDIN
$$$$

170 ZHONGZHENG RD., SEC. 2 TIANMU

TEL 02/2877-1178

Le Jardin specializes in southern French and Provençal cuisine. You'll find the thick fish soup with garlic saffron sauce hearty. Rack of lamb in rosemary sauce and pan-fried beef filet with creamy anchovy sauce are as rich as they sound.

🪑 80 💳 All major cards

🍴 PASTA WEST EAST
$$$$

7 ANHE RD., SEC. 1

TEL 202/2721-0029

As its name suggests, this place concedes some Italian authenticity to Asian tastes. The *pasta alle vongole* (spaghetti with a creamy sauce, fresh clams, and basil) is a popular choice. Try the homemade breads.

🪑 60 💳 All major cards

PORTOFINO

$$$$

2F, 323 DUNHUA SOUTH RD., SEC. 1

TEL 02/2755-5580

A taste of northern Italy, starting with heavenly fresh bread accompanied by piquant dip—capers, black olives, and fresh tomatoes. Pasta that smacks of freshness and flavor is enlivened with nice sauces.

90 All major cards

SALSA BISTRO

$$$$

9 LANE 141, ANHE RD., SEC. 1

TEL 02/2700-3060

South American decor accents this small spot. Try the fresh fish marinated in lemon juice as a refreshing appetizer before tucking into the baked corn and meat pastry entrée. A wide selection of Chilean wines.

35 All major cards

SHANGHAI STORY

$$$$

2F, 25 XINYI RD., SEC. 4

TEL 02/2702-1566

Shanghai of the 1920s and '30s is the backdrop in which to enjoy Shanghai soup buns and authentic Jiangsu and Zhejiang cuisine. The chefs excel in their creation of the must-try scallop and shrimp streamed dumplings. Other dishes, like shrimp with vegetables, succeed because of unpretentious preparation.

70 All major cards

SHINTORI

$$$$

B1, 191 ANHE RD., SEC. 2

TEL 02/2735-2288

Salmon roe, soft-shell crabs, salmon, and tuna come from Japan to maintain the authenticity of the Kaiseki cuisine. Dishes are presented with such meticulous detail that you feel a bit guilty about eating the work of art in front of you.

218 All major cards

SOMMELIER

$$$$

553 MINGSHUI RD.

TEL 02/2532-4707

Both imaginative and familiar Continental cuisine is served in this town-house-style spot. Shrimp, scallops, squid, and other seafood come sautéed in butter and enhanced with spices and Pernod. Sautéed shrimp and wild mushrooms in garlic sauce has a more Asian background. The wine list is varied and reasonable.

60 All major cards

SOWIESO

$$$$

88 SIWEI RD.

TEL 02/2705-5282

While labeled Italian, this place is known to wander off the culinary trail. Grilled abalone with frog legs and truffles is one example. The patio is very popular.

100 Closed Sun. All major cards

TIEN HSIANG LO

$$$$

LANDIS TAIPEI HOTEL

B1, 41 MINQUAN EAST RD., SEC. 2

TEL 02/2597-1234

A top-notch restaurant that serves Hangzhou cuisine—known for it subtle taste and presentation. The specialties are fish and crustaceans, though the chicken and wonton soup is a favorite. For something different, try the shrimp fried with tea leaves.

90 All major cards

TOSCANA ITALIAN RESTAURANT

$$$$

THE SHERWOOD

111 MINSHENG EAST RD., SEC. 3

TEL 02/2718-1188, EXT. 3001

Floor-to-ceiling windows separate the indoor and alfresco sections. The kitchen specializes in Italian cuisine with some variations. The porcini mushroom soup is delicious as are the imported smoked Italian meats. The poached Maine lobster on a bed of couscous salad can be enjoyed as an appetizer or main course.

120 All major cards

TRADER VIC'S RESTAURANT

$$$$

7F, 135 MINSHENG E. RD., SEC. 3

TEL 02/2545-9999

www.tradervics.com

Here, the rattan furnishings evoke a South Seas theme, as does the *bongo bongo:* creamy oyster soup served in a seashell. Other good bets are the sweet pork spareribs and the crispy chicken. Finishing the delicious mud pie is a chore, but worth the effort.

150 All major cards

ZIGA ZAGA

$$$$

GRAND HYATT TAIPEI

2 SONGSHOU RD.

TEL 02/2720-1200, EXT. 3198

The selections at this excellent buffet vary daily and include a large range of salads, pastas, seafood, and meat dishes. Pizza is the specialty. Desserts are irresistible. Diners linger to dance to the bands and DJs.

120 All major cards

BAMBOO VILLAGE

$$$

81 NANJING EAST RD., SEC. 2

TEL 02/2551-1838

Desire delicious dim sum in the wee hours? This place stays open until 3 a.m. (it opens at 5:30 p.m.). This Cantonese restaurant also places emphasis on fresh seafood.

110 All major cards

CAFÉ ASTORIA

$$$

2F, 7 WUCHANG ST., SEC. 1

TEL 2/02/381-5589

This renowned heritage spot, opened after World War II by a White Russian émigré from Shanghai. Long beloved by

President Chiang Ching-kuo and his Russian wife, it has an old Russian salon decor and serves traditional borscht and more. No spoken English.

🛏 132 🚫 All major cards

SOMETHING SPECIAL

🍴 HONG YUN CANTONESE RESTAURANT
$$$

2F, 275 NANJING EAST RD., SEC. 3
TEL 02/2713-3877
An innovative and extremely long menu keeps this 24-hour establishment busy. Chefs create wonderful dim sum, including asparagus and codfish dumplings. The yam and snow-clam soup is the equivalent of clam chowder. For dessert, chrysanthemum cake with matrimony vine—a traditional Chinese herb—is not only delicious but is said to soothe both body and mind.

🪑 120 🚫 All major cards

🍴 JAKE'S COUNTRY KITCHEN
$$$

705 ZHONGSHAN NORTH RD., SEC. 6, TIANMU
TEL 02/2871-5289
This restaurant, popular with expatriates and Western visitors, serves up an array of Mexican favorites—enchiladas, quesadillas, and tacos. Breakfast served all day. Generous portions and reasonable prices.

🪑 80 🚫 All major cards

🍴 MING GARDEN
$$$

AMBASSADOR HOTEL
63 ZHONGSHAN NORTH RD., SEC. 2
TEL 02/2100-2100, EXT. 2183
The buffet has a "Chinese cuisines area" where you can sample an extensive mix. Western dishes are laid on in equal abundance. At the afternoon tea buffet, the food tends to be a little lighter but abundant.

🪑 120 🚫 All major cards

🍴 MOROCCAN RESTAURANT
$$$

1 LANE 165, DUNHUA NORTH RD.
TEL 02/2719-4469
One of the best of Taipei's limited number of Middle Eastern/African restaurants. The Harira soup combines lamb, paprika, saffron, tomatoes, beans, and lime juice. Lamb and chicken dominate the entrées. Lamb, stewed with olives, almonds, vegetables, and beans, is served on couscous. Try the sweet mint tea.

🪑 176 🚫 All major cards

🍴 PENG YUAN
$$$

2F, 380 LINSEN N. RD.
TEL 02/2551-9157
The original in the locally renowned "Peng's Garden" chain. Expansive and always busy. The Hunanese food's the thing here. The best selection is Hunan ham cooked with honey—rich and smoky. You'll need a Chinese speaker in your group.

🪑 122 🚫 All major cards

🍴 PIAO LIU MU (DRIFTWOOD) ABORIGINAL RESTAURANT
$$$

4 ALLEY 9, LANE 316, ROOSEVELT RD., SEC. 3
TEL 02/2365-7413
Some of the island's best aboriginal artists painted the murals that depict scenes from legends. The excellent grilled wild boar is served with a special sauce and wild vegetables. Aboriginal performers take to the stage on weekends at 9 p.m.

🪑 50 🕐 Closed Mon. 🚫 All major cards

🍴 SHIN YEH RESTAURANT
$$$

34-1 SHUANGCHENG ST.
TEL 02/2596-3255
The main branch of a popular chain that serves Taiwanese fare to a bustling clientele

of locals and travelers. The seafood—squid, grilled eel, fried shrimp rolls, and grilled clams—is excellent and a good value.

🪑 120 🚫 All major cards

SOMETHING SPECIAL

🍴 TAINAN TAN TSU NOODLES
$$$

31 HUAXI ST.
TEL 02/2308-1123
At the north end of Huaxi St. Tourist Night Market. The signature dish is a traditional specialty, *danzai mian/tan tsu mian,* or passing-the-lean-months noodles. They might be Taiwan's priciest noodles, served on Wedgwood china. The seafood is also praised.

🪑 140 🚫 All major cards

🍴 TANDOOR INDIAN RESTAURANT
$$$

10 LANE 73, HEJIANG ST.
TEL 02/ 2509-9853
The excellent menu includes mixed grill of chicken, lamb kebab, fish, and prawns sizzling on a bed of onions. The ovens turn out an assortment of unleavened breads to complement the range of rich curries.

🪑 80 🚫 All major cards

🍴 TAPAS BAR
$$$

50 HEPING WEST RD.
TEL 02/2362-8777
Western expatriates crowd the cozy place where waiters circulate explaining the dishes. If you are in a group, call ahead and order paella. French food is also available.

🪑 30 🕐 Closed Mon. 🚫 No credit cards

🍴 VUVU ROCK ABORIGINAL RESTAURANT
$$$

3 ZHISHAN RD., SEC. 2

TEL 02/2880-3043
Stucco walls, sculptures, and murals are a little overdone, but diners don't seem to mind, tucking into some unusual aboriginal dishes. The betel-nut flower with either beef or pork is popular, as is the mixed stir-fry that includes wild boar and seasonal flying fish. Sweet red rice wine can be ordered by the pitcher, and enjoyed while aboriginal artists perform.

🛏 105 🔲 All major cards

🍴 FANG FAMILY RESTAURANT
$$
136 XINYI RD., SEC. 4
TEL 02/2754-1658
Basil, spring onions, garlic, soy sauce, ginger root, and other savory items are added to beef dishes. Some feature various innards. Try the Jiangzhe selections, such as pea shrimp, cabbage pot, and beef brisket.

🛏 85 🔲 No credit cards

🍴 TIEN XIANG HUI WEI
$$
2F, 16 NANJING EAST RD., SEC. 1
TEL 02/2511-7275
The litany of spices added to the hot pots makes this chain a favorite. The herbs are mixed with other special ingredients to create warming and flavorful hot pots. Try the fish balls.

🛏 186 🔲 All major cards

🍴 OLD ZHANG'S BEEF NOODLES
$
19 LANE 31, JINSHAN SOUTH RD., SEC. 2
TEL 02/2396-0927
Beef noodles, introduced by north Chinese soldiers in the late 1940s, are one of Taiwan's most popular dishes. Order it with a light broth or a thick, slightly spicy broth.

🛏 60 🔲 No credit cards

🍴 ZHEN XIANG BEEF NOODLES
$
198 SONGREN RD.
TEL 02/2720-9089
This small, unassuming eatery serves up noodles with distinction. That accounts for the crowds of diners. Chunks of tender beef swim in a rich broth. Dry beef noodles (without the broth) are also available. For about U.S. $2 you can buy what regulars consider the best beef noodles in Taipei.

🛏 30 🔲 No credit cards

■ AROUND TAIPEI & THE NORTH

BEITOU

🏨 SPRING CITY RESORT HOTEL
$$$$
18 YOUYA RD.
TEL 02/2897-7245
www.springresort.com.tw
It's a short taxi ride from the nearby MRT station, making this a viable alternative to Taipei hotels, especially during the week when room rates halve. Decor mixes art deco with Asian. Deep in-room pools are filled with hot water piped in from the springs.

ⓘ 95 🔲 🔲 🔲 🔲 🔲 All major cards 🚇 Xinbeitou

🏨 WHISPERING PINE INN
$$
21 YOUYA RD.
TEL 02/2895-1531
This is one of only a few traditional Japanese-style inns remaining in the area. Large Western and tatami rooms and slate-floor hot-springs bathing rooms are set amid tranquil Japanese gardens. There have been recent concerns that renovations are needed.

ⓘ 20 🔲 All major cards

ZHONGLI

🏨 KUVA CHATEAU
$$$
398 MINQUAN RD., TAOYUAN COUNTY
TEL 03/281-1818
FAX 03/281-1616
www.kuva-chateau.com.tw
Located 15 minutes from Taiwan Taoyuan airport, and 25 minutes from Taipei, this is the only deluxe hotel in the area. It is aimed at the corporate traveler. There is an airport shuttle.

ⓘ 248 🔲 🔲 🔲 🔲 🔲 All major cards

KEELUNG

🏨 EVERGREEN LAUREL HOTEL
$$$
62-1 ZHONGZHENG RD.
TEL 02/2427-9988
FAX 02/2422-8642
www.evergreen-hotels.com
On the edge of Keelung Harbor, some rooms offer harbor and ocean views. Room size, decor, and amenities justify its four-star status. An indoor heated pool, steam room, and sauna are found in the health center.

ⓘ 140 🔲 🔲 🔲 🔲
🔲 All major cards

NORTH COAST

🏨 HOWARD BEACH RESORT GREEN BAY
$$$
17 FEICUI RD., WANLI TOWNSHIP, TAIPEI COUNTY
TEL 02/2492-6565
FAX 02/2492-6588
www.howard-hotels.com.tw
Multistory hotel right on the beach with recreational facilities, including indoor and outdoor pools, a spa, and all sorts of beachside accoutrements for rent.

ⓘ 241 🔲 🔲 🔲 🔲
🔲 All major cards

🔲 Elevator 🔲 Indoor Pool 🔲 Outdoor Pool 🔲 Health Club 🔲 Credit Cards

TAOYUAN

🏨 HONGXI TA SHEE RESORT
$$$$

166 REXIN RD., DAXI TOWNSHIP
TAOYUAN COUNTY
TEL 03/387-6688
FAX 03/387-5288
In the hills 40 minutes south of Taipei, 20 minutes east of the airport. The key attraction is the adjoining Ta Shee Golf & Country Club. Hotel guests have special access.
🛏 208 🅿 🔁 🏊 🍷
🏧 All major cards

🏨 EVERGREEN TRANSIT HOTEL
$$

4F, TERMINAL 2, TAIWAN TAOYUAN INTERNATIONAL AIRPORT, TAOYUAN COUNTY
TEL 03/383-4510
FAX 03/383-4610
www.evergreenhotels.com
The Evergreen Transit Hotel was officially opened in 2003. There is a limited but state-of-the-art range of recreational facilities in the small facility.
🛏 21 🅿 🍷 🏧 All major cards

YANGMINGSHAN

🏨 LANDIS RESORT YANGMINGSHAN
$$$$

237 GEZHI RD.
TEL 02/2861-6661
FAX 02/2861-3885
www.landisresort.com.tw
This boutique hot-springs resort in Yangmingshan National Park has serene modern Japanese decor. Water from the nearby hot springs is piped into the deep soaking pools in guest-room baths.
🛏 47 🅿 🔁 🏊 🍷
🏧 All major cards

■ EAST COAST

HUALIEN

🍴 EMERALD GARDEN
$$$$

CHINATRUST HOTEL
2 YONGXING RD.
TEL 03/822-1171
At this popular European-style buffet, the most popular dinner dish is the honey chicken leg, but the chef's favorites are the seafood marinara and filet of sole meunière.
🪑 125 🏧 All major cards

🍴 LOTUS RESTAURANT
$$$$

CHINATRUST HOTEL
2 YONGXING RD.
TEL 03/822-1171
The restaurant specializes in Cantonese fare. The most popular dish is the Fugui prawn ball, but the head chef's recommendation is the harbor-fresh seafood dim sum. The large facility is almost always bustling.
🪑 140 🏧 All major cards

HUALIEN COUNTY

🏨 PROMISED LAND RESORT
$$$$$

1 LIXIANG RD.
SHOUFENG TOWNSHIP
TEL 03/865-6789
FAX 03/865-6555
www.plcresort.com.tw
Located in the East Rift Valley, about 25 minutes south of downtown Hualien, are luxury cottages surrounding a lagoon where you can take boat rides. After dark, lounge by the poolside bar and enjoy the nighttime star extravaganza.
🛏 260 🅿 🔁 🏊 🍷
🏧 All major cards

🏨 HUALIEN FARGLORY HOTEL
$$$$

18 SHANLING, YANLIAO VILLAGE
SHOUFENG TOWNSHIP

PRICES

HOTELS
An indication of the cost of a double room in the high season is given by $ signs.

$$$$$	Over $235
$$$$	$185–$235
$$$	$120–$185
$$	$70–$120
$	Under $70

RESTAURANTS
An indication of the cost of a three-course meal without drinks is given by $ signs.

$$$$$	Over $50
$$$$	$25–$50
$$$	$12–$25
$$	$5–$12
$	Under $5

TEL 03/812-3999
FAX 03/812-3988
www.farglory-hotel.com.tw
The plush Victorian Farglory–takes care of every need you might desire. Hotel guests enjoy special rates at the Hualien Ocean Park theme park. Shuttle pickups from the airport and train station.
🛏 391 🅿 🔁 🏊 🍷
🏧 All major cards

🏨 SHIN KONG CHAO FENG RANCH AND RESORT
$$$/$$

20 YONGFU ST., LINRONG WARD FENGLIN TOWNSHIP
TEL 03/877-2666
FAX 03/877-1433
In the middle of the broad north end of the East Rift Valley, a perfect place to spend the nights gazing at the stars from the verandas of the Dutch-style cabins. This resort is perfect for families with its bird park, animal area, and water-fun arena. Bike and golf cart rentals available.
🛏 122 🅿 🏊 🏧 All major cards

TAITUNG

🏨 FORMOSAN NARUWAN HOTEL & RESORT
$$$$$

66 LIANHANG RD., TAITUNG
TEL 089/239-666
FAX 089/239-777
www.naruwan-hotel.com.tw
The aboriginal-theme decor and spacious well-appointed rooms embellished with dark wood-panel inlays work well in this young hotel, which offers aboriginal song and dance performances weekends. A pleasant lobby lounge bar looks out over a sparkling swimming pool. Wonderfully relaxing outdoor spa. A shuttle bus runs to the National Museum of Prehistory nearby.

🛈 276 🅿 ⬆ 🌊 💪
🚫 All major cards

🏨 HOTEL ROYAL CHIHPEN
$$$$$

23 LANE 113, LONGQUAN RD., WENQUAN VILLAGE, BEINAN TOWNSHIP
TEL 089/510-666
FAX 089/510-678
www.hotel-royal-chihpen
.com.tw
One of a few so-called upscale hotels in the popular Zhiben hot-springs resort town. Facilities are aimed at the soaking crowd, with various indoor, outdoor, and in-room hot-springs options.

🛈 183 🅿 ⬆ 🌊 💪
🚫 All major cards

🍴 ESOD VEGETARIAN RESTAURANT
$$

320 ZHONGXING RD., SEC. 1
TAITUNG CITY
TEL 089/232-106
Vegan fare in the heart of the city, amid simple and straightforward decor. The wide-ranging menu centers on rice, noodle, and pasta dishes. The ramen is especially tasty. The sundry teas and shaved-ice treats are also popular.

🍴 45 🚫 All major cards

TAROKO GORGE

🏨 SILKS PLACE TAROKO
$$$$

18 TIAN TIANXIANG RD., XIULIN TOWNSHIP, HUALIEN COUNTY
TEL 03/869-1155 OR 02/2560-3266 (TAIPEI)
FAX 03/869-1160
A low-rise hotel in the magnificent Taroko National Park. The setting makes it an ideal place to stay if you plan to spend a few days. Rooms open to balconies and splendid views. Lots of aboriginal-motif decor in the lobby. Completely refurbished; upgraded in 2009. Shuttle service provided from Hualien airport or railway station.

🛈 225 🅿 ⬆ 🌊 💪
🚫 All major cards

■ THE SOUTH

DONGGANG

🍴 CHANG FAMILY RESTAURANT
$$$

65-1 GUANGFU ROAD, SEC. 2, PINGTUNG COUNTY
TEL 08/833-7251
In a fishing port known for its fresh seafood, this large and bustling place stands out. Buses full of Japanese tourists are common. Be sure to try the town's specialty, the "three treasures of Donggang"—shrimp with sliced cabbage sautéed in chicken broth, ribbon fish eggs marinated in Shaohsing wine, and otoro, from the belly section of the bluefin tuna.

🍴 150-plus 🚫 No credit cards

HENGCHUN

🏨 YOHO LANDIS BEACH CLUB
$$$$

27-8 WANLI RD.
TEL 08/886-9999
FAX 08/886-9998

www.yoho.com.tw
Located on the beachfront in Kenting National Park, some of the rooms offer ocean views. Huge seaview swimming pool is the main attraction. Also has a special Kids' Club and Kids' Pool. The hotel's glass-walled Seaview Restaurant affords ocean panoramic views. The club is a bit removed from Kending Town but has scheduled shuttle service to Kaohsiung airport.

🛈 415 🅿 ⬆ 🌊 💪
🚫 All major cards

🍴 BOSSA NOVA CAFÉ
$$

100 NANWAN RD., PINGTUNG COUNTY
TEL 08/889-7137
Located in South Bay or Nanwan, this small establishment serves up tasty sandwiches and simple Asian and Western meals (chicken burritos, spicy Thai chicken, spaghetti). The idyllic spot has a big front patio with shaded tables.

🍴 45 🚫 No credit cards

🍴 CHAO LI
$$

98-1 HEPING DISTRICT, NANWAN WARD, PINGTUNG COUNTY
TEL 08/889-6587
Located in a shady grove along the main highway (no. 26), this was the first (and still best) of a clutch of well-known roadside restaurants serving up a Hengchun specialty, puffer fish—locally caught. Most dishes here are Hengchun-based, using local seafood and vegetables. Also try the parrot fish with Hengchun chili peppers.

🍴 50 🕐 Closed Mon.
🚫 No credit cards

KAOHSIUNG

🏨 GRAND HI-LAI HOTEL
$$$$$

266 CHENGGONG 1ST RD.
TEL 07/216-1766

⬆ Elevator   🏊 Indoor Pool   🌊 Outdoor Pool   💪 Health Club   🚫 Credit Cards

FAX 07/216-1966
www.grand-hilai.com.tw
The lobby and public areas are furnished in a neoclassical European style, while the spacious guest rooms are more subdued. There is a quality gym, pool, and squash courts, but the harbor and ocean views are the treat. The huge family rooms are furnished with two king-size beds. Thirteen food & beverage outlets spread throughout the hotel provide for every hunger pang.

🛈 540 🅿 🔁 🏊 📺
⬧ All major cards

🏨 THE SPLENDOR KAOHSIUNG
$$$$
1 ZIQIANG 3RD RD.
TEL 07/566-8000
FAX 07/566-8080
www.gfk.com.tw
Rising 85 stories from the edge of Kaohsiung Harbor, this is one of the world's tallest hotels. Needless to say, the views are spectacular. Guest rooms (including 92 suites) are comfortably appointed, and all bathrooms come with an inviting soaking tub. The Palace Club on floors 77–79 bills itself as the highest health club in the world.

🛈 592 🅿 🔁 🏊 📺
⬧ All major cards

🏨 AMBASSADOR HOTEL
$$$
202 MINSHENG 2ND RD.
TEL 07/211-5211
FAX 07/201-0348
www.ambhotel.com.tw
This international-class hotel features American maple wood furnishings and neutral European wool carpets. The Japanese duvets and Spanish marble bathrooms with German fittings complete the multinational contributions. Most rooms have harbor views. The pool is set in tropical gardens, and the rooftop garden provides grand views.

🛈 453 🅿 🔁 🏊 📺
⬧ All major cards

🏨 GRAND HOTEL—CHENG CHING LAKE
$$$
2 YUANSAN RD.
KAOHSIUNG TOWNSHIP
TEL 07/370-5911
FAX 07/370-4889
www.grand-hotel.org
The scaled-down sister of Taipei's landmark Grand Hotel is located on Chengqing Lake parklands. Guests become temporary members of the Yuan Shan Sports Club, with a night-lit driving range, tennis, squash, well-equipped gym, sauna, and Olympic-size pool.

🛈 107 🅿 🔁 🏊 📺
⬧ All major cards

🏨 HOWARD PLAZA HOTEL
$$$
311 QIXIAN 1ST RD.
TEL 07/236-2323
FAX 07/235-8383
www.howard-hotels.com
It's a little difficult finding the check-in counter (on the fifth floor), but once you do, you can settle into a comfortable guest room. It's worth paying extra for the Rosewood Club executive floors, with bigger rooms and more attentive service. Six food and beverage outlets, including a popular breakfast, lunch, and dinner buffet in the atrium lobby. Fee for pool and fitness center use.

🛈 328 🅿 🔁 🏊 📺
⬧ All major cards

🍽 ARTIST
$$$
CORNER OF WUFU 3RD RD. & ZHONGHUA RD.
TEL 07/282-9777
This popular 24-hour eatery turns out pizzas, casseroles, hot pots, salads, soups, and Chinese stir-fry dishes.

🪑 60 ⬧ All major cards

🍽 BRASS RAIL TAVERN
$$$
21 WUFU 4TH RD.
TEL 07/533-5747
This bar/restaurant is famous for pizza, especially its seafood variety. Other favorite dishes include the U.S. prime filet and fish-and-chips. The restaurant also serves noodles, rice, stir-fry meats, and seafood dishes. There's a large variety of international beers and a surprisingly extensive wine list.

🪑 70 ⬧ All major cards

🍽 MAYADA
$$$
226 MINGCHENG 2ND RD.
TEL 07/558-1099
A tasteful Southeast Asian ambience replete with Thai wood carvings, pottery, and other ornaments sets the tone for some authentic Thai dishes, including lemongrass shrimp with raw shrimp dipped in a piquant sauce.

🪑 50 ⬧ All major cards

🍽 ROOF LOUNGE BAR & CAFÉ
$$$
15F, 165 LINSEN 1ST RD.
TEL 07/241-6666
As the name suggests, the restaurant sits high in the sky. The ambience is casual and comfortable and the Southeast Asian menu has dishes from Thailand, Malaysia, Indonesia, and Yunnan Province in China.

🪑 55 ⬧ All major cards

🍽 EASTERN VS. WESTERN MUSIC RESTAURANT
$$
490 HEDI RD.
TEL 07/954-6406
An interesting fusion—or jumble—of Eastern and Western decor. The food is mainly Western, though, with famous Texas roast ribs that are cooked over imported walnut and acacia charcoal. You'll find

southeast Asian dishes on the menu, too.

🔁 75 🀫 All major cards

🍴 LIU FAMILY STICKY RICE DUMPLINGS
$$

171-2 ZUOYINGDA RD.
TEL 07/588-9885
Dumplings resembling tamales and called *rouzong* are stuffed with delicious meat, mushroom, and seafood fillings. This place is so inexpensive that you can easily feast on a wide variety of these tasty morsels.

🔁 55 🀫 No credit cards

🍴 MUSHROOM KITCHEN
$$

197 MINGHUA 1ST RD.
TEL 07/556-1821
A refreshing and comfortable place with garden dining. Mushrooms, as the name suggests, dominate the menu. Chicken, fish, or various meats are added to hot pots filled with a staggering array of mushrooms for a savory and fulsome taste. A nice touch are the drawers in the dining tables that contain napkins, spoons, chopsticks, and toothpicks. Talk about attention to detail: Different dishes, spoons, chopsticks, and pots are used for vegetarian customers.

🔁 45 🀫 All major cards

🍴 NAKA BASHI
$$

23 QIXIAN 2ND RD.
TEL 07/285-2843
Crowds flock here during the late evening to enjoy generous portions of Japanese-style hot pots and barbecues. Hot pots incorporate chicken, pork, beef, and seafood with a broad range of vegetable and tofu accompaniments. A sweet rice dessert follows each meal. The model train whizzing around the restaurant makes for an interesting diversion.

🔁 60 🀫 All major cards

KENTING

🏨 CAESAR PARK HOTEL
$$$$

6 KENTING RD.
TEL 08/886-1888 OR
02/2717-5125 (IN TAIPEI)
FAX 08/886-1818
www.caesarpark.com.tw
Smaller and more intimate than the neighboring Howard Beach Resort, the rooms here are furnished for comfort and relaxation. Glass doors to balconies with views of either the ocean or an expansive swimming pool set amid tropical gardens. The hotel's buffet breakfast (usually complimentary) is excellent.

ℹ️ 245 🅿️ 🔁 🏊 🀫
🀫 All major cards

🏨 HOWARD BEACH RESORT
$$$$

2 KENTING RD.
TEL 08/886-2323
FAX 08/886-2359
www.howard-hotels.com
Located at the east end of Kending Town, you will find no end to the facilities at this sprawling resort. A handy tunnel connects the hotel to Small Bay. Rooms are large enough for more than two people, making it a favorite with families. Try for a room with the balcony overlooking the swimming pool and Kending Beach; then settle there to watch the sunset.

ℹ️ 405 🅿️ 🔁 🏊 🀫
🀫 All major cards

🍴 CACTUS CAFÉ
$$

126 DAWAN RD.
TEL 08/886-2747
A nice and inexpensive place for a hearty North American–style breakfast. Choose from eggs, home fries, bacon, burritos, French toast, buttermilk pancakes, and fruit and yogurt. Lunch, dinner, and bar menus are available throughout the day. Ocean views are free.

🔁 35 🀫 All major cards

🍴 MAMBO
$$

46 KENTING R4
TEL 08/886-2878
This crowded shopfront restaurant serves up a full range of Thai dishes in a densely tabled, casual, unaffected atmosphere. In keeping with its location at one of Taiwan's most popular beach resorts, the menu has a wide selection of seafood. If you are with a group, share the sea bass with sweet chili, steamed garoupa in lemon, and prawn satay. No matter what, don't miss the justly popular shrimp cakes.

🔁 120 🀫 All major cards

▨ STRAIT ISLANDS

JINCHENG

🏨 HOTEL RIVER KINMEN
$$

100 XIHAI RD., SEC. 3
TEL 082/322-211
FAX 082/323-322
The best of the bunch on these isolated islands, the Hotel River Kinmen has large, clean rooms and your standard budget hotel facilities. The travel service in the hotel is good for booking trips around the islands.

ℹ️ 122 🅿️ 🀫 🀫 All major cards

NANGAN ISLSAND

🏨 SHENNONG HOTEL
$$$

84-2 QINGSHUI VILLAGE
TEL 0836/26333
FAX 0836/26330
The Matzu islands are just finding their feet in terms of tourism resources, and this hotel is one of the few choices. It sits on a high point near the middle of the island and provides fine ocean views from the upper floors. Rooms are clean and bright, and the staff aims to please but nonetheless can be unfamiliar with the expectations of international travelers.

ℹ️ 63 🅿️ 🔁 🀫 All major cards

🔁 Elevator 🏊 Indoor Pool 🏊 Outdoor Pool 🀫 Health Club 🀫 Credit Cards

GRANDMA'S EATERY
$$$/$$

143 NIUJIAO RHINO HORN
VILLAGE

TEL 0836/26125

In this lovely restored inn-style residence made of local stone, the cuisine is north Fujian-style with an emphasis on seafood. The most unusual dish is barnacles, which the staff will teach you how to eat. Beyond the Chinese beer, the spirits are all made on the islands.

50 No credit cards

PENGHU

HOTEL EVER SPRING
$$

6 ZHONGZHENG RD.,
MAGONG

TEL 06/927-3336

FAX 06/927-2112

http://everspring.hotel
.com.tw

Options here are limited to budget tourist hotels. At the Hotel Ever Spring, you will find a clean room, a comfortable bed, satellite television, free Internet, and a bar fridge. What else do you need? The bar fridge will be empty, by the way, so you will need to stock it with supplies.

85 All major cards

CENTRAL WEST

ALISHAN

ALISHAN HOUSE
$$$$

16 ALISHAN, XIANGLIN VILLAGE
ALISHAN TOWNSHIP,
CHIAYI COUNTY

TEL 05/267-9811

FAX 05/267-9596

www.alishanhouse.com.tw

A small, charming hotel perched high in the mountains and set amid lovely gardens. Rooms are elegant. All have views. Choices in Alishan Forest Recreation Area are limited, so best to book early because it is small and can fill quickly.

There's a lovely outdoor café and mountain-view patio, among other top-flight amenities.

35 MC, V

CHIAYI

CHIAYI CHINATRUST HOTEL
$$

257 WENHUA RD.

TEL 05/229-2233

FAX 05/229-3998

www.chinatrust-hotel. com.tw

You will likely need to stay in Chiayi overnight if you want to catch the morning train to Alishan. This hotel is typical of those run by Chinatrust around the island. The rooms may lack the elegance of large city decor, but they are dependably clean and comfortable.

170 All major cards

WU LI MUSEO STORICO DEGLI SPAGHETTI
$$$

29-1 CHUIYANG RD.

TEL 05/223-8941

Standard Italian fare of pasta, seafood, and fowl dishes. Roast chicken with lemon and butter sauce is a popular choice, as in one of the tasty varieties of pizza. The cappuccino, latte, and au lait are the best you'll find in the city.

40 All major cards

SUN MOON LAKE

SOMETHING SPECIAL

THE LALU
$$$$$

142 ZHONGXING RD., YUCHI
TOWNSHIP, NANTOU COUNTY

TEL 049/285-5311

FAX 049/285-5312

www.thelalu.com.tw

This resort hotel is in the gold standard league for Taiwan. Dark wood floors, glass curtain windows, and minimalist,

PRICES

HOTELS

An indication of the cost of a double room in the high season is given by $ signs.

$$$$$	Over $235
$$$$	$185–$235
$$$	$120–$185
$$	$70–$120
$	Under $70

RESTAURANTS

An indication of the cost of a three-course meal without drinks is given by $ signs.

$$$$$	Over $50
$$$$	$25–$50
$$$	$12–$25
$$	$5–$12
$	Under $5

sharp-lined modern furnishings create a super-stylish simplicity. Suites have balconies with uninterrupted views of the lake, while one- and two-bedroom courtyard villas come with their own swimming pools and an outdoor dining pavilion. The China Tea House serves dim sum and the Japanese Restaurant offers teppanyaki. Guests are charged extra to use the tennis courts.

71
All major cards

TAICHUNG

EVERGREEN LAUREL HOTEL
$$$$

6 TAICHUNG GANG (HARBOR
RD., SEC. 2

TEL 04/2313-9988

FAX 04/2313-8642

www.evergreen-hotels.com

Rosewood furniture and neutral tones add a pleasant

feel. All rooms have four-star accoutrements, including an personal safe-deposit box, satellite television, and marble-clad bathroom. A nice, and for Taiwan unusual, addition is a squash court.

🛈 354 🅿 🖹 ♨ 🍸 ♿
🅂 All major cards

🏨 HOWARD PRINCE HOTEL
$$$$
129 ANHE RD.
TEL 04/2463-2323
FAX 04/2463-3333
www.howard-hotels.com
The picture windows allow in plenty of natural light to the well-furnished, spacious rooms. The French, East/West buffet, Cantonese, and Shanghainese restaurants are well patronized, and the lobby bar is a friendly, chatty place. The Business Center is conveniently open 24 hours.

🛈 135 🅿 🖹 ♨ 🍸
🅂 All major cards

🏨 TEMPUS TAICHUNG HOTEL
$$$$
9 TAICHUNG GANG (HARBOR) RD., SEC. 2
TEL 04/2326-8008
FAX 04/2326-8060
www.tempus.com.tw
The guest rooms use woods and gold hues to sync with its modernist furniture and fittings in an understated and agreeable style. The cool, crisp bed linens and lightweight goose-down duvets are a delight. Good outdoor pool and spa facilities.

🛈 260 🅿 🖹 ♨ 🍸 ♿
🅂 All major cards

🍽 BA BU
$$$$$
61 WUQUAN WEST 1ST ST.
TEL 04/2372-0777
Located inside a mansion surrounded by courtyard and garden, Ba Bu's atmosphere flows from its polished floors

to crisp linen. Add to that black truffles! European style is reflected in its combination of French, German, Swiss, and Italian dishes. Examples include pan-fried prawn and scallops served with mushroom rice, sablefish filet meunière, and knuckle of veal Aargau style. The shark's fin and abalone are worthwhile departures from the European influence.

🍴 60 🅂 All major cards

SOMETHING SPECIAL

🍽 SERIOUS DAVID SHEN'S STEAK & SEAFOOD HOUSE
$$$$$
277 MINQUAN RD.
TEL 04/2322-6156
David Shen is certainly serious about presentation and taste in this high-end establishment. Wood floors, leather furniture, and attentive tuxedo-clad service staff lend a cigar-smoking, brandy-sipping ambience to the place. The restaurant uses only Australian and USDA prime beef. Carnivore delights include a petite 8-ounce New York steak, 12-ounce rib-eye steak, an improbable 30-ounce Porterhouse, and, the house special, pig's knuckle. The restaurant's "surf and turf" meals mix steak with lobster.

🍴 90 🅂 All major cards

🍽 FIVE-CENT DRIFTWOOD HOUSE
$$$$
SHIZHENG NORTH 3RD RD.
TEL 04/2254-5678
Antique pottery, carvings, sculptures, faux cave, trees, and even a carp-filled mini-lagoon embellish the restaurant's elegance. Once seated, you can tuck into innovative Chinese cuisine. The "Simple Meal" lets you combine a variety of dishes, including fish, beef, pork, lamb, goose, shrimp, and crab. Popular among the à la carte dishes are goose in a

wine sauce and tender lobster slices with mayonnaise.

🍴 110 🅂 All major cards

🍽 CHILI'S GRILL & BAR
$$$
1F, 120 HENAN RD., SEC. 3
TEL 04/3602-8838
Chili's serves up huge portions of Tex-Mex food in a convivial atmosphere. Diners munch on tangy buffalo wings with blue cheese dressing, baby back ribs, and chicken, followed by generous salads for starters. Other favorites include the big burgers, including one topped with blue cheese and bacon. Desserts are big here—you may find trouble fitting them in after the starters and main course.

🍴 110 🅂 All major cards

🍽 SPOOL RESTAURANT
$$$
154 DALONG RD.
TEL 04/2329-9590
This restaurant is located amid beautiful tropical gardens, while the inside is adorned with palms, ferns, and Asian art (many pieces are for sale). A sizable Western menu renowned for its attention to detail is available, along with a large selection of chilled tropical alcoholic and non-alcoholic drinks.

🍴 75 🅂 All major cards

🍽 WU GUO JIE RESTAURANT
$$$
191 DONGXING RD., SEC. 2
TEL 04/2472-6200
Nicknamed "No Frontiers" to indicate the range of food choices available. Chefs here can create Chinese and European dishes with equal flair. Popular Chinese entrées include rock-sugar pig's feet and vinegar fish, while butter bream, roasted lamb chops, and special German-style pork chops are favored European meals. Set-course dinners are available.

🍴 65 🅂 All major cards

🛗 Elevator 🏊 Indoor Pool 🏊 Outdoor Pool 🍸 Health Club 🅂 Credit Cards

🍴 GU JIN SHAO
$$

94 JINGMING 1ST ST.
TEL 04/2328-9228

Gu Jin Shao is a small, unob-trusive eatery with a big reputation. The restaurant imaginatively combines Chinese and Japanese cuisine into its own creations. Its Japanese chicken rolls, crispy oyster rolls, and shrimp rolls make delicious starters. The surprisingly inexpensive juicy tender pork has all the fat removed and is simmered in soy sauce. It comes with all the extras. Tasty and various noodles, rice dishes, fish and beef hot pots, and dumplings are also available.

🪑 30 💳 All major cards

🍴 ZEN CURRY
$$

299 TAICHONGGANG RD., SEC. 1
B1 SOGO STORE
TEL 04/2329-9222

A stylish, relaxing, and con-temporary place that, as its name suggests, serves up a wide variety of Japanese curries. You can order them in varying degrees of spiciness and heat. Reasonably priced set meals are available.

🪑 50 💳 All major cards

TAINAN

🏨 TAYIH LANDIS
$$$

660 XIMEN RD., SEC. 1
TEL 06/213-5555
FAX 06/213-5599
www.tayihlandis.com.tw

Another classy offering from Taiwan's Landis group. Large, stylish rooms, efficient staff, and complimentary services that you usually have to pay for at other hotels are standard here. The lobby Deli Corner sells tasty gourmet sandwiches, savories, and cakes to go, making for a tasty mobile meal while on a walking tour of the nearby temples.

ℹ️ 257 P 🪑 🏊 🎾 ♿
💳 All major cards

🍴 TYCOON RESTAURANT
$$$$

258 SHIMEN RD., SEC. 4
TEL 06/251-2706

Traditional Chinese decor sets the scene for quality Cantonese and Hunanese cuisine. House specials are extensive, with the prawn salad, black pepper steak, and garlic steamed *yudai* top-ping the list. Wallet-depleting abalone is available for those who wish to impress their guests. Ginseng chicken and Peking roast duck need to be ordered in advance. Guests are entertained by costumed musicians between 7 p.m. and 9 p.m.

🪑 110 💳 All major cards

🍴 TERRAZZA RISTORANTE
$$$

7F, 52 GONGYUAN RD.
TEL 06/223-2698

The plush—even somewhat pretentious—decor belies the reasonable prices in this top-notch Italian restaurant. Large varieties of pasta and risotto dishes are on the menu. Delicious salads incorpor-ating such tasty items as wild mushrooms, beef, and smoked salmon are mandatory starters.

🪑 40 ⊘ Closed Mon.
💳 All major cards

🍴 HUNDRED HOUSE FRA-GRANCE VEGETARIAN RESTAURANT
$$

15 CHANGRONG RD., SEC. 3
TEL 06/208-6928

An MSG-free vegetarian res-taurant with fresh, simple, and healthy meals delivered to your table quickly and without fuss. For a delicious surprise of a dessert, try the gel-milk cubes, sweet potato balls, or peanut tofu.

🪑 40 💳 All major cards

🍴 PLEASURED TREASURE VEGETARIAN RESTAURANT
$$

15 FUQIAN RD., SEC. 1
TEL 06/213-3405

One of Tainan's most frequented vegetarian restaurants, with homey atmo-sphere and friendly service. An extensive menu of fried vegetables, tofu, rice, noodles, and stews are prepared here. Rice cakes accompany the tasty selection of soups, including the restaurant's spicy noodle concoctions.

🪑 35 💳 All major cards

WULING

🏨 HOYA RESORT
$$$

3-16 WULING RD., HEPING
TOWNSHIP, TAICHUNG COUNTY
TEL 04/2590-1399
FAX 04/2590-1118

Located at Wuling Recreational Farm high in the mountains with magnificent scenery, this high-end facility was opened in 2003 and is often jam-packed on weekends, when room prices shoot up. Forty of the rooms are designated as family guest rooms, oversized with a separate room for the kids. The farm offers numerous hiking paths.

ℹ️ 143 P 🪑 🏊
💳 All major cards

🏨 Hotel 🍴 Restaurant ℹ️ No. of Guest Rooms 🪑 No. of Seats P Parking 🚇 Metro ⊘ Closed

Shopping in Taiwan

Taipei's shopping scene is extensive and vibrant, with upscale boutiques, modern shopping centers, discount stores, and lively and colorful night markets. During the evening in some sections of the city, shopping possibilities expand even further when thousands of small-time vendors lay claim to a patch of sidewalk or roadside to hawk their low-priced, often knockoff goods. Shopping outside Taipei in the small towns can be a source of quality goods.

Fashions and consumer goods are no cheaper here than in other Asian cities, and possibly more expensive than you would find in the West. However, department store sales offer huge discounts.

Remember that Asian sizes are smaller than Western. A T-shirt with a tag reading XL will likely be equivalent to a medium (M) back home. Sleeves are shorter. Fit around the hips and rear is tighter.

Good buys can be had on products that are not readily available anywhere else (see Specialized Shopping p. 261). Among the locally made items, you'll find carved jade jewelry, silks, wood carvings, calligraphy scrolls, tea sets, lacquerware, and foodstuffs.

For inexpensive knickknacks try the **Antique Market,** a collection of small shops at the corner of Bade and Xinsheng Roads. For a more extensive range, try the government-run **Chinese Handicraft Mart** (see Antiques & Artifacts).

Rip-offs are refreshingly rare in Taiwan. What you buy is what you get. Staff who speak English, a rare commodity, are usually friendly and helpful.

Shopping Areas
Zhongxiao East Rd., Sec. 4
A popular locale in the Dinghao area with department stores, high- and mid-end shops, music stores, and restaurants.
Renai Circle/Dunhua South Rd.
Designer-label shops are found in this area just south of Zhongxiao East Rd., Sec. 4.
Ximending
This area in western Taipei just north of Wanhua is bounded

by Zhonghua, Zhongxiao West, Huanhe South, and Chengdu Roads. Here are movie theaters, chic stores, camera shops, and hundreds of tiny shops. Pedestrian streets draw young hordes.
Xinyi District
Around the Taipei World Trade Center, this large concentration of department stores and shopping malls with entertainment facilities is a favorite of young people and families.

Antiques & Artifacts
Cherry Hill Antiques
6 Lane 77, Zhongshan North Rd., Sec. 2, tel 02/2541 7575, www.cherryhill.antiques.com.tw
Imported and restored wood furniture, panels, and mirrors from mainland China. Other items include porcelain figurines and silk embroidery.
Chinese Handicraft Mart
1 Xuzhou Rd., tel 02/2393-3655, www.handicraft.org.tw
This government-run emporium is an ideal place to shop for arts, crafts, and antiques. The store has everything from small gifts to expensive artifacts.
Pacific Cultural Foundation Art Center
38 Chongqing South Rd., Sec. 3, tel 02/2337-7155, www.pcf.org.tw
Contemporary art, ink painting, oil, watercolor, photography, sculpture, and mixed media.
Bai Win Antiques
2 Lane 405, Zhongshan North Rd., tel 02/2874-5525, www.baiwinantiques.com
Carries quality items from Taiwan, China, and Southeast Asia, mostly from the Han, Ming, and Qing dynasties.

Arcades & Malls
The Taiwanese often make shopping a family outing—eating and relaxing. Malls generally have a department store, smaller shops, and restaurants and food courts. Many have cinemas and other entertainment facilities. Most open daily around 10–11 a.m. and close 9–9:30 p.m.
Breeze Center
39 Fuxing South Rd., tel 02/6600-8888
Busy mall with mid- and upscale fashions and accessories.
Core Pacific City Living Mall
138 Bade Rd., Sec. 4, tel 02/3762-1888
The striking, globe-shaped exterior and circular interior atrium provide a stunning layout for these shops. Besides retail outlets, you'll find a cinema complex and restaurants.
Formosa Regent Boutiques
B1, Lane 39, Zhongshan North Rd., Sec. 2, tel 02/2256-9121
A comfortable, ritzy ambience with lots of expensive price tags carrying luxury fashions and accessories—a favorite of Japanese tourists.
Taipei Metro (The Mall)
203 Dunhua South Rd., tel 02/2378-6666
Skylights, greenery, ponds, and fountains set the tone in this mall. Famous brand-name stores are featured, along with outlets selling jewelry, watches, trendy home furnishings, and endless fashionable accessories.

Books
Caves Books
103 Zhongshan North Rd., Sec. 2, tel 02/2599-1169
You'll find a large range of

English-language fiction, non-fiction, travel, textbooks, and foreign magazines.

Eslite Bookstore
245 Dunhua South Rd., Sec. 1, tel 02/2775-5977
Taiwan's biggest bookstore chain has a large selection of English-language fiction and nonfiction. The adjoining coffee shop and 24-hour operation make this a favorite haunt for night owls.

Department Stores

Department stores tend to have shorter hours than shopping centers, about 11 a.m. to 9:30 p.m.
Pacific SOGO
45 Zhongxiao East Rd., Sec. 4, tel 02/2776-5555
A popular Japanese-style department store loaded with upscale and brand-name fashions and accessories. Eagerly awaited big-discount sales.
Shin Kong Mitsukoshi
66 Zhongxiao West Rd., Sec. 1, tel 02/2388-5552
This branch of the Japanese department store is near Taipei Main Train Station. Name fashions share floors with mid-price clothing, accessories, electronics, etc.

Food & Drink
Nanmen Market
1 Nanmen Market, 8 Roosevelt Rd., Sec. 1, tel 02/2321-8069
Taipei's largest traditional day market, with preserved and packaged sausages, hams, pastries, and other Taiwan and China goods.
G&G Delicatessen
435 Zhongshan North Rd., Sec. 6, Tianmu, tel 02/2876-8557
Fresh breads and imported cheeses and meats, along with wines. The deli also has a café.
Maison Alexandre Sandwich Shop
756 Zhongshan North Rd., Sec. 6, Tianmu, tel 02/2876-1229
Imported and hard-to-find gourmet foods and groceries.
Tien Mu Grocery
39 Zhongshan North Rd., Sec. 7, Tianmu, tel 02/2871-4828
Stocks a multinational array of

foods, groceries, and wines. The owners speak English.

Markets
Dihua Street Traditional Dried Goods Market
Mid-morning–evening
Taiwan's oldest dry-goods, herbs, and traditional crafts market. Sealed foods make good gifts.
Huaxi Street Tourist Night Market
6 p.m.–1 a.m.
The once famous Snake Alley has cleaned up its red-light act, but the snake-handling shows still attract crowds. You can try snake, and drink snake's blood, in the snake blood-and-bile soup. There are also a number of seafood restaurants, foot massage places, and footwear shops.
Raohe Street Tourist Night Market
6 p.m.–1 a.m.
Crowded market with vendors selling herbal medicines, handicrafts, and Taiwanese snack foods (corn on the cob, squid on a stick, steamed peanuts, chicken feet). It's very colorful.
Shilin Night Market
Off Wenlin Rd. northwest of Jiantan MRT station, 4 p.m.–1 a.m.
Taipei's largest night market. It's a great place to try Taiwanese food. Hundreds of shops and market vendors compete for business in and around the packed market. Retailers sell cheap clothing, shoes, souvenirs, toys, CDs, gifts, tools, kitchenware, and more.
Taipei Holiday Flower Market
Under the Jianguo elevated expressway, south of where it passes over Renai Road.
10 a.m.–6 p.m. Sat. & Sun.
Adjacent to the Holiday Jade Market. Vendors sell a wide variety of flowers and plants.
Taipei Holiday Jade Market
Under Jianguo elevated expressway, north of Renai Road overpass.
10 a.m.–6 p.m. Sat. & Sun.
Plenty of good-quality jade. Lots of cheap trinkets, too. Vendors

also sell Chinese macramé, Buddhist prayer bead bracelets, flashy costume jewelry, and jewelry supplies.

Specialized Shopping

Taiwan has numerous towns and regions that specialize in certain products. In some cases, the whole town is built around the manufacture and sale of a particular product.
Jiufen This quaint town north of Taipei (avoid on weekends) has become an artists enclave, and much of their work is displayed and sold in boutique galleries, primarily along the narrow streets off Jishan Road.
Kaohsiung–Tailian Street For sheer numbers and variety, the city's famous "Shoe Street" is in a league of its own. If it fits on a foot, the retailers have it. The range is staggering and the prices the lowest in Taiwan.
Lugang–Zhongshan Road
This historic town has numerous factory shops, some more than a hundred years old, turning out traditional, quality handicrafts, including wood carvings, tinware, fans, lanterns, and pottery.
Sanyi The center of Taiwan's wood-carving industry, with hundreds of outlets selling a staggering variety of wood products from delicate sculptures to solid furniture. See wood-carvers sculpting away in their workshops.
Yingge This is the pottery center of Taiwan–south of Taipei. Here, streets are lined with factories and shops turning out and selling everything from miniature clay tea sets to porcelain toilet bowls. You'll find a variety of pottery objects, including simple earthenware products, musical instruments, Ming and Qing dynasty reproduction pieces, and exquisite glazed porcelains.

Entertainment & Activities

Taiwan's Chinese heritage is celebrated in drama and art. The country's museums hold priceless collections, while galleries sell works by contemporary artists. Hollywood movies compete with the region's active film industry. The major cities have no shortage of nightlife options—from karaoke bars to trendy clubs. All entertainment venues listed here are in Taipei. Throughout Taiwan, outdoor activities abound—from hiking to rafting, windsurfing to hang gliding.

Entertainment Centers

National Concert Hall
21-1 Zhongshan South Rd.,
tel 02/3393-9888, www.ntch
.edu.tw
Home of the Taipei Symphony
Orchestra, the hall also hosts
international orchestras and other
large-scale music concerts. Also
housed here is the Recital Hall for
chamber music, workshops, and
lectures.

**Sun Yat-sen
Memorial Hall**
505 Renai Rd., Sec. 4, tel
02/2758-8008, www.yatsen
.gov.tw
Musical performances and drama,
both local and international. Also
available are a number of galleries, a café, and exhibits dedicated
to Sun Yat-sen.

National Theater
21-1 Zhongshan South Rd.,
tel 02/3393-9888
Along with the National Concert
Hall, this imposing building forms
the National Chiang Kai-shek Cultural Center. Productions of Chinese opera, traditional Chinese
folk arts, Western opera, drama,
ballet, and other dance forms.

Novel Hall for Performing Arts
3 Songshou Rd., tel 02/2722-
4302, www.novelhall.org.tw
Holds regular performances of
various forms of Chinese drama,
including the Beijing, Taiwanese,
and Liyuan opera.

The Red House
10 Chengdu Rd., tel 02/2311-
9380, www.redhouse.org.tw
Opened in 1908 as a market, the
Red House now has a second-
floor performance area under a
beautiful timber-domed ceiling
that welcomes small productions,
including puppetry and children's
theater.

Cinema

The Taiwanese love movies, especially first-run Hollywood films.
Most cinemas have several theaters, and are in or near shopping
centers. Local English-language
papers have daily listings.

Ambassador Theater
88 Chengdu Rd., tel 02/2361-1222
Powerful surround-sound makes
the 1,500-seat cinema popular.

Lux Theater
85 Wuchang St., Sec. 2, tel
02/2311-8628
Four cinemas. digital audio system.

President Cineplex
4F, 59 Zhonghua Rd., Sec. 1, tel
02/2388-5576
Ergonomic seats and an impressive sound system.

Spring Cinema Galaxy
10F, 52 Hanzhong St., tel
02/2381-1339 or 2381-1399
The cinema's two theaters show
art-house movies.

Vie Show Cinemas
18 Songshou Rd., tel 02/8780-
5566 or 2757-2345 (reservations)
A 17-theater cineplex located in a
retail/entertainment complex.

Nightlife

There is no shortage of pubs,
bars, and nightclubs in Taipei,
from British-style pubs to trendy
dance clubs. Opening hours
vary from 11:30 a.m. for lunch
to 5 p.m. Most close between
1 and 3 a.m.—some not until
dawn. A small bottle of imported
beer or glass of wine costs
between NT$150–200, with
mixed drinks around NT$200
or higher.

Bliss
148 Xinyi Rd., Sec. 4, tel 02/2702-
1855, www.bliss-taipei.com
Features strong local bands and
solid imported groups. Sessions are mostly rock, and start
about 10 p.m. Wednesday has
Girl's Night Out specials, with
free champagne for ladies and
NT$100 highballs.

Blue Note
4F, 171 Roosevelt Rd., Sec. 3,
intersection of Shida Rd.,
tel 02/2362-2333
A popular jazz club with local
and international performers. It is
small so get there before 9 p.m. if
you want a table. Pleasant service.
Minimum charge.

Carnegie's
100 Anhe Rd., Sec. 2, tel
02/2325-4433
Among the most popular bars in
Taipei, it carries a staggering list
of 300 shooters. Long lines of
people outside on weekends.

Brown Sugar
101 Songren Rd., tel 02/8780-
1110, www.brownsugar.com.tw
International and local jazz and
blues bands perform in an intimate, lively atmosphere.

Indian Beer House
196 Bade Rd., Sec. 2, tel 02/2741-
0550
Dinosaur Beer House would be an
appropriate name given the Jurassic decor and the roof's dinosaur
skeleton. Long tables, flowing
beer, scurrying waiters, and cheerful patrons make for a lively and
loud atmosphere. Feed on the
Taiwanese and Chinese snacks.

Luxy
5F, 201 Zhongxiao E. Rd., tel
02/2772-1000, www.luxy-taipei
.com
One of Taiwan's glitziest dance

clubs. Two areas, each with its own DJ music and ambience. Cover Wed.–Sat., free entry before 11 p.m. Wed. (Ladies' Night).

My Other Place
303 Fuxing North Rd., tel 02/2718-7826
This welcoming pub serving British beer is downtown. It draws expatriates and business people mainly for its generous lunch and early evening happy hour.

The Ploughman Inn
8 Lane 232, Dunhua South Rd., Sec. 1, tel 02/2773-3268
One of Taipei's oldest pubs, it draws expatriates and locals equally. The friendly staff makes you feel welcome. Special theme every night with cheap drinks for those who dress right. Many take advantage of the Mongolian BBQ in the basement. Cover.

Q-Bar
16 Alley 19, Lane 216, Zhongxiao East Rd., Sec. 4, tel 02/2771-7778, www.qbartaipei.com
Chic after-work spot with inexpensive imported beers that belie its up-market ambience. The staff is friendly. the patrons, chatty.

The Tavern
415 Xinyi Rd., Sec. 4, tel 02/8780-0892, www.tavern.com.tw
Nautical theme attracts foreign and local businessmen here to enjoy the extensive range of beers. A giant TV shows international sporting events, while pool tables keeps patrons occupied.

The Zone
Often also called the Combat Zone. Cheek-by-jowl bars that were once favored by U.S. troops on R & R during the Vietnam Wars. Some bars have been refurbished, while others have changed little since the 1970s. Mainly expatriate male clientele. To enter the Zone, head to the neon-lit lanes along Shuangcheng Street, behind the Imperial Hotel.

Active Sports

Taiwan presents numerous opportunities to get involved with sports. The sporting associations and clubs are well organized, helpful, and generally welcoming to visitors—although language problems may be encountered. The most popular and accessible outdoor pursuit is hiking. There are numerous quality golf courses and some good beaches for swimming. Adventure sports like diving, paragliding, white-water rafting, and rock climbing can be organized with relative ease.

Cycling & Mountain Biking

Taiwan's compact size and beautiful scenery make it ideal for mountain biking and cycling. The hilly terrain makes for some long and exhilarating downhill rides, along with challenging climbs. Numerous off-road possibilities exist. Any cycle shop will put you in touch with a biking/cycling club. Good info on routes and services is available in the Let's Go Cycling section of the Taiwan Tourism Bureau website, *www.taiwan.net.tw*.

Golf

Courses are open to guest membership for foreign visitors. this can usually be arranged at the hotel concierge desk or through travel agencies. Excellent courses can be found on the outskirts of major cities. Clubs and shoes are available at most clubs.
ROC Golf Association
12F-1, 125 Nanjing East Rd., Sec. 2, Taipei, tel 02/2516-5611

Hiking & Mountaineering

Hiking is one of the favorite activities of the Taiwanese. There are many hiking clubs that take busloads of hikers to the mountains for day or overnight trips. If you prefer more solitude, registered guides can be hired. In some cases, mountain permits are needed—generally for ascents above 9,800 feet (3,000 m) and for protected areas. Contact the National Police Administration *(tel 02/357-7377)* or go to the Taiwan Tourism Bureau website for a downloadable permit application form. Other sources:
Alpine Association
10F, 185 Zhongshan North Rd., Sec. 2, Taipei, tel 2594-2108, wwwmountaineering.org.tw
Chinese Taipei Mountaineering Association
50-A Longjiang Rd., Taipei, tel 02/2751-0938, www.alpineclub.org.tw

Hot-Air Ballooning

Colorful hot-air balloons float in the southern sky over Pingtung and Kaohsiung Counties.
Shyang An Enterprises Co., Ltd.
68-6 Zhongshan Rd., Yangpu Township, Pingtung County, tel 08/793-8827

Kayaking

Taiwan's mountains and heavy rainfall contribute to some good runs, mainly during the wet season and especially after a typhoon. The most popular areas are the East Coast's Xiuguluan River in Hualien County and Laonong River in Kaohsiung County.
Chinese Taipei Aruba Kayaking Association
1F-1, 3 Lane 238, Yangping Rd., Yonghe, Taipei County, tel 02/2552-8000
Chinese Taipei Canoe Association
260 Guangming St., Xindian, Taipei County, tel 02/2918-5151

Martial Arts

After a few lessons you can join the tens of thousands of people at dawn who practice tai chi in temple courtyards and parks around the island. The most popular places for tai chi in Taipei are 2-28 Peace Park, Chiang Kai-shek Memorial Plaza, and Sun Yat-sen Memorial Plaza.

National Tai Chi Chuan
Association
6F, 20 Zhulun St., Taipei,
tel 02/2778-3887

Paragliding

The three most popular paragliding launch sites are on the north coast at Green Bay and in the mountains at Luye Plateau fronting tea plantations, in the Taitung County's East Rift Valley, and at Saijia Aero Sports Park in Sandimen Township, Pingtung County. Solid information in English is found on the Wings Taiwan website (*http://wingstaiwan.com*).

Chinese Taipei Aero Sports
Association
9F, 20 Zhulun St., Taipei,
tel 02/2775-8755
Taipei Aero Sports Association
10 Alley 5, Lane 305, Yuandong Rd., Zhonghe, Taipei County,
tel 02/2247-5905

Rock Climbing

The sea cliffs of Longdong on the northeast coast are regarded as the best for climbing because of the surface variations.

Taipei Rock Climbing
Association
1F-1, 3 Lane 238, Yanping Rd., Yonghe City, Taipei County,
tel 02/8923-5476
Shao Hu Tz Rock
Climbing Enterprise
(XHZ Adventure Life)
1 Lane 16, Alley 60, Shuangcheng St., Xindian City, Taipei County,
tel 02/2215-9019
Rock Wall Climbing
Taipei Youth Activity Center
9F, 917 Renai Rd., Sec. 1, Taipei
tel 02/2343-2388

Snorkeling & Diving

The corals fringing Kenting, Green Island, and the Penghus host excellent dives. Kenting has a number of dive shops offering PADI courses for a reasonable fee.
PADI Dive Centers and Resorts
www.padi.com

Inner Space Dive Center
1F, 55 Bade Rd., Sec. 5, Taipei,
tel 02/2767-1124

Surfing

An enthusiastic and welcoming surfing community makes the best of the swells off the island's east coast. The popular spots are the northeast coast's Honeymoon Bay and Fulong Beach, and the Kenting National Park's east coast. The best conditions are after a typhoon.

Chinese Taipei Surfing
Association
5F, 11 Alley 20, Lane 155, Bade Rd., Sec. 3, Taipei, tel 02/2577-1666
Spider Surf Club/Shop
96 Binhai Rd. (coastal highway), Toucheng, Yilan County, tel 03/978-1809, www.spidersurfing.com

Swimming

The best beaches by far are in Kenting National Park in the south. The better hotels have swimming pools.

White-water Rafting

The most popular area is the Xiuguluan River in Hualien County, the only river on the island that carries enough water year-round for white-water rafting. The wet season, however, is the best time to hit the water. After a typhoon, the rivers swell and deliver plenty of thrills. Full-day rafting trips including transportation and equipment can be booked through travel agents.

Nansen Amusement Co., Ltd.
Taipei, tel 02/8809-4688
Hualien, tel 03/833-4369
Wanjiang Amusement Co., Ltd.
138-6 Guolian 1st Rd., Hualien City, tel 03/835-6285
Baumay Rafting
1 Zhongzheng Rd., Boalai Village, Liugui Township, Kaohsiung County, tel 07/688-2580

Windsurfing

Windsurfing gear can be rented from popular beaches around the island. The best conditions for the sport are found on the windswept Penghu Archipelago in Taiwan Strait between October and April.
Liquid Sports
36 Huimin 1st Rd., Magong, Penghu, tel 06/926-0361, www.liquidsport.com.tw

Spectator Sports

Spectator sports in Taiwan do not draw big crowds to stadiums or arenas, although some have a large television following. Outdoor stadiums are generally small, with the largest only holding 10,000 spectators. Baseball attracts the largest, most vocal, and fanatical crowds, although attendance per game is not high. There is also a basketball league. Big-event regional and international martial arts and table-tennis competitions draw larger crowds.

Taipei Arena
2 Nanjing E. Rd., Sec. 4,
tel 02/2578-3536
www.taipeiarena.com.tw
This state-of-the-art sports complex opened in 2005, seating up to 15,000 depending on configuration. Many international sporting events are staged here, and it serves as home base for the professional Super Basketball League, with mostly local players. An ice-hockey league is also based here, with local and foreign players—and with thousands attending playoff games.
Tianmu Baseball Stadium
77 Zhongcheng Rd., Sec. 2, Taipei,
tel 02/2873-6548
Weekend games are often staged here during the 9-month season. The stadium holds 10,400. Crowds are generally only a few thousand except for the season's opening game and at playoff time, so you can always get a ticket by just turning up.

INDEX

ILLUSTRATIONS CREDITS

National Geographic
TRAVELER

Taiwan

Published by the National Geographic Society
John M. Fahey, Jr., *President and Chief Executive Officer*
Gilbert M. Grosvenor, *Chairman of the Board*
Tim T. Kelly, *President, Global Media Group*
John Q. Griffin, *Executive Vice President; President, Publishing*
Nina D. Hoffman, *Executive Vice President; President, Book Publishing Group*

Prepared by the Book Division
Barbara Brownell Grogan, *Vice President and Editor in Chief*
Marianne R. Koszorus, *Director of Design*
Barbara A. Noe, *Senior Editor*
Carl Mehler, *Director of Maps*
R. Gary Colbert, *Production Director*
Jennifer A. Thornton, *Managing Editor*
Meredith C. Wilcox, *Administrative Director, Illustrations*

Staff for This Book
Sheila Buckmaster, *Project Editor*
Kay Kobor Hankins, *Art Director*
Linda Makarov, *Designer*
Jane Sunderland, *Copy Editor*
Connie Binder, *Indexer*
Michael McNey and Mapping Specialists, *Map Production*
Katherine Brazauskas, Lynsey Jacob, *Contributors*
Robert Waymouth, *Illustrations Specialist*

Manufacturing and Quality Management
Christopher A. Liedel, *Chief Financial Officer*
Phillip L. Schlosser, *Senior Vice President*
Chris Brown, *Technical Director*
Nicole Elliott, *Manager*
Rachel Faulise, *Manager*
Robert L. Barr, *Manager*

National Geographic Traveler: Taiwan (Third Edition)
ISBN: 978-1-4262-0717-4

The National Geographic Society is one of the world's largest nonprofit scientific and educational organizations. Founded in 1888 to "increase and diffuse geographic knowledge," the Society works to inspire people to care about the planet. It reaches more than 325 million people worldwide each month through its official journal, *National Geographic,* and other magazines. National Geographic Channel. television documentaries. music. radio. films. books. DVDs. maps. exhibitions. school publishing programs. interactive media. and merchandise. National Geographic has funded more than 9,000 scientific research, conservation and exploration projects and supports an education program combating geographic illiteracy. For more information, visit nationalgeographic.com.

For more information, please call 1-800-NGS LINE (647-5463) or write to the following address:

National Geographic Society
1145 17th Street N.W.
Washington, D.C. 20036-4688 U.S.A.

For information about special discounts for bulk purchases, please contact National Geographic Books Special Sales: ngspecsales@ngs.org.

For rights or permissions inquiries, please contact National Geographic Books Subsidiary Rights: ngbookrights@ngs.org.

The information in this book has been carefully checked and to the best of our knowledge is accurate. However, details are subject to change, and the National Geographic Society cannot be responsible for such changes, or for errors or omissions. Assessments of sites, hotels, and restaurants are based on the author's subjective opinions, which do not necessarily reflect the publisher's opinion.

Printed in Hong Kong

10/THK/1

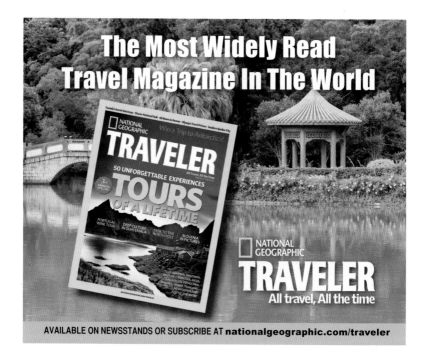